Australia in a Nutshell

A Narrative History

REGULATIONS WITH A VENGEANCE

Mr McKean: "Then there's the licence fee, and the surveyor's fee, and the half year's rent, which will come to about fifteen pounds besides—"
Free Selector. "Beg your pardon, Sir, hope no offence, but it seems to me as this new act is only for them with lots of money and lots of time to waste."

Contemporary cartoon commenting on how free selection favoured those with money. See pages 126-9. (Australian History Museum, Macquarie University)

Australia in a Nutshell

A Narrative History

Frank G. Clarke

Rosenberg

First published in 2003 by Rosenberg Publishing Pty Ltd
P.O. Box 6125 Dural Delivery Centre NSW 2156 Australia
Phone 02 9654 1502 Fax 02 9654 1338
Email rosenbergpub@smartchat.net.au
Web www.rosenbergpub.com.au

The front cover shows (*top*) the 13th Australian Light Horse on the way to the
front in August 1918 (Australian War Memorial #E02979) and (*bottom*) a
nineteenth century cartoon of an emu hunting scene.
Cover design by Highway 51 Design Works.

National Library of Australia Cataloguing in Publication Data
Clarke, F. G. (Francis Gordon), 1943- .
Australia in a nutshell : a narrative history.

Bibliography.
Includes index.
ISBN 1 877058 13 0.

1. Australia - History. I. Title.

994

Set in AGaramond 11 on 13 point
Printed in Malaysia through SRM Production Services Sdn. Bhd.

Contents

Preface

A narrative history is an attempt to tell the story of a people—in this case, the story of the Australian people which begins with the arrival of the first Australians between 100 000 and 60 000 years ago. It involves honouring the achievement of Aboriginal Australians in the way they came to terms with a unique environment and in their understanding of the country and the rhythms of existence it imposed. It also includes the study of the ways this continent became caught up in the international rivalries of the great powers of Europe at the end of the eighteenth century, and the resulting settlements established by Britain after 1788. Great power antagonisms have continued to affect Australia's development ever since and, although Australians might have felt isolated from the wider world after 1788, history shows that this was more psychological than real.

The narrative then becomes a study of the way in which a continuing flow of new arrivals attempted to come to terms with the country and its people, and of the manner in which the country stamped its uniqueness upon them and made them and the succeeding generations into something different from what they had been when they arrived. It necessarily involves a study of the contributions made to this course of development by a continuous process of accommodation that the environment forced upon Europeans who had imagined that they could impose their way of life and culture upon a continent that was manifestly unsuited to sustain it. The attempts to master and subdue the country and its original inhabitants constitute a significant part of the narrative, and the processes of accommodation have still not run their course at the beginning of the third millennium of the modern era. But perhaps at long last, Australians are beginning to understand why they have failed and, in the light of that dearly bought knowledge, to recognise the wisdom of the indigenous people.

Wherever possible, I have attempted to illustrate the broad general themes of the narrative with individual exemplars—with the stories of men and women whose experiences and contributions to the history of this country can be seen as representative of wider forces than themselves. In some ways this means concentrating on the movers and shakers of society, and this involves the risk of losing sight of ordinary Australians—settlers and native-born— who actually made the history. However, without such a selection process, the narrative of a people would become uncontrollable, and general history could not be written at all. All history involves selection and, to that extent, all history is biased. I hope readers can see those prejudices of which I am aware, and also those of which I am not. I am conscious that I share a common Australian predilection in favour of the underdog and in sympathy with the democratic and egalitarian ethos of modern Australia; and perhaps this has rendered me less tolerant of the forces of conservatism and patrician pretentiousness that have always existed in this country. Wherever a social pyramid exists, there will be those who aspire to position themselves at its summit, and their story is as much a part of the narrative as is anybody else's.

I am grateful to my friends and colleagues in the Department of Modern History at Macquarie University for their continued encouragement and support; to my students for their endless capacity to ask questions and to force me to think again about many issues I had thought were well settled; and to my wife Jan who bravely put up with my preoccupation and abstraction as the project unfolded. My friend and editor, Ross Gilham, has been invaluable. This is the third book on which we have worked together and I have come to rely heavily on the coolness of his judgment and to benefit from his expertise as the nonpareil of editors.

Frank G. Clarke
Macquarie University
January 2003

1

Aboriginal Australia

Aborigines, the first Australians, have lived in this country for at least 60 000 to 70 000 years, and the dating of human remains and artefacts keeps extending the period of time for which evidence of human occupation of Australia can be unearthed. Archaeologists prefer to date occupation from the hard evidence of human bones and tools, but other scientists—using the evidence of carbon deposits in geological core samples and abandoned camp sites— have suggested that the original human occupiers of Australia arrived well over 100 000 years ago. Some Aboriginal spokesmen have even suggested that their people have always been present, and they deny that their ancestors were immigrants.

Until recently, the oldest archaeological sites discovered had been in the south of the continent, but much older sites are being uncovered in the northern regions of Australia, from where most scholars believe the flow or trickle of population worked its way down the face of the country into the southern regions. Aborigines are thought to have found their way here during the period when the south-eastern shores of Asia were much closer to Australia, and when New Guinea and Tasmania were still part of the Australian continental land mass.

During this last Ice Age, the level of the seas around Australia and throughout the Asian region are estimated to have been between 130 and 200 metres lower than at present, and the

Australian shoreline of that period—with all the evidence of early human arrival—is today well beneath the sea. By walking, and by short voyages across the shallow seas, the first native Australians filtered into the large and unpopulated continent's northern regions. Over thousands of years, by natural increase and successive migrations, the people of early Australia finally reached the southern extremity of the continent, now known as Tasmania. When the Ice Age ended and the seas slowly rose, New Guinea and Tasmania became separated from the mainland of Australia, and this brought to an end the movement of people overland into northern Australia and also into Tasmania. Both mainland Australia and Tasmania then began a long period of isolation from the rest of the world—a period of isolation that remained unbroken, as far as is known, until the 1400s, when Indonesian traders and fishermen re-established contact with the continent and the unique people who had developed during those millennia. When European explorers landed several hundred years after the Indonesians, they too were struck by the singularity of the now numerous peoples whom they encountered.

Tribes and territories

By the time that European observers arrived on the scene, Australian Aborigines had developed a fairly rigid pattern of clan and tribal territories, but this could not always have been the case. Obviously, with people moving from the northern regions into new and unoccupied territories further to the south, the close links between land and tribe, so noticeable in the eighteenth and nineteenth centuries, must have been non-existent or considerably more flexible. Nor can it be said that Aboriginal peoples constituted a unified people in any social or political sense. The small groups were divided by a staggering diversity of languages and customs. Oral communication between natives from different regions was to prove impossible in the nineteenth century, and it seems likely that this differentiation had existed for many thousands of years. For example, on the island of Tasmania there were five distinct languages spoken, all of which were different from one another, and none of which had anything in common with languages spoken in the Port Phillip district of the adjoining mainland.

Tribal territorial boundaries must have been more adaptable in the earlier years of occupation than they had become by the time that the Europeans arrived. Adjustments would have been necessary to accommodate the migration of clans or tribes moving further south through the territory of tribes already settled, and those people who lived in the territories now beneath the seas must also have been absorbed into the tribes living in adjacent and unsubmerged lands. It seems a more accurate representation of traditional life in Aboriginal Australia to think in terms of several hundred independent republics, rather than of a continent occupied by a single Aboriginal nation.

Estimating the size of the Aboriginal populations in pre-colonised Australia has been notoriously difficult, and demographers still are in substantial disagreement. Current opinion is that the Aboriginal population of Australia on the eve of the first European arrivals, was probably between 600 000 and 1 000 000 people. It cannot be assumed, however, that this was a stable population level for most of the history of Black Australia. In earlier times, before the desertification of much of inland Australia, far larger populations of Aborigines might have lived out their lives here. The fossil record of inland regions supports the proposition that there were times when quite large populations of Aborigines lived around a huge inland lake system that provided ample game and plants for food-gathering.

Whenever it was that Aborigines arrived in Australia, the fossil records make it plain that they existed for thousands of years alongside a wide variety of now extinct flora and fauna. Giant kangaroos, a species of giant wombat the size of a water-buffalo, marsupial lions and tigers, and giant snakes, lizards, and emus are but some of the species of megafauna of which there are fossil remains. A question that still remains unresolved is the extent of Aboriginal involvement in the disappearance of these animals. Were they, as suggested by some zoologists, hunted to extinction, or did they disappear as a result of some natural calamity or climatic change? Perhaps it was a combination of hunting and the slow process of inexorable climatic change that produced the loss of species over the millennia.

The pressure on these giant animals would have been much greater had Aboriginal numbers grown geometrically but, judging from practices in the eighteenth and nineteenth centuries, Aborigines consciously managed their population sizes so as to avoid putting undue strain on food supplies or way of life. The population was widely dispersed throughout the continent, and even the inhospitable inland desert regions carried small numbers of Aborigines who were able to live a comparatively comfortable existence in that harsh environment. Along the river systems and in the coastal regions the density of population increased, as the fertile land was capable of carrying more people. The balance of population and the capacity of the tribal territory to support the population seems to have been carefully preserved. Unwanted children or children who could not be suckled—as a result of multiple births, or the death of the mother—were killed. Children were kept on the breast for several years, both for survival and to increase the time between births. An Aboriginal mother could care for only one infant at a time because she had to participate in the normal food-gathering activities of the tribe, and carry her share of the camp chattels during seasonal movements. Infanticide was an important measure in the overall control of Aboriginal population. It also seems clear, that in some parts of Australia, Aboriginal women were able to procure reliable and safe abortifacients, and that these were sometimes used to end unwanted pregnancies.

The very nature of the Aboriginal way of life and their

traditional economy made managing population size necessary. Women played a vital role in food-gathering activities, and they were unable to enjoy the luxury of full-time mothering. Aboriginal males hunted the larger animals for their meat, and provided fish when these were available, but the women's regular gathering of seeds, fruits, roots, and small animals provided approximately two-thirds of the daily food intake. This was the basis of traditional Aboriginal life and, consequently, anything that affected the activities of the women impacted directly on the general wellbeing of the tribe—indeed, on its ability to survive at all. Too many babes in arms, too many women marrying outside the clan, or too many women being abducted by surrounding tribes, all had profound implications for the long-term ability of the tribe to maintain its population at a level sufficient to secure its survival and its traditional territory.

Kinship, religion, and the land

It is not known at what stage of the occupation of Aboriginal Australia that the rigid definition of tribal territories became established. By the time that Europeans arrived, these territorial divisions had existed since time immemorial, and tribal lands had become integrated into an intricate and detailed set of religious beliefs and practices that governed all aspects of traditional Aboriginal life. As in so much of Aboriginal Australia, there were significant regional variations but, in general terms, Aborigines believed that the physical structure of their tribal territory—its geological features, and the plants and animals that existed within the territory—embodied spiritual entities of great antiquity which overshadowed the land and preserved and protected it. Because the land was the physical expression of these spirit ancestors, and because they were also the progenitors of the Aborigines themselves, the land and the people who lived on it were indissolubly connected in a mutually dependent relationship. Aborigines therefore did not own their land in any European sense of that term but, instead, existed upon it and were responsible for maintaining it as part of their continuing relationship with the spirit presences embodied within it. The land was central to any sense of personal identity, and this must have reinforced the natural human disinclination to move into unfamiliar areas. Over thousands of years this resulted in a culture so closely linked to its geographical territory that it was unable to survive when Europeans forcibly transplanted it to other locations.

Aboriginal culture was also non-expansionist, as the territory of another tribe had little or no significance or meaning to Aborigines in adjoining areas. This meant that wars over land involving the expansion of one tribe's territory at the expense of another's were unknown. Aborigines believed that the spirit ancestors had established the territory within which their successors should live, and they felt no link with or desire to possess the lands of other tribes. This does not mean that conflict between tribes was non-existent. Indeed, violent clashes were certainly quite common as Aboriginal tribes raided one another for women, sought revenge for earlier raids, or responded to deaths that they attributed to malefic sorcery from another tribe. Nevertheless, such conflict did not normally involve the appropriation of territory. Nor was domestic discord within the clan or tribe unknown and, occasionally, an untimely end resulted from such internal family quarrels. By and large, however, traditional Aboriginal society was introverted, peaceful, and possessed of a respect for custom and familiar ways of doing things.

Within the tribal territory there could exist several small groups or clans that moved systematically from place to place in search of food. These clans would periodically come together as a larger unit for the purposes of celebrating an important festival, for trade, for arranging marriages, and for important religious rites and ceremonies. When gathered together in such a way the tribe could number hundreds of people, but the smaller clans or family groups could be as small as one or two dozen. Because of the relationships between the spirit ancestors at the time of creation, nearly every person with whom an Aborigine came in contact during the course of a lifetime would be some sort of relative. This made for strict and involved marriage customs to avoid inbreeding, and traditional Aboriginal law dealt harshly with violation of the marriage laws.

Because women were so vital to survival in traditional society, the older, more powerful men of the tribe tended to secure the youngest girls as wives. This was important insurance in a harsh environment for, when a man grew too old to hunt, he could survive on the mainly vegetable foods gathered by his young and vigorous wives. Thus it was quite common in traditional Aboriginal society for very young girls to be given in marriage to comparatively old men—a custom abhorred by European observers in the nineteenth century.

Membership of a tribe involved detailed and specific rights and duties. The sharing of resources was one of the primary obligations incurred and, in traditional Aboriginal society, no one was ever alone. There were always the wider relationships upon which people could depend in times of stress or need. Everything was shared with one's kin—including wives, food, hunting implements and tools, trade goods, and valued ceremonial articles. Such items were freely given as part of a reciprocal system of sharing that reinforced familial bonds. Individual acquisitiveness was not an admired character trait, and loyalty to clan and tribe overrode individual advancement.

Traditional economy

Aborigines did not exist in a state of introverted self-absorption and, just as the clans that made up a tribe or language group met together periodically, so too did tribes in adjoining territories come together at certain times for the purposes of trade and religious ceremonies. The extent of the trading network can be gauged by the finds that archaeologists have made of materials thousands of kilometres away from their place of origin. Pearl shells are the best-known items of this type, but other artefacts introduced by Indonesian fishermen in the extreme north have also been found far inland, and stone implements have been unearthed at considerable distances from the area in which the stone was quarried. Some tribes with special skills in the manufacture of boomerangs or ceremonial belts of human hair supplied these items to other tribes that did not bother to manufacture them for themselves. Such specialisation also occurred for more obvious geographical reasons—because the ceremonial clays and ochres did not occur naturally in all parts of Australia, and the stone preferred for spearheads and seed-grinding was also restricted to a number of limited locations. The tribes in these fortunate situations were in a strong position to trade advantageously with those in less well-endowed areas.

The traditional economy of Aboriginal Australia was, however, not centred on trade. Rather, it was structured on subsistence husbandry that was delicately attuned to the breeding cycles of food animals and the seasonal variations in vegetation. For a long time it was assumed by scholars that this way of life could accurately be described with the label 'hunter–gatherer', and Aborigines were depicted as a species of passive parasites who wandered the countryside utilising the bounty of nature without changing the environment. This romanticised vision led to a twentieth-century revival of the myth of the noble savage, in which the Aborigine was said to have lived an idyllic existence in harmony with nature and in an unchanging world.

Fire-stick farming

Recently a more realistic assessment has begun to prevail. In this assessment Aborigines are viewed as being far from passive in the management of their country. As more information becomes

Tjingilli man—heavy scarring indicates a fully initiated male. (Australian History Museum, Macquarie University)

known about traditional Aboriginal life, it becomes clearer that Aborigines practised a form of animal and agricultural husbandry more accurately described as 'fire-stick farming' than as 'hunter–gathering'. What emerges is that Aborigines were anything but the passive exploiters of nature, and it is now becoming clear that they managed their tribal territories very carefully. In so doing, they exploited to the limits of their technology the countryside in which they lived, and produced irreversible and ineradicable change in the Australian environment.

Perhaps the most noteworthy means by which such change was brought about is the way Aborigines used fire. Early European navigators repeatedly commented on the fires that they saw burning as they approached the coastline of Australia, and the smoke from some of these conflagrations was visible far out to sea. Although a number of such bushfires could well have been caused by random lightning strikes, they cannot all be explained in this way. Moreover, the evidence of early European settlers throughout Australia is agreed on the widespread use of fire by the Aborigines as a method of more fully exploiting their tribal territories. Aborigines regularly set fire to the bush in a deliberate attempt to expand the grasslands and to attract the grass-eating animals that provided an important constituent of their protein intake. There is also evidence that Aborigines used fire as a hunting technique to enclose animals in a confined space where they could be more easily killed. Occasionally, fire became a weapon, and there are many accounts by Europeans of Aboriginal use of fire to kill the stock of the colonists and to destroy their crops.

Gippsland Aboriginal family in front of mia mia. (Taken from Jack Cato, *The Story of the Camera in Australia*, Melbourne, 1955)

Because Aborigines possessed no methods of controlling the fires that they had started, or of fighting fires that were out of control, any escaped fires burnt until rain came or until they burnt themselves out. Regular burning of this type over thousands of years might well have caused major ecological change, particularly when associated with climatic change of the interior of the continent. It is known that inland Australia was once far more fertile and carried much larger populations of animals and people than it did by the time Europeans arrived. As the climate slowly dried out the interior, regular burning of the bush, accompanied by progressively lower rainfall, would have accelerated the process by which the inland became desert. Eventually a time would have occurred when the regenerative powers of nature could no longer cope with the twin processes of fire-stick farming and increasing aridity.

As a technique of control and development, the use of fire in those parts of the continent better served by rainfall proved to be very efficient. The wide grasslands burnt easily and, once rain fell, the ashes were a good foundation for the new shoots of tender

Aboriginal man in full ceremonial paint. (Taken from Jack Cato, *The Story of the Camera in Australia*, Melbourne, 1955)

green grass that grew up in the devastated areas. These new grasses encouraged the kangaroos and wallabies to move into the area and enabled the overall populations of such animals to increase.

The ecological changes thus produced were major, and extended beyond the eradication of large areas of closely timbered land and its replacement by open forest and grassland. The Aborigines increased the capacity of the land to support certain favoured species of animals, and reduced the populations of animals more at home in a closely forested terrain. Fire-stick farming over thousands of years produced a land in which fire-resistant species of plants prospered at the expense of species less capable of adapting to regular burning. Prolonged use of fire also robbed the soil of nitrogen and, in a time of climatic change in the sparser woodland of the interior, encouraged the development of the great inland deserts of today. Some of the early explorers and pastoralists recognised the paradox that it was the farming methods of the Aborigines that had been primarily responsible for preparing the country so well for the introduction of their sheep—for it was the grasslands and the open forest areas cultivated over the millennia by the Aborigines that proved most attractive to the colonial sheep farmers of the nineteenth century.

Fire-stick farming was far from being a passive existence, and a question often raised in the more than two hundred years of European settlement is why Aborigines never developed any form of tillage or cultivation of cereal grains or fruit. Seeds, grains, and fruits occurred naturally throughout Australia, and Aborigines collected them in season and either ground them into flour for cakes or ate them in their natural state. Yet they never seem to have made any attempt at cultivation of these food items in a systematic way. In the north of Australia it is known that Aborigines occasionally accompanied the Indonesian fishermen back to their homeland where they would have seen a society based upon the cultivation of rice. They would also have encountered the yam as an edible root-vegetable, and the coconut, as well as domestic animals such as pigs and dogs. Aside from an enthusiastic acceptance of dogs, the Aborigines never attempted to develop a similar economy by borrowing technology and expertise from the Indonesians. The plants grew well enough in Australia, and Aborigines would harvest and consume them when they found them, but they did not adopt an agrarian model.

There are two conjoined reasons for this. First, the Aborigines' long occupation of this country had given them a profound understanding of the vagaries of the El Niño phenomenon and its impact on the climate and rainfall patterns of the continent. The El Niño phenomenon makes rainfall notoriously unpredictable in Australia, and any form of cultivation that depended on rainfall could not be sustained over the long term. There were periods of drought that went for years on end, and would have spelt disaster to a people who had placed their reliance on growing and harvesting crops for their survival. Unlike the predictable climatic cycles of Europe and North America, where seasonal change and climatic variation are severe but regular, the El Niño cycles are impossible to forecast, and a period of severe drought can last for almost a decade. Long experience had taught Aborigines that their method of existence worked best in this country.

Secondly, Aborigines appear to have made a deliberate choice not to embrace the agricultural way of life because of its demands on time and energy. One of the most apparent aspects of agriculture is the intensity of effort required over long periods to produce any

Aboriginal males with traditional weapons. (Australian History Museum, Macquarie University)

worthwhile result. In the meantime, life has somehow to be supported. It is typical of the agricultural peasant farmer to labour from sunrise to sunset in his fields, but Aborigines were able to maintain their way of life without this continuous and backbreaking toil. Several hours of hunting, fishing, and collecting by the clan would usually be sufficient for the supply of that day's foodstuffs.

The remainder of the time was given over to leisure. So long as the population was kept within limits so as not to overstrain existing food supplies, there was no need for Aborigines to change to the far more arduous way of agriculture. It was in maintaining food supplies with a minimum of effort that traditional Aboriginal society most closely approximated the more leisured way of life of today's developed nations. There were places and seasons in Australia where Aborigines were able to sustain a comfortable way of life with an ease that appalled European observers, who tended to equate hard work with godliness. William Dampier's dismissive observations in 1688 of coastal Aborigines in the north-west of

Western Australia drew attention to their lack of the accoutrements of a 'civilised' culture, but also commented upon the ease with which the Aborigines were able to feed an entire tribe by merely visiting an elaborate fish-trap that they had built nearby. When the tide receded, all that was required was for them to walk down to the beach and collect the fish which were immediately cooked and eaten. This process occurred after each high tide:[1]

> . . . their chiefest dependence is upon what the sea leaves in their Wares; which, be it much or little they gather up, and march to the place of their abode. There the old People, that are not able to stir abroad, by reason of their Age, and the tender Infants, wait their return; and what Providence has bestowed on them, they presently broil on the Coals, and eat it in common. Sometimes they get as many Fish as makes them a plentiful Banquet; and at other times they scarce get every one a taste . . . When they have eaten they lye down till the next low water, and then all that are able march out, be it night or day, rain or shine, 'tis all one; they must attend the Wares, or else they must fast: For the Earth affords them no Food at all.

Similar observations were made by other Europeans—who regarded the Aboriginal disinclination to embrace a life of small-scale farming on a more recognisable European pattern as evidence that an incorrigible laziness lay at the heart of Aboriginal culture. It never seems to have occurred to the Europeans that Aborigines might have assessed and then rejected the model of European or Indonesian agriculture and animal husbandry in favour of their own traditional and comparatively leisured style of living. After more than two centuries of experiencing the ravages of El Niño on rural production since first settlement in 1788, there are now many Australians who see the need to reassess the way humans relate to the land, and to look again at a way of life that proved to be sustainable over thousands of years.

Invasion and the conflict between cultures

When contact between the two races did eventually occur, the cultural gap yawned alarmingly between a people who valued a way of life that was non-acquisitive and communal, with few social and political distinctions based upon birth or possessions; and a people whose values embraced individual acquisitiveness and a system of preferment favouring those who acquired possessions or were born into the ruling gentry. Because both Aborigines and Europeans rejected one another's cultures as having little to offer, the opportunities for misunderstanding became tragically enlarged. In other parts of the world colonised by the British, the subject races had adopted at least some of the customs and trappings of British civilisation. In the Pacific area, for example, the Maori eagerly accepted firearms and participated enthusiastically in trading with the European interlopers. In Australia, however, the British found themselves confronted by Aborigines who were not prepared to alter their traditional way of life beyond the superficial acceptance of iron implements, and a fondness for the more portable of European-style foodstuffs such as flour, tea, and sugar. Trading between Blacks and Whites was not usual, and a cultural intransigence marked the attitudes of both peoples to each other. Each felt that the other race was uncouth and did not know how to behave properly or lawfully, and the original dispute over the invasion and the unauthorised occupation by the British of Aboriginal lands quickly developed into a wider cultural conflict of truly tragic consequence in the history of Australia.

The obvious preference of Aborigines for their own culture was interpreted by the British as evidence that Aboriginal culture was irretrievably buried in the stone age. This view proved much easier to sustain in Australia, because Europeans were able to settle here without having to adapt to local conditions by accepting Aboriginal food-gathering techniques and climate-coping strategies, as had been necessary when the British settled the North American continent. Settlers therefore saw little or nothing of value in the culture they had come to supplant in this country, and imagined that they had nothing to learn from the original inhabitants of their new land. The Aborigines came to be despised as a rural pest, whereas the First Nations of North America and the New Zealand Maori were admired and feared as brave and noble exemplars of an admirable warrior culture.

Why did the closeness of Aboriginal links with the land escape the notice of early settlers? How did the British come to be so blind as to be unable to recognise that Aborigines were connected with their tribal territories by religious and psychic ties that were qualitatively different from those of other native peoples whose lands they had taken? It is too easy to escape into the realm of racial stereotyping and cultural defamation at this point and to dismiss the British people as a race of predatory thugs usurping Aboriginal lands, regardless of the consequences of such freebooting behaviour. The record shows that this would produce an historical distortion out of all contact with reality. But well-intentioned British administrators and statesmen did quite genuinely believe that Aboriginal links with the land were of such a nature as not to amount to ownership in the eyes of Europeans.

The British regarded Australia as *terra nullius*, a land owned by no one, and therefore capable of being claimed by any power that was prepared to utilise the land for farming. This doctrine never meant that the British claimed that the continent was uninhabited. From Dampier's visit onwards, European navigators had met with and studied the Aborigines and, in 1770, James Cook had even pronounced them happier than Europeans. The key to understanding the British official view lies in the criteria generally accepted throughout Europe in the eighteenth and early nineteenth centuries of what constituted an effective occupation by a nation of its territories. In this question, the primacy accorded to agriculture was paramount. European jurists agreed that God had intended that mankind should populate the earth, but how was an increasing population to be fed except through agriculture?

As the population of the world increased, more and more land would be needed for agriculture to maintain the increase, and when agricultural nations became too confined at home, they had a right to move into parts of the world where the land was not being tilled for crops and to appropriate that 'waste land' for their own use. A way of life such as that of Australia's Aborigines was believed to be against God's will because hunting animals and gathering fruits and seeds involved too great an expanse of territory. Agriculture gave a nation title to its territory, and the lack of agriculture similarly was taken to show that the land, although it might be occupied, was not owned by the occupiers if they merely wandered over the surface of the country and did not exploit it in recognisably European ways. Wherever the British encountered native peoples who engaged in agriculture, they went through a treaty-signing protocol that recognised that ownership of the land lay in the hands of the indigenes. North America and New Zealand are cases in point. Australia became an exception to this practice because Aborigines already knew that agriculture was an insecure basis for a long-term sustainable life-style in a country so at the mercy of El Niño.

Thus it was that when Europeans came to settle Australia, they were sent by a government that firmly believed that the Aborigines did not own their lands, and that therefore treaties of occupation with the native inhabitants of the continent were not necessary to secure title. The way of life that had evolved over more than 60 000 years of unbroken occupation in Australia was not recognised as constituting an effective ownership of the continent. The Aboriginal rejection of agriculture as a way of life meant that they were regarded as nomadic occupiers of the country but not its lawful possessors. Herein can be found the seeds of more than two centuries of conflict between Blacks and Whites in Australia, concerning who owned the country then and who owns the country now. And flowing from that is the question of whether any form of legal or moral obligation exists for the descendants of the Whites to apologise to, and to compensate, the descendants of the Blacks for the invasion and loss of their country after 1788.

2

In Search of
the Great South Land

Although the earliest non-indigenous visitors to Australia were Indonesian fishermen, there is some evidence that European explorers arrived only a century or so later. Recent work in the area of historical geography indicates a possibility that the Portuguese might well have been the first of the Europeans to discover the continent. There is speculation that the Portuguese undertook a secret voyage of discovery around 1524 that resulted in their mapping the eastern coastline. If this speculation proves to be well founded, the Portuguese deserve the credit for the courage and vision they demonstrated.[1]

European nations were interested in discovering the Great South Land that they believed existed in this region of the world. *Terra Australis Incognita* ('the Unknown South Land') had been the name given to this country of the imagination, and a belief in its existence became a commonplace assumption of most educated Europeans in the sixteenth, seventeenth, and eighteenth centuries. Speculation blossomed concerning the value of such a land because of the latitudes in which it was presumed to lie. Scholars surmised that if lands in similar latitudes in known parts of the world were fertile and temperate, these characteristics would be shared by a land in the same latitudes in the unknown southern hemisphere. Moreover, since the time of Marco Polo, European venality had been whetted by rumours of an unknown southern continent of staggering riches. It was therefore not surprising that, as European nations took increasingly to the sea over the next few centuries in the search for empire, trade, and plunder, Portugal, Holland, Spain, France, and England all made attempts to discover and claim this unknown southern continent. It was not until James Cook's second expedition (1772–75) that the myth of the Great South Land was finally laid to rest. But before then considerable exploration activity by the rival European powers, especially the Spanish and the Dutch, slowly established the existence of the Australian continent.

The English

England, although a comparatively late starter in the search for overseas empire, had also expressed an early interest in discovering the Great South Land. Vincent Harlow claims that the instructions drawn up for Sir Francis Drake's famous circumnavigation in 1577 originally envisaged that he would enter the Pacific, search for *Terra Australis Incognita* and claim it for England. Drake converted this ambitious and far-sighted plan into a piratical expedition in search of Spanish plunder and, in this latter aim, proved eminently successful. Future English expeditions into the Pacific region tended to be voyages in search of loot, although both Cavendish in 1586 and Hawkins in 1593 also hoped to discover the Great South Land.[2] Their efforts were in vain, and it was not until the wreck of the *Triall* early in the seventeenth century, and then William Dampier's successful landing on the west coast of Australia in 1688, that Englishmen actually set foot on Australian soil.

In 1622, the English ship the *Triall* was wrecked, out of sight of the land, on a reef to the north-east of the Monte Bello Islands—thereby becoming the first confirmed European vessel to come to grief on the Australian coastline. Forty-six of the crew reached the Dutch colony of Batavia, but another ninety seamen were abandoned on the wreck and also became the forerunners of many who found an early grave on the rugged shores of New Holland. The English did not reappear in Australian waters until the

William Dampier. (Australian History Museum, Macquarie University)

buccaneer adventurer, William Dampier, decided to forgo the pleasures of roaming the Spanish Main and, in 1685, joined the *Cygnet* under the command of Captain Swan. When they failed in their plan to intercept the rich Manilla galleons carrying spices and treasure to Spanish America, the crew deposed Captain Swan and marooned him, before sailing off under Dampier's command to the South China and Java seas. Eventually, they reached the west coast of New Holland where the ship was careened in a lonely inlet. The *Cygnet* lay beached for about six weeks, and Dampier became the first European to spend a prolonged period in New Holland and to survive to write about it. His impressions of the land and its people were anything but favourable. He described the land as being dry, sandy, and destitute of water, and stated that there were no animals for food and that the sea was not plentifully stocked with fish. The people of the country were so primitive that, in Dampier's view, setting aside their human shape, 'they differ but little from Brutes'.[3]

A useless country?

Dampier's voyages served to reinforce the view made public by the Dutch that nothing advantageous was to be gained from New Holland and that its climate and terrain rendered it obviously unsuitable for settlement. Such a conclusion derived from men with a first-hand experience of the inhospitable west coast of the continent, but they did not succeed in persuading everybody that

New Holland had nothing to offer. This conflict between theory and practical experience can be witnessed in the next episode of Australian contact with Europe, an example that was to be repeated many times during the colonial period when the work of speculative theorists appeared to contradict the experience of those with first-hand knowledge.

The sheer size of Australia led geographers to doubt whether the observations made by explorers were typical of the country as a whole. After all, Australia lay in latitudes that, in the known parts of the world, had produced regions renowned for their fertility and mineral wealth. How could New Holland be different? Mariners had seen only a very small portion of the continent and might have viewed unrepresentative tracts of territory. Jean Pierre Purry, a Swiss writer, perpetuated this belief in the 1720s when he published a proposal to establish a colony in a portion of South Australia visited by the Dutch explorer Peter Nuyts in 1627, and named Nuytsland after himself. Purry's scheme had originally been addressed to his employer, the Dutch East India Company but, in the face of its uninterest, Purry also attempted to persuade both the French and the English.[4] His argument based on climatic analogy was a powerful one, and it continued to affect both official and private British attitudes towards Australia by making them unrealistically optimistic until well into the nineteenth century. Purry's ideas passed into the conventional wisdom of the age, and arguments based on geographical analogy and climate that favoured the colonisation of New Holland appeared in a variety of European languages around the middle of the eighteenth century.

British–French rivalry

As the eighteenth century unfolded, the quickening French and British interest in *Terra Australis* can be situated within the wider imperial rivalry between the great powers of Europe. For hundreds of years Britain's traditional enemy in Europe had been France, or the alliance between France and Spain. Centuries of warfare and dispute had resulted in a deep distrust between Britain and France, and national antagonisms ran deep. European great power rivalries had been transferred to the New World and, in America, the West Indies, and India itself, the British found themselves confronted and confined by their old enemy, France. Anglo–French wars were endemic during the seventeenth and eighteenth centuries, and the periods of peace between hostilities were regarded by both sides as mere truces in a continuing battle for supremacy that either would resume whenever advantage beckoned.

One of the major episodes in this incessant warfare, an episode that had profound significance for the British settlement of Australia, began in the early months of 1756 when the French attacked British-held Minorca. The Seven Years War followed. Unlike earlier wars European nations had fought with one another, the Seven Years War was ominously 'modern'. It was a global conflict. Fighting took place on the soil of Europe, America, India, the West Indies, and the Philippines. As a result of Britain's victory in that war, the strategic balance of power was temporarily altered heavily in Britain's favour. France lost most of her North American possessions and considerable territory in India to Britain but, more importantly, the British emerged from the war with unparalleled naval superiority over France, Spain, and all other European powers. Moreover, the defeat of both France and Spain had been so complete that for a time, Britain was freed from the usual concern to match the French presence in all parts of the globe, and was able to turn her attention to breaking into the Pacific and disputing Spain's claims to complete control over the area. The lure of the Great South Land and the riches of India and the South Seas proved to be potent magnets in what historians have come to describe as the Swing to the East by the great powers of Europe.[5]

Despite their recent heavy defeats, the French and the Spanish were not about to defer to Britain or to hand the Pacific region over to British control without a struggle. The Spanish withheld all cooperation from the British and, during the final decades of the eighteenth century, dispatched a series of expeditions to shadow British explorers and to check up on their activities. The French launched a series of voyages led by famous mariners such as Bougainville, d'Urville, Marion Dufresne, St Allouarn, and La Perouse; and the British were represented by Anson, Byron, Carteret, Wallace, and the incomparable James Cook. It was Cook's first expedition aboard HMS *Endeavour* which, in 1770, finally brought a representative of one of these imperial rivals to the eastern coastline of Australia. Cook promptly annexed and claimed the territory on behalf of his sovereign, George III, under the name of New South Wales. But the French were not too far behind and, in 1772, the explorer St Allouarn aboard his ship the *Gros Ventre* made landfall at Turtle Bay on the western coast of Australia and claimed the country in the name of the French monarch, Louis XVI.[6]

James Cook

The ostensible reason for the voyage led by James Cook was to convey a party of scientists—members of the prestigious Royal Society—to Tahiti where they could observe the rare astronomical phenomenon of the transit of the planet Venus across the face of the sun. The British Admiralty, however, refused to allow the expedition to be commanded by Alexander Dalrymple, an experienced hydrographer employed by the British East India Company and well known for his speculative writings on the subject of the Great South Land, despite Dalrymple's being the leader chosen by the Royal Society. Instead, the Admiralty insisted on appointing a royal naval officer, the newly commissioned Lieutenant James Cook, to his first command aboard HMS *Endeavour*. Cook, the son of a Yorkshire labourer, had earlier worked on the ships carrying coal along the English coast, before joining the Royal Navy as an able seaman. Despite his lack of connections and his humble origins, his abilities soon brought him to

James Cook proclaims New South Wales to be British territory in 1770. (Australian History Museum, Macquarie University)

prominence during the Seven Years War, and it was Cook who charted the St Lawrence River in Canada and then piloted General Wolfe's successful expedition up the river to capture Quebec from the French.

Nevertheless, why did the Royal Navy overlook a senior and experienced mariner such as Dalrymple in favour of the junior and comparatively unknown Cook? Perhaps part of the explanation might lie in the public reputations of both men. Alexander Dalrymple was a widely recognised publicist and enthusiast for expanding Britain's empire in the Far East. He also favoured the discovery and exploitation of the Great South Land by Britain. Confirmation of his appointment to lead the expedition would have amounted to an unmistakable signal to France and Spain that England was embarking upon a program of territorial expansion in the South Seas. Thus forewarned, England's enemies could have mounted their own expeditions to frustrate and pre-empt British plans. The appointment of an unknown junior lieutenant to command the expedition effectively played down the territorial aspect of the voyage and concentrated attention on the scientific events associated with the transit of Venus. Cook, however, received secret instructions that, when the astronomers had finished their work on Tahiti, he was to search for and claim the Great South Land for Britain. Secret written instructions on this point were given to Cook and are available in the records. It is also known that the British Admiralty had given earlier mariners such as Commodore Anson secret oral instructions relating to territorial claims in the Pacific. A combination of reasons like this could well explain Cook's annexation of New South Wales in 1770.[7] What is certain, is that junior lieutenants in the Royal Navy did not blithely wander around the globe annexing countries 'willy-nilly'—not if they were hopeful of any sort of a career in the navy.

Certainly the Spanish showed alarm at Cook's activities, and the French had already embarked upon a series of explorations in the South Seas. In 1768 Cook left on his first voyage of exploration and, in that same year, a French expedition under Bougainville set out for the Pacific and arrived at Tahiti slightly behind Cook. Between 1770 and 1774, three Spanish voyages were mounted into the Pacific to check up on the activities of the English and to search for the Great South Land and claim it for Spain.[8]

Even Britain's ally Portugal did not believe that the observation of the transit of Venus was the real reason for the voyage of the *Endeavour*. The Viceroy at Rio, where Cook called to gather provisions and water on his outward journey, commented that he felt 'the greatest distrust' that astronomy was the main purpose of the voyage. He felt convinced that observing Venus masked some deeper British design in the South Seas.[9] The annexation of New South Wales demonstrated that Spanish fears and Portuguese suspicions were indeed well founded.

Certainly, Cook's discovery of New Zealand flax and (on his second voyage) of Norfolk Island with its pine trees—seemingly so suitable for ships' masts—was to give added value to his annexation of the east coast of New Holland in the minds of strategically orientated observers in the next two decades. But it also appears that both Cook in 1770 and St Allouarn in 1772 were engaging in pre-emptive annexations in promising latitudes—annexations that were designed to forestall rivals rather than to gain immediately useful territories for their respective sovereigns. Neither mariner could have been much impressed by what he had seen of Australia, and Cook was less than enthusiastic in his assessment of the utility of New South Wales. It *might* prove fertile enough to sustain life, was the bleak response of the botanist Joseph Banks. Moreover, despite the strategic and potential value of both the eastern and western coasts of the continent to rival imperial powers, neither France nor Britain moved quickly to exploit their new acquisitions. The motivation behind both annexations was therefore more likely to be the desire to deny an enemy a new territory that might, at some future time, prove to be worthwhile—rather than the value of any immediate productions of the land itself. Thus Australia became a pawn in the global confrontation between rival European empires, both of which were prepared to claim the territory first and worry later about how they might obtain some use from it.

In 1770, when Cook sailed away from Australia never to return, he believed that his discoveries and annexation were of no particular importance in themselves, and of marginal relevance only in the global context of empire. That the British authorities tended to see Australia in precisely this way, rather than as a valuable acquisition to be immediately exploited, can be gauged by the fact that eighteen years were to elapse between Cook's annexation and the arrival of the first British settlers. There was obviously no urgency to play the imperial pawn.

Britain's preoccupation elsewhere during these years can be easily understood. From 1776 to 1783 she was locked in conflict with her American colonists in the American War of Independence. France and Spain soon came into the war on the side of the Americans, and the hostilities quickly took on the global character already noted in the Seven Years War. Britain was vanquished in the American War of Independence and, in addition to losing the thirteen American colonies, she also had to confront a resurgent France and Spain. The defeat was comprehensive, and the government of William Pitt the Younger faced a serious French threat to Britain's empire in India, while coping at the same time with the urgent necessity of rebuilding the shattered morale and military effectiveness of the army and the navy. Pitt and his ministers recognised that a continued British presence in the East and access to the enormous wealth of that part of the world, provided perhaps the only hope of eventual British recovery. The maintenance and extension of the eastern trade was therefore considered to be a vital component in this rebuilding program.[10] The core of the problem lay in the fact that, in India, Britain came face to face with France in the form of a reconstituted French East India Company. At the conclusion of the War of Independence, the Treaty of Versailles in 1783 had included an agreement whereby France and Britain were to limit the size of their war fleets in Indian waters. But, following the peace, the French government decommissioned a number of 64-gun ships-of-the-line and leased them to the new French company as merchantmen. These sailed to the East without technically violating the treaty, but both sides knew how easily and quickly they could be reconverted to their original purpose as warships whenever hostilities between the two countries resumed.

In addition to the threat in the East, Britain found that French diplomatic activities with Russia jeopardised continued supplies of flax and timber from the Baltic. In 1786 Russian agents, acting with the permission of Catherine the Great, purchased all available supplies of Baltic hemp, thereby securing a monopoly of the British market. The price was forced up by more than 50%; more importantly, Britain's vulnerability had been amply demonstrated. Supplies of hemp for the manufacture of ropes and sails, were as vital to a naval power in the eighteenth century as are supplies of microchips and digital circuitry to a military power in the modern world. During the War of Independence, the British naval squadron in Indian waters had suffered considerable difficulties in remaining seaworthy and battle-ready due to a chronic shortage of naval supplies to repair and refurbish ships damaged in battle. Britain's reliance on an unstable source only increased the government's recognition of the need to gain access to alternative sources of flax and timber.[11]

The road to Botany Bay

This imperial component of Australian settlement follows naturally from the strategic rivalries inherent in the original British and French annexations, and displays a continuity of motive quite distinct from the spur of the moment decision-making that is traditionally associated with the British decision to found a convict colony in its territory of New South Wales. Convicts provided an ideal source of human capital for such ventures, and all European colonising nations used convicts in their overseas ventures. In law, convicts sentenced to death, and then sent to the colonies as exiles, were regarded as legally dead. They possessed no rights until the period of transportation had run its course. This made them ideal colonising material and, if they returned to Britain before the period of the sentence had been completed, the original death sentence came into force. The criminals sent to Australia provided the means for the British government to realise the military and strategic objectives of precluding a settlement by the French, of gaining access to the naval resources discovered by Cook on Norfolk Island in 1774, of breaking through the Spanish pretensions to sole control of the South Seas, and of providing a port of call where British warships could refresh and refit in time of war before sailing off to attack Spain's colonies in South America, and the Dutch and French bases in the Far East. Britain was a world power. British fleets operated in all the oceans of the world, and provided British governments with a global strategic reach. The British government and its rivals had no option but to think globally not locally, and the decision to send a fleet to New South Wales must be seen as fitting into this global strategic perspective. The convicts sent to Australia in the First Fleet were a means to an end, and it should be remembered that, although Australia was settled *by* the convicts, it was not settled *for* the convicts.

The transportation dilemma

This is not to deny that the government faced a considerable domestic problem concerning what to do with increasing numbers of criminals condemned to transportation. The roots of this dilemma went back to Elizabethan times, when various classes of socially undesirable people—the sturdy beggars, as well as criminals—had been sentenced to be transported abroad. Since then, a large variety of capital sentences had been remitted to exile, as an act of mercy. In the later years of the eighteenth century, Britain transported about a thousand criminals a year to her colonies in North America. The prisoners were sold as indentured servants for the term of their sentences—thereby preserving the fiction that it was the indenture, not the person, that was sold. The government was not directly involved in this transportation, except insofar as it made a profit out of selling the indentured prisoners to the shipping contractors, who then onsold them to those American colonists who desired their labour.

When the American War of Independence broke out, the passage of convicts to North America was no longer possible and, as a temporary measure, the British government elected to house prisoners awaiting transportation on old unseaworthy ships moored in the Thames, and at Portsmouth and Plymouth. These receptacles, known as the 'hulks', proved to be considerably more than the temporary expedients originally planned, and remained in service until 1868.

As the American war dragged on, rumours concerning the

overcrowded conditions aboard the hulks abounded. They were mostly wrong, and convicts on the hulks were, in fact, well looked-after and received adequate medical care and attention, but the rumours caused considerable public unease. Thousands of convicts inhabited the hulks, and the possibility that infectious diseases such as typhoid and cholera might break out and sweep through the wider community ensured continued public scrutiny. Indeed, the foremost justification for the establishment of a convict colony in New South Wales in 1788 begins with an expression of official concern:[12]

> The several gaols and places for the confinement of felons in this kingdom being in so crowded a state that the greatest danger is to be apprehended, not only from their escape, but from infectious distempers, which may hourly be expected to break out amongst them, His Majesty, desirous of preventing by every possible means the ill consequences which might happen from either of these causes, has been pleased to signify to me his royal commands that measures should immediately be pursued for sending out of this kingdom such of the convicts as are under sentence or order of transportation.

It is noteworthy that Lord Sydney had expressed such concern in almost identical terms more than a year previously when justifying to the Treasury the proposal to establish a convict colony in Africa.[13] The possibility of escapes and outbreaks of disease were clearly a useful political device when requesting funds for the establishment of convict colonies abroad.

Maintaining British power

Something undoubtedly had to be done about the convicts, and public fears had to be allayed. But these domestic interests fade into relative insignificance when measured against the greater concern to preserve Britain's status as a major power *vis-à-vis* other European nations. The Pitt administration was determined to protect Britain's possessions in the East and to make them the basis for rebuilding the strength of the empire to the pre-eminence that it had enjoyed prior to the War of Independence. An Australian settlement could assist in securing Britain in the East, deny France access to potentially useful naval stores, and put pressure on Spanish America—thus providing sufficient reasons to proceed with the scheme. If, at the same time, the plan also helped to resolve current domestic political difficulties, the proposal was rendered even more attractive.

In studying the motivations for the settlement of New South Wales, care must be taken not to be misled by justifications produced after the decision had been taken. An explanation designed for public consumption and to vindicate a large government expenditure might well be expressed in terms of relieving an urgent and pressing domestic problem. Similarly, eventual outcomes should not be confused with initial intentions. Such explanations would certainly eschew any detailed discussion of the Cabinet's strategic plans and assessments of Britain's strength relative to her enemies and rivals. All the intelligence coming in from British diplomats and secret agents throughout Europe pointed to a combined Dutch, French, and Spanish attack on Britain that was believed to be imminent between 1784 and 1786. British diplomats worked desperately during these years to avert such hostilities until Britain had recovered from the debacle of the War of Independence, and British spies operated in all the main port towns across Europe keeping a constant watch on French and Spanish naval preparations, and the building of new French battleships. One professional spy who drew up detailed maps of Spanish ports in South America for the British Admiralty to facilitate an invasion, and who undertook several clandestine missions in France was a British naval captain who would play a considerable role in the early history of Australian colonisation. His name was Arthur Phillip.[14]

In such a climate of opinion, when the maintenance of Britain as a first-rate power hung in the balance, the disposal of criminals overseas became an insignificant worry unless it could somehow be connected with the overriding problem of securing the survival of Britain as a great power.[15] It is in this context that an assessment should be made of the various plans and proposals brought before the British government for the settlement of New South Wales and Norfolk Island between 1783 and 1786. It was not until the Pitt administration had ruled out other apparently more attractive strategic sites for a convict settlement that New South Wales was chosen, and the clear inference to be drawn from the government's procrastination is that strategic benefit greatly outweighed the immediate problem of disposing of criminals. The convict colony of New South Wales became a reality after 1786 when the British government realised that this large territory claimed for Britain in 1770 by Cook could play the role of strategic outpost to the Indian empire and, at the same time, provide British fleets in Indian waters with useful supplies of naval stores such as flax and timber.

From 1783 to 1788, a series of proposals for the colonisation of Australia and Norfolk Island, either as a convict colony or a free settlement, had appeared for the consideration of the secretary of state for War and the Colonies. In 1783 James Matra, who had served with Cook aboard the *Endeavour*, proposed to settle American loyalists in New South Wales, and adapted his plan, at Lord Sydney's request in the following year, to include convicts. Lord Sydney received similar suggestions from Admiral Sir George Young and the businessman Sir John Call in subsequent years. These blueprints all stressed the strategic benefits that would flow to Britain from such a settlement—the colonies of Britain's enemies could be powerfully annoyed in time of war, the new colony would prove valuable by augmenting the nation's naval resources and, given its latitude, New South Wales had the potential to grow tropical luxuries.

The race for New South Wales

After the failure of two attempts to establish convict colonies in the preferred strategic location of Africa, and following disturbing news from France that the French explorer La Perouse was already at sea and en route to the Pacific carrying convicts with whom to settle New Zealand, the tide of events left the Pitt administration with little alternative but to turn its attention to New South Wales. Haste now seemed to become a factor in the government's behaviour, as it confronted a crisis in Europe and the East, with France moving onto a war footing. The importance of buttressing British power in the East seemed greater than ever, and the use of a convict colony in New South Wales as a strategic outpost appealed to Prime Minister Pitt. By August 1786 it had become obvious that a decision could be delayed no longer. On 21 August Sir Evan Nepean, the permanent under-secretary in the Home Office and a close confidant of the prime minister, drafted a letter to the Treasury seeking the release of the necessary funds to implement Pitt's tactical design for New South Wales. Unfortunately, the Lords of the Treasury—without whose permission no government expenditure could be undertaken—had adjourned for a two-months' break only three days earlier. But so urgent had the matter become that Nepean backdated the letter, and the accompanying document entitled 'Heads of a Plan', to 18 August. With Pitt's support, the secretaries at the Treasury obligingly recorded that they had received the documents in the morning of 18 August, and that the Lords of the Treasury had approved the request for funds to establish New South Wales before they had adjourned.[16]

Thus the origin of the much-debated document 'Heads of a Plan', under Lord Sydney's signature, renders all the paperwork associated with the decision highly suspect. It is a document produced in extraordinary circumstances and deliberately confected for insertion into the public record. It is falsely dated to make it appear that the decision to found a convict colony in New South

Wales had received mature consideration and Treasury approval in the normal way. For obvious reasons, such a document will not contain a full discussion and appreciation by Pitt's inner Cabinet of Britain's strategic position and vulnerability in the East. Not surprisingly the 'Heads of a Plan' concentrates on the immediate domestic problem of easing the overcrowding in the jails with a final paragraph or two in which various commercial possibilities from the Australian settlement are raised to suggest possible offsets to the establishment costs. Such documents cannot be taken at face value, and a more sceptical epoch has become wary of placing too much weight on such a suspicious and prefabricated explanation.

Captain Arthur Phillip and the First Fleet

Arthur Phillip. (Australian History Museum, Macquarie University)

In keeping with its overriding imperial concerns, the British government recalled one of the Admiralty's most senior spies and trusted strategic advisers from a clandestine mission in France, and appointed him as leader of the expedition and governor of the new colony. Captain Arthur Phillip had been employed by the Royal Navy as an intelligence operative for a number of years, and he had extensive knowledge of Spanish capabilities in South American waters—in addition to the detailed information he had gathered in two missions to France where he had reported on the state of the dockyards and the naval stores at Toulon. Phillip is also thought to have carried convicts to the Portuguese colony at Rio during his time serving as a captain in the navy of Britain's ally Portugal. This experience, together with his other obvious accomplishments, made him a sound choice as governor of a new colony with such high strategic value to Britain. Who better than such a trusted adviser to monitor French and Spanish activities in the Pacific?

The First Fleet under Phillip's command set sail from Portsmouth on 13 May 1787 on its voyage of 12 000 miles (about 19 000 kilometres) to Botany Bay. The departure had been delayed several times as Phillip fought a fumbling and inefficient bureaucracy to obtain improved supplies and conditions for his charges. Lower-level officials saw the Botany Bay scheme as a convenient way to dispose of convicts who had become a burden on the rates because age or infirmity precluded their working, whereas Phillip wanted to have convicts who were obviously diseased or insane removed from the expedition. On the eve of embarkation, the seamen went on strike and refused to leave England until they had obtained and spent a special monetary advance on their salaries. They needed the money to support their families while they were away, and also to buy goods for the voyage. Some of the money, however, went in a night of drunken riot and celebration, and the First Fleet was washed out of England on a wave of drunkenness. The fleet eventually washed up in New South Wales with a similar bacchanalia. It set something of a pattern for European settlement in Australia.

British convicts sentenced to transportation. (Australian History Museum, Macquarie University)

Accompanying Phillip were 443 seamen, 568 male convicts and 191 female convicts (with 13 children), 160 marines, 51 officers and non-commissioned officers (NCOs), 27 soldiers' wives (with 19 children), and 9 members of the governor's personal staff. The lieutenant-governor and second-in-charge was Major Ross, the commanding officer of the marines, and Captain David Collins was appointed deputy judge-advocate, the colony's foremost legal officer. The spiritual welfare of the new settlers was under the care of the Reverend Richard Johnson, an Anglican chaplain appointed to the colony on the suggestion of William Wilberforce.

In addition to the regular officers of the marines, the expedition also included Lieutenant Dawes, who had been recommended to the under-secretary, Nepean, as a man with abilities that could prove useful in working the New Zealand flax plant. Among the convicts were hempdressers, ropemakers, and weavers, and the equipment carried included a machine for dressing flax with the necessary hackles, combs, pins, and brushes, together with a loom for weaving the flax thread into canvas. So widespread was the knowledge of British government interest in the New Zealand flax plant that the precursor of the *Times* indulged a penchant for gallows-humour:[17]

> It has been asserted by those who have visited Botany Bay that its immediate neighbourhood produces a species of Hemp of so firm and infrangible a texture, that a cable of it, of the common size used by cutters of several tons, would be sufficient to hold a first rate man of war. It will therefore, become a very proper object for the consideration of Government, to employ the convicts transported thither in manufacture of packthread, strong enough to hang their more unfortunate brethren in England.

The First Fleet straggled into Botany Bay between 19 and 20 January 1788; but Phillip soon became dissatisfied with the site as the location of a permanent settlement. He deemed the harbour unsatisfactory and dangerous, and the provision of fresh water inadequate. To add a spur to activity, six days after the British arrival, the French expedition under La Perouse also sailed into Botany Bay. Phillip had only just beaten La Perouse to New South Wales. Within a few days Phillip ordered the fleet to remove to Port Jackson wherein he had discovered a harbour to delight an imperial strategist's heart—one sufficiently large to permit a large war fleet. As Phillip described it: ' . . . the finest harbour in the world, in which a thousand sail of the line may ride in the most perfect security'.[18]

Perhaps it was also a response to the appearance of the French that Phillip moved quickly to implement his instructions to annex Norfolk Island. Less than three weeks after the first landing at Port Jackson, he sent Lieutenant Philip Gidley King RN to establish a settlement on Norfolk Island, and instructed him to 'proceed immediately to the cultivation of the flax plant'. This marked the first of many such extensions of British territory in the South Seas as Britain attempted to pre-empt real or imagined French threats of settlement.

The military nature of the new colony of New South Wales did not occur as a matter of chance or coincidence. Captain Arthur Phillip received two commissions establishing him as governor of New South Wales, and the first, in October 1786, shows that insofar as the Pitt administration was concerned the military and strategic aspects of the settlement outweighed all other considerations. It makes no mention whatsoever of convicts or prisons, but stresses that the colony must be subject to 'the rules and discipline of war' and makes specific reference to 'towns, garrisons, castles, forts and all other fortifications or other military works, which now are or may be hereafter erected upon this said territory'.[19] In April 1787, a second commission more civil in character laid greater stress on the rule of civil law and the establishment of those parts of British civil government appropriate for a settlement colony. Even so, this commission also contained no specific reference to convicts, and it was not until the issue of instructions setting out the ways these commissions were to be implemented is there, at last, some mention of the convicts.

Foundations

On 25 and 26 January, Phillip ordered the transports to sail from Botany Bay to Port Jackson and, on the second day—now observed as Australia Day—the British flag was unfurled, toasts were drunk, and volleys of musket fire announced to the rest of the world, and to any Aborigines who witnessed the event, that New South Wales was now a British colony. On 7 February the formal proclamation of the colony took place, and Phillip was proclaimed captain-general and governor-in-chief over His Majesty's territory of New South Wales. The limits of the colony were greatly extended with the formal announcement that the longitude of the inland boundary lay at 135 degrees (Greenwich) East, whereas the longitude of Cook's annexation in 1770 had been 142 degrees (Greenwich) East. These extra seven degrees of longitude 'cribbed' by England in 1788 added to New South Wales a piece of territory more than a thousand kilometres wide.[20] If merely establishing a receptacle for convicts had been the aim of Phillip's expedition, sufficient space for hundreds of years of convict transportation lay in the area annexed by Cook in 1770. The grab for thousands of square kilometres more in 1788—to which Britain had no valid claim by right of prior discovery—provides further evidence of the imperialist nature of this undertaking. New South Wales in 1788 encompassed approximately half of mainland Australia, and the boundary extended seawards at least to Norfolk Island.

Early difficulties

Phillip's first task was to ensure the survival of his people. There had been almost a week of raging thunderstorms before the official proclamation and, on the night before, five sheep and a pig from the colony's tiny stock of animals had been killed by lightning. Housing and feeding the populace became the first priority, and food shortages were recognised as constituting a major danger. Phillip had warned in his proclamation speech that anyone who stole food would be hanged and, as rations had to be progressively reduced when supply ships failed to appear, this finally occurred. The failure of the British government to supply the colony has led to the view that New South Wales could not have been regarded as of much importance if its survival was paid such scant regard in England. But the record clearly shows that the Pitt administration did attempt to send food and additional livestock to New South Wales. In September 1789, HMS *Guardian*, under the command of Lieutenant Edward Riou, was loaded with supplies, nine agricultural supervisors, and twenty-five convicts experienced in building, gardening, or farming, and dispatched to New South Wales. On the outward-bound voyage, the vessel loaded livestock for the colony at the Dutch colony at the Cape of Good Hope. Unfortunately, on 13 December, the ship struck an iceberg and became a floating disaster. Eventually Riou worked the hulk back to the Cape colony, but there it was wrecked in a storm. By the time that news reached England another convoy was already being prepared, but it did not appear in New South Wales until well after the arrival of the Second Fleet in June 1790. The Second Fleet brought some supplies, but also brought 733 convicts, nearly 500 of whom were sick. A total of 267 had died on the way out as a result of the private contractors' negligence and greed.

Providing for these new arrivals, together with the existing population, put great strain on the colony's limited resources. Gardening and farming with the equipment and seed grains taken aboard the First Fleet at the Cape proved very unsatisfactory, and Phillip believed that the Dutch had knowingly sold poor-quality grain and stock to the expedition. Furthermore, the agricultural implements—axes, spades, and shovels—proved woefully inadequate, and no plough was to be found in the colony until 1796 when the enterprising John Macarthur imported the first one. In the meantime, the settlers attempted to grow crops on the infertile soils around Sydney with tools that allowed them to make use of only the first few centimetres of top soil. There were insufficient stock animals to provide manure to enrich this poor soil, and the labour came from a convict workforce that was characterised by a desire to do as little hard work as possible on the government farms that Phillip had established to feed the colony. Agricultural returns were poor, and Phillip found himself forced progressively to reduce the rations. The hardships of these early years have produced some colourful anecdotes of settlers eating maggot-ridden mutton and dining out on the haunch of a dog. To make matters worse, the supply ship *Sirius* was wrecked off Norfolk Island in February 1790 and the colony faced severe rationing. The stores contained salt meat sufficient to last until 2 July, flour until 20 August, and rice or dried peas until 1 October.

Phillip dispatched the last ship in the colony, appropriately named *Supply*, to Batavia to procure emergency food. In the meantime, he implemented a series of dramatic policies to eke out supplies. All small boats in the colony were sent fishing each day, and their catch was issued in place of salt meat wherever possible. All officers in the colony volunteered to man these boats every alternate night. The best marksmen among the marines (and even those from the ranks of the convicts) were armed with muskets and sent out into the bush to hunt kangaroos and wallabies. Despite the welcome additions to the diet produced by these activities, the short rations produced their inevitable effects of weakness, lassitude, and sickness. Concern grew apace to keep knowledge of the vulnerable state of the settlers from the Aborigines. The Aborigines might become very troublesome if they realised how hunger-induced weakness had eroded the settlers' ability to defend themselves. Thus the irony occurred of the Aborigine named Bennelong being fed on a much more generous ration than that allocated to the Whites. A week's normal rations proved insufficient to satisfy Bennelong for even a day, and he received constant increments in his food supply in the form of fresh fish and ground cornmeal. Despite these supplements, it was observed that the captive Bennelong often became furious and melancholy through want of food.[21]

The stealing of food became, at this time, one of the most serious crimes in the colony, and subject to severe punishment. A convict found stealing potatoes from a garden received a sentence of three hundred lashes and six months in irons. Moreover, it was ordered that his allowance of flour be stopped for six months— which meant that he had to survive on only two pounds of pork (one kilogram) and two pounds of rice a week.[22] Others detected in the theft of supplies were also treated very harshly as Phillip sought to deter both convicts and marines from such antisocial self-indulgence. Indeed, the colony's first official hangman was appointed as part of Phillip's attempts to crack down on this pilfering of food. In the early weeks of settlement the convicts James Freeman and James Barrett, with additional accomplices, were apprehended stealing from the stores. Freeman and Barrett received death sentences, and the others were sent off to Norfolk Island. As no executioner had been sent out with the First Fleet, who was to carry out the sentence? It was decided to pardon Freeman on condition that he become the colony's hangman. Freeman accepted the pardon, and his first official duty on 27 February 1788 was the hanging of his confederate James Barrett.[23]

The sufferings endured by the first colonists during this early period were great. Captain Watkin Tench commented that the need of the 'lower classes' (meaning the convicts) for clothes was almost as distressing as their other wants. The stores were exhausted, winter was approaching and, by 1790, clothing was in desperately short supply. Tench mentioned the ingenuity of the female convicts in patching, repairing, and salvaging the pitiful remnants of their clothing. Many of the marines were also without boots or shoes, and it became quite common for guard parties to number more soldiers without footwear than with.[24] Such general hardship demonstrates that the colony was quite literally in danger of coming apart at the seams. And to make matters worse, the Aborigines were becoming threatening.

Aboriginal reactions

The colonists were aware of their vulnerability to attack, and the Aborigines must have noticed opportunities. Why then did they fail to take advantage of their superior numbers? The answer probably lies in one of the most tragic episodes of interracial contact in the colonial period. Phillip had been instructed to treat the natives with friendship and to live in peace with them. Cook and Banks had claimed that there were few Aborigines and, because they seemed to be nomadic, it was felt that there was no need to negotiate a treaty with them as had been the normal approach of British expansionists in the seventeenth and eighteenth centuries. The lands of Australia were regarded as *terra nullius*—owned by no one—and therefore open to annexation and exploitation by any nation on the basis of discovery and occupation. Australian natives had resisted the Europeans since they had first arrived. Convict working parties and stragglers were attacked, and Phillip himself received a serious spear wound in the side; but resistance was greatly weakened by a terrible outbreak of the disease smallpox. Early in 1789, observers commented on an 'extraordinary calamity' among the Aborigines. Colonists began to report their finding, in the coves and inlets around Port Jackson, 'the bodies of many of the wretched natives of this country'.[25]

The disease was quickly identified as smallpox by the colony's surgeons, who also observed the extreme susceptibility to it of the Aborigines. The death rate among Aborigines in the area during this outbreak has been estimated at approximately 50%.[26] This devastation of the natives of Sydney Cove helps to explain the lack of any large-scale resistance to White settlement. Phillip had been quick to appreciate that the Aboriginal population was very much larger than Cook and Banks had estimated, and certainly enough to constitute a significant threat to the fledgling colony. Other colonists also felt at risk, and recognition of this deep-seated fear among the settlers has led to an acrimonious debate concerning the possibility that smallpox was deliberately introduced to the Aborigines to eliminate such a worry.[27] British military officials are known to have discussed such a use of biological weaponry in the American colonies during the Pontiac Wars, and it cannot be entirely ruled out in New South Wales. Once the disease had swept through the Aborigines of the Port Jackson region, the dispirited remnant was no longer capable of being more than an occasional nuisance to the spread

Bennelong. (Australian History Museum, Macquarie University)

of settlement. Certainly, they were unable to threaten its survival.

Aboriginal people developed a variety of responses in their attempts to cope with the European presence. Resistance fighters were led by the warrior Pemulwuy and his son Tedbury, among others, and their raids terrified colonists who established their small properties along the banks of the Hawkesbury River. Some Aborigines, such as Bennelong, collaborated with the Europeans and attempted to ingratiate themselves by cooperating with the newcomers. Bennelong eventually travelled to Britain with Arthur Phillip in 1792 where he was treated kindly and introduced to George III. He also became something of an outcast and ended being rejected by both Blacks and Whites. Some, such as Colbey, practised a form of mediation between the races, by which he became trusted by the Whites yet retained the confidence and affection of his own people. Colbey was able to warn Aborigines of punitive raids by Whites, and to impede the progress of European expeditions when they became lost in the bush. Another Aboriginal reaction to the European presence was to use the sexual services of

Aboriginal women in an attempt to assimilate the newcomers—in conformity with Aboriginal law—and involve them in a reciprocal relationship between the races, with rights and responsibilities on both sides.

The New South Wales Corps

The marines who had accompanied Phillip were responsible for protecting the colony from attack, either by Aborigines or by rival European powers. Major Robert Ross, the commanding officer of the marines, proved to be an exceedingly troublesome individual from Phillip's perspective. Ross took the view that the marines were a force of soldiers whose primary responsibility was to protect the colony against aggressors; they were certainly not jailers, and he refused to permit his men to fulfil the role of overseers and prison guards as Phillip had expected. The governor was forced to the expedient of appointing guards, overseers, and police from the ranks of the convicts themselves—with all the obvious difficulties and problems involved in such a procedure.

Phillip's complaints eventually bore fruit and, in June 1789, the British government moved to raise a special army corps for service in the colony. The New South Wales Corps was to consist of four companies of men—each with its usual complement of officers and NCOs. Many of the privates in the new regiment came from the Savoy military prison, and the calibre of the officers was not much better. Among the officers destined to become notorious in New South Wales was a young lieutenant named John Macarthur, who distinguished himself even before the Corps had set sail with the Second Fleet by fighting a duel with the captain of the ship on which he and his wife were to travel. The remainder of Macarthur's life was to be characterised by similar episodes of hubris and lack of self-control, and he was to prove a thorn in the side of many governors from Phillip to Darling.

Rum and the colonial economy

As France exploded into a revolution that would bring military intervention from the other European monarchies and the resumption of Anglo–French warfare, Phillip nursed the new settlement through its difficult first years. By 1792 he could look back on a considerable achievement. Food supplies had become adequate, provision of land grants for free settlers and former convicts had received British endorsement, and the granting of land to officers in the New South Wales Corps and to civil officers was soon to be legalised.

A basic economic structure had begun to emerge that worked with reasonable efficiency, given the endemic shortage of currency in the colony. The government commissary purchased the produce of the colonists and paid for it with store receipts. These became accepted as a form of legal tender within the colony, so settlers could purchase supplies from the merchants with them. Once sufficient store receipts had been accumulated, they could be exchanged for a treasury bill or sterling money order which was accepted by visiting ships as negotiable currency in payment for cargoes of imports. Since initially only the civil and military officers were paid in treasury bills, it also followed that they possessed a fortuitous monopoly over the means to purchase the cargoes of incoming ships. Wholesaling did not violate the code of the officer and gentleman, but retail trading certainly did. Consequently, a number of merchants and middlemen began to appear as retail traders within the colony. The wholesaling officers enjoyed profit margins of 50–400% or more as they grew wealthy on the fruits of this unplanned monopoly. However, their favoured position did not last long and, by the turn of the century, the monopoly had been broken by the retail traders who also collected the store receipts, purchased treasury bills with them, and then broke into wholesaling in opposition to the officers. By the time that Phillip left the colony in 1792 the basic economic pattern had emerged, and subsequent developments during the time of governors

Hunter, King, and Bligh can be viewed as logical extensions of the original structure rather than departures from it.[28]

When Arthur Phillip left the colony because of illness in 1792, command passed automatically to the commanding officer of the New South Wales Corps as the second-most senior official. Major Grose took over and, after two years, his successor Captain Paterson became chief administrator. During this period, before the arrival of Governor Hunter in September 1795, land was freely granted to the officers of government who were also generously endowed with ten convict labourers plus personal servants—all clothed and victualled from the government store. More importantly, John Macarthur was given charge of public works and convict labour in the entire area encompassed by Parramatta, Toongabbie, and the Hawkesbury River.

Convicts working for private entrepreneurs soon found themselves offered inducements in the form of spirits, tobacco, sugar, and tea—all of which the officers had begun to import before Phillip's departure. Because of the association of the Corps' officers with the importation and the distillation of spirits, and their responsibility for the degradation it was to bring to colonial society, the Corps became known as the 'Rum Corps', and its coup d'état against Governor Bligh in 1808 has gone down in history as the 'Rum Rebellion'.

By the time of Hunter's arrival in 1795, the Corps was entrenched in power. Its officers owned extensive landholdings, they speculated in the wholesale trade, they flooded the settlement with hard liquor (which quickly assumed economic importance as the prime medium of exchange on the labour market), and they controlled the colony's courts in their capacity as magistrates and jurors. John Macarthur, in particular, had prospered, and had begun to accumulate a substantial fortune. By 1801, Governor King estimated Macarthur to be worth £20 000—quite an achievement for a man who, only ten years before, had arrived in the colony substantially in debt.[29]

Both Hunter and King confronted the problem of Macarthur and the New South Wales Corps, and essentially both governors proved unable to cope. The use of rum as a payment for labour was the most visible difficulty, but it was by no means the only one. The colony of New South Wales appeared to these jaundiced observers to float upon a sea of rum. No work could be extracted from the convicts without rum and it rapidly became a necessary inducement if a colonist hoped to secure any services or labour at all. For colonists across the social spectrum—from unknown convicts to the judge-advocate and the governors—rum provided a form of anaesthetic whereby loneliness, despair, sickness, and a numbing sense of exile could be rendered more bearable or temporarily blotted out. If the strictures of the governors and clergymen in New South Wales are to be believed, the men and women of the colony sought what comfort they could in those traditional forms of pleasure and relief afforded by alcohol and sex. The consolation of religion came a poor third to these in the early decades of European settlement, and a reputation for alcoholic overindulgence became established at that time. Subsequent generations of Australians have never been able entirely to shake it off.

Convict troubles

Similarly, the convict women of Australia have traditionally been regarded as a vile and degraded group of prostitutes who had no option but to continue an existence of reluctant promiscuity to secure the basic necessities of life. Recent work has shown that the images of hard-drinking and loose women are not really reflections of historical reality, but are elaborate fictions based upon biased and ill-informed criticism by settlers who intentionally falsified the true position to blacken the reputations of governors, officials, and social groups.[30] Generations of historians have uncritically accepted these judgments and repeated them, thereby perpetuating the myths. In fact, consumption of alcohol on a per capita basis was lower in New South Wales than in England. When the role of women in the early colonial economy is subjected to a similar close analysis, it quickly emerges that women were far from the whores they have been painted as being, and that many of them made significant contributions to the economic and social life of the colony.[31]

From the early days of settlement, both male and female convicts enjoyed a reputation for laziness and a poor attitude towards work that occasionally became the despair of colonial officials. Many convicts came from environments in the British Isles where work was avoided in favour of crime. A twelve-hour shift in a factory or down a mineshaft was dangerous, dirty, and poorly remunerated, whereas a quick burglary or episode of pick-pocketing brought a greater financial reward together with the luxury of idleness between crimes. Phillip found such people a most unsatisfactory workforce:[32]

> Experience, sir, has taught me how difficult it is to make men industrious who have passed their lives in habits of vice and indolence. In some cases it has been found impossible; neither kindness nor severity have had any effect; and tho' I can say that the convicts in general behave well, there are many who dread punishment less than they fear labour; and those who have not been brought up to hard work, which are by far the greatest part, bear it badly. They shrink from it the moment the eye of the overseer is turned from them.

Disapproval of convict behaviour was often expressed in moral terms, and never more so that when the deportment and sex lives of the female convicts were under discussion. The prurient interests of the Reverend Samuel Marsden—the Anglican chaplain to the colony—are reflected in his somewhat obsessive preoccupation with the private behaviour of the female convicts and former convicts. His commentaries provide a greater insight into the mind of Samuel Marsden than they shed light on the true state of affairs concerning women in New South Wales. The same point can be made about many of the opinions presented by contemporary

Reverend Samuel Marsden. (Australian History Museum, Macquarie University)

observers in the colony. They amount to snap moral judgments, made by men from the bourgeois and gentry classes, concerning the sexual mores and behaviour of lower-class women who lived by a very different moral code from that espoused by the observers.

Part of the basis for this disapproval lay in fear. The convicts frightened 'respectable' people in the colony both by their numbers and by their clannishness. The bulk of the convicts came from the lower levels of British society, and the French Revolution had shown what such people were capable of doing. Moreover, from the very beginnings of settlement, it was apparent that the gulf between the convicts and the officials who accompanied the First Fleet was exacerbated by language. Watkin Tench reported that an interpreter was frequently needed to translate the deposition of a witness or the defence of a prisoner in the colony's law courts. This was necessary because the convicts spoke a 'flash' language (or distinct dialect) among themselves that was incomprehensible to outsiders.[33] After the failure of yet another Irish rebellion in Ireland in 1798, this problem was compounded by the arrival of hundreds of Gaelic-speaking Irishmen, and the existence of separate languages among the convicts caused considerable unease to settlers and officials who felt threatened by their inability to understand what convicts were saying to one another. Sedition and violence were suspected, and such a view was not entirely wide of the mark—as demonstrated by the rising of the Irish convicts at Castle Hill in 1804.

The degree to which fear affected official behaviour can be seen in the treatment of prisoners suspected of involvement in a planned uprising by the Irish convicts. As early as 1800, the Reverend Samuel Marsden tortured an Irish prisoner named Paddy Galvin from 28 to 30 September in an attempt to extract information from him about a suspected rising. In 1804, the judge-advocate, Richard Dore, awarded punishments ranging from a hundred to five hundred lashes to nine Irish convicts suspected of involvement in the plan. In both of these cases, the men were flogged without being found guilty of any crime, and the 'innocent 'til proven guilty' dictum clearly did not extend to the Irish. Galvin was the victim of a Marsden atrocity, receiving an unspecified number of lashes upon his back, and when that proved incapable of taking any more punishment, he was flogged on the backside and the backs of his legs. This was the climate of opinion in which moral judgments on convicts were made. Riot, rebellion, and sedition were in the air, and attitudes were coloured accordingly. Ironically, the successful rebellion and sedition were to come four years after the abortive convict rising at Castle Hill in 1804 (which was put down easily by the New South Wales Corps). But, in 1808, the successful overthrow of the settlement's government was to come not from below but from above, and it would be led by the officers of the New South Wales Corps themselves.

Fighting off the French

As the tensions that produced these scenes of domestic unrest and excitement built up in New South Wales, the old enmity between France and Britain again played a vital part in British expansion in the antipodes. During the time of the first Napoleon, the French demonstrated a continuing interest in Australia. Maps were published in France naming the continent 'Terre Napoleon', and placing the names of the emperor's wife and family on prominent geographical features. In 1802, Governor King became alarmed at rumours that the French scientific expedition led by Baudin intended to fix on a place in Van Diemen's Land for a settlement. King responded by dispatching a local expedition from Sydney which found the French scientists at work on King Island and ran up the British flag under their noses, claiming the territory for the crown and announcing the intention of establishing a settlement there. King's justification for this initiative to his superiors in London was expressed entirely in terms of pre-empting the French, and they gave their unreserved approval to his actions. Later on, King was also to laud the utility of a second settlement that would enable him to divide the convicts, to secure useful timber resources, to raise grain, and to promote the seal fishery; but these themes were clearly secondary to the overriding strategic necessity of denying the French access to any part of New Holland.[34]

A third settlement at Port Phillip, on the mainland across Bass Strait from Tasmania, was also mounted from Britain to shut out the French. Governor King had mentioned the fertility of the soil in that district and had suggested that the French were also interested in the region. When hostilities again resumed between the two great rivals, the imperial authorities responded to King's prompting by noting the strategic value of controlling Bass Strait.[35] Accordingly, Lieutenant-Governor David Collins—like Governor King, another veteran of the First Fleet—was sent early in 1803 with a party of marines, 19 free settlers and their families, 308 convicts, 17 convicts' wives, and 18 children to form a new colony at Port Phillip. After choosing a site very injudiciously, Collins reported to King that Port Phillip was totally unsuitable for any settlement, and received King's permission to transfer the embryo colony across Bass Strait to Van Diemen's Land. On 30 January 1804 Collins sailed for the Derwent River, and established his settlement on a site he named Hobart Town. Both of these new settlements and the incorporation of the island known as Van Diemen's Land into New South Wales, demonstrate the readiness of the British government to undertake expense to forestall a French claim to any part of the Australian continent. It was a motivation that remained essentially unchanged until 1829 when, with the final annexation of Western Australia, the entire continent passed into British control.

Whaling, sealing, and wool

In the meantime, the colony of New South Wales was beginning to pay its way. Whaling and sealing were the industries that provided the first staples from the colony, and exports in these areas were not exceeded in value by wool until the 1830s. Colonial traders such as Robert Campbell and the former convict, Simeon Lord, diversified into shipbuilding and sealing, and found that handsome profits could be turned from such ventures. The seal skins and the oil were sold in China and the United States, and most of the colonial sealers and whalers tended to establish themselves in Van Diemen's Land because of its proximity to the seal rookeries and the southern fisheries. Hobart quickly developed into the most important port for whalers and sealers in the southern hemisphere. The trade was intensely competitive, and colonial ventures were carried out in the teeth of rivalry from American, British and, occasionally, French interests.

Sealers lived a hard and dangerous life. They ranged from New Zealand to what was to become South Australia in search of the seals' breeding grounds. Baby seals were clubbed to death, the smaller females were killed with lance or harpoon while sleeping, and the large bulls were dispatched with a musket. Sealers often kidnapped Aboriginal women as sexual partners, or purchased them from rival tribes who abducted women to trade with sealers for dogs, liquor and tobacco, iron implements, and flour. Stories abound of the cruelties inflicted on female Aborigines and the unfortunate menfolk who tried to protect their women. On the other hand, there are also accounts of long-lasting relationships between sealers and their Aboriginal and Maori women, and there is some evidence to suggest that, occasionally, Aboriginal women sought out the sealers as a way of escaping from the hardships and rigours of their traditional way of life.

Although economic primacy remained with sealing and whaling, the foundations of the wool industry were also laid in these early years. In June 1798, Captain Waterhouse had shipped the first flock of Spanish merinos to New South Wales, and several settlers had purchased stock from this pioneering venture. The Reverend Samuel Marsden had begun selective breeding with some of these sheep in the following year, and other colonists, including John Macarthur, were quick to follow suit. The colonial economy continued to grow and diversify over the next few decades, despite all the conflict and political agitation caused by the colourful personalities involved in colonial public life at that time. In November 1801, Governor King shipped Macarthur off to England to face a court-martial for fighting a duel in which he wounded his commanding officer. Macarthur swept back in triumph in June 1805, with an order from the secretary of state for a grant of 10 000 acres (4050 hectares) and thirty convict labourers to work it. Macarthur had turned defeat into victory and, far from being disgraced, he had so interested the British government in the economic prospects of Australian wool that the local governor was ruthlessly humiliated and abandoned by the authorities, who obviously placed a higher priority on profit than on loyalty to a subordinate in a supremely difficult position. It would not be the last time that governors in New South Wales found themselves sacrificed on the altars of political and economic expediency, particularly when they became embroiled with John Macarthur.

Governor King had sarcastically suggested that Macarthur be made governor of New South Wales to legitimise the power he exercised in the colony. The full extent of John Macarthur's influence was to be felt by the fourth of the colony's naval governors, the hapless William Bligh.

3

Australia All Over: Completing the Conquest

Governor Bligh

On 8 August 1806, a figure of some notoriety landed at Sydney Cove and assumed the office of governor of New South Wales. William Bligh had demonstrated courage and determination in piloting the loyal crew members of HMS *Bounty* across half the Pacific following the mutiny of most of his crew and the loss of his ship. He had been chosen for the position of governor precisely because of those qualities of strength and self-sufficiency. But he possessed characteristics of a different kind that made his appointment somewhat dubious. William Bligh was also well known as a man with a violent temper, who had been officially reprimanded by the British Admiralty and admonished to modify the insulting and intemperate language he habitually directed at those with whom he was displeased.

Bligh had been chosen, on the recommendation of Sir Joseph Banks, because stories of the intemperate and immoral society allegedly coming into being in New South Wales had begun to cause embarrassment and concern to the British authorities. They sought to rectify the situation by sending out a martinet such as Bligh, who was bound to run up against the well-established and powerful John Macarthur. The latter, however, was a man who would not brook interference from anybody, especially a foul-mouthed, blustering sailor.

The rough edge of the new governor's tongue was soon felt by people of all ranks and positions in colonial society. When his goods were being unloaded on the Sydney quayside, Bligh astounded a local shipmaster with the breadth and strength of his mastery of invective, leading the man to comment admiringly: 'By God, I thought I could swear with any man but I give it up to the governor who should have a patent for swearing as he beats every man I ever knew'.[1] The soldiers of the New South Wales Corps were described by the governor as 'wretches' and 'gaolbirds' and as virtually indistinguishable from the convicts. The officers of the Corps were, in the governor's view, so compromised by their associations with male and female convicts that they could not be trusted with rendering impartial justice in the colony's law courts. The sensitivities of John Macarthur were outraged when Bligh commented that he believed Macarthur had gained his grant of land at Camden by means of false representations to the British authorities, and that he would make it his business to ensure that Macarthur did not keep it. The even-handedness of the governor's abuse of power was demonstrated by his arbitrary jailing of the great emancipist traders Lord, Kable, and Underwood, who found themselves jailed for a month because of a critical (although polite) letter that they had written to Bligh.

By the end of 1807, Bligh's high-handed behaviour had effectively isolated him from the main power groups in colonial society. He did receive support and gratitude from the small farmers on the Hawkesbury—for his efforts to help them when the river flooded them out in 1806—but they were too far from Sydney to be able to render any practical assistance to Bligh when he really needed them.

Bligh had come to New South Wales with instructions to prohibit the use of rum as a medium of exchange. He believed that rum was grossly overvalued, and that it distorted the labour market by pricing labour out of the reach of those without spirits, thereby forcing them into debt.[2] Therefore he attempted to kill two birds with one stone when he tried to bring John Macarthur before the courts for the illegal importation of stills for the manufacture of rum in the colony. He also charged Macarthur with sedition, as the registered owner of the vessel, when the master and crew of Macarthur's ship *Parramatta* landed illegally at Sydney. On 26 January 1808, the soldiers of the New South Wales Corps marched—with fixed bayonets—under the orders of their commanding officer Major Johnston, to Government House, and there placed Bligh under arrest. Major Johnston styled himself 'lieutenant-governor' of the colony, and John Macarthur was rewarded by the rebel administration with the post of colonial secretary of the colony. The degree of Bligh's self-inflicted isolation was demonstrated by the fact that, when the troops marched into Government House, the only person who sought to deny them entrance was Bligh's daughter Mrs Putland. She had confronted the drunken rabble and demanded that they respect the life of her father. For her pains, she shared his imprisonment.

Bligh remained under arrest in New South Wales for more than a year, before giving his word as an officer and a gentleman that he would sail directly to England if he were released, and would not call into any of the outlying settlements. The rebel junta thereupon released Bligh, who immediately broke his parole and sailed to Hobart where his intemperance made Lieutenant-Governor Collins' life extremely difficult until news arrived that his successor Major Lachlan Macquarie had probably already arrived at Sydney Cove and that his moment of vindication was at hand.

The Age of Macquarie

Britain was at war with France, and the British government was singularly unimpressed with officers who mutinied and overthrew their legitimate superiors. Major Johnston's explanation that he had acted to forestall an insurrection and to protect Bligh from the furious masses was obviously a self-serving lie, and the government was determined to punish those involved in the coup.

Lachlan Macquarie came as commanding officer of his own regiment, and the New South Wales Corps was shipped back to England in disgrace. Major Johnston was placed under arrest and sent to England to face court-martial. Macquarie had been ordered to reinstate Bligh as governor for a period of one day before he took over the administration of the colony, but Bligh was not in Sydney when Macquarie arrived, and so missed out on the satisfaction of reinstatement. Macquarie's investigations into the causes of the rebellion found that Bligh had done nothing to warrant the military acting as it had. But he also discovered that personal dealings with the angry and emotional Bligh were a real strain, and he felt some understanding of the former governor's unpopularity among the higher ranks of colonial society. John Macarthur, now a civilian, travelled to England to give evidence on Johnston's behalf at the court-martial but, despite this support, the commanding officer was found guilty and sentenced to be

Elizabeth Macarthur. (Taken from Penny Russel (ed), *For Richer for Poorer*, Melbourne, 1994)

cashiered. Macarthur himself was not granted permission to return to New South Wales until the end of 1816 as a punishment for his role in the rebellion. So, from 1811 to 1817, the business interests of the Macarthur family were in the capable hands of Mrs Elizabeth Macarthur, where they prospered exceedingly well. Elizabeth Macarthur is one of the prominent businesswomen who made a profound impact on the economic development of colonial New South Wales.

When the new governor took office in 1810 the colony had degenerated into a sorry state. The rebel period seemed characterised by a determination to do nothing until Bligh's successor should arrive. It was as though their involvement in a mutiny paralysed the officers, and Macquarie described the colony's condition when he arrived in the most unflattering terms:[3]

> I found the Colony barely emerging from an infantile imbecility and suffering from various privations and disabilities, the country impenetrable, agriculture in a yet languishing state; commerce in its early dawn; public buildings in a state of dilapidation and mouldering to decay; the few roads and bridges formerly constructed almost impassable; the population in general depressed by poverty; no public credit, no private confidence; the morals of the great mass of the people in the lowest state of debasement and religious worship almost totally neglected.

Expansion and construction

Some measure of Macquarie's achievements in rectifying this state of affairs can be gauged from the basic arithmetic of his period in office. The population had been 11 590 when he arrived and stood at 38 778 upon his departure. Cattle had increased from 12 500 to 103 000, and sheep numbers had risen from 25 900 to 290 000. Land under cultivation had expanded from 7600 acres (3040 hectares) to 32 270 acres (13 069 hectares). The area of settlement itself had grown twenty times in size as the governor encouraged a series of land explorations that successfully opened up New South Wales for farming and grazing. Many new towns had been established, and nearly 300 miles (480 kilometres) of roads constructed—not the least important of which lay across the Blue Mountains and unlocked the rich Bathurst Plains to the west. In all, the penetrated area of the mainland increased from 2500 square miles (647 500 hectares) to 100 000 square miles (25 900 000 hectares) during these years. Sydney itself was drastically altered from a straggling makeshift town to a properly laid-out city with wide straight streets and soundly constructed and attractive public buildings. All in all, Macquarie's time as governor of New South Wales was marked by rapid expansion and construction, and yet these achievements were often accomplished in the teeth of extraordinary opposition from the upper levels of colonial society and from within the ranks of the colonial administration itself. The governor's social policies lay at the heart of this conflict.

Society in New South Wales had become highly stratified, and the normal economic divisions between rich and poor were complicated by another set of divisions between those who had come free to the colony and those who had come out as convicts. The free settlers and their descendants regarded themselves as socially and morally superior to those who had arrived in New South Wales as felons, or whose parents had been felons, and they gloried in the sobriquets of 'pure merinos' or 'exclusives' or 'sterling'—to distinguish themselves from the criminally tainted 'emancipists' or their native-born children, the 'currency lads and lasses'. It was considered perfectly acceptable for exclusives to conduct business with emancipists, but it was decidedly unacceptable for there to be any social intercourse outside of business. Former convicts, irrespective of their current economic status, were not considered fit people to hold office or with whom a gentleman could associate. Macquarie announced his determination to break down these barriers in his very first dispatch from the colony and, to this end, he began inviting wealthy emancipists to dine with him at Government House, and also to make them magistrates. The exclusives were stung by this code of behaviour, which threatened their social and political pre-eminence, and they reacted with bitter hostility when they were given the opportunity to attack the governor during investigations held by Commissioner John Thomas Bigge in the final years of Macquarie's time in office.

By the end of the Macquarie period in New South Wales, the convict system had produced a considerable degree of ambivalence towards the colony in the minds of British administrators and observers. On the one hand they admired the obvious progress so readily apparent by 1821 when New South Wales seemed to be on the threshold of a prosperous and assured future. The colonial economy was thriving, with the settlement comfortably self-sufficient in foodstuffs. Visitors to Sydney saw a settlement humming with vitality, for Macquarie had abolished the use of rum as an inducement to labour, and had paid particular attention to improving the morals of the community by strictly enforcing church attendance on the convicts and by encouraging settlers with common-law marriages to regularise their situations. The early days of barter and the widespread circulation of promissory notes had long since departed, and the governor had introduced a makeshift currency for internal use within the colony. There were strict sanctions against any ships' captains found leaving the colony with the coins known as 'holey dollars' and 'dumps' on board.

On the other hand, the popular sense of the convict system as a section of the penal code that permitted great cruelties to be perpetrated against the convicts made New South Wales, or 'Botany Bay' as it was still known in Britain, a byword for degradation and horror. British observers believed that the population of Australia was criminally tainted or corrupted by association with criminals, that the native-born Australians carried hereditary criminality in their blood and that, as a consequence, the human breeding stock of the colony was so corrupted and degenerate that several generations of crime-free lives were needed before any native-born Australians should be considered eligible for official positions.

Convicts: punishment and reformation

Convicts were undoubtedly punished in Australia. They endured exile and the loss of liberty. They were subject to the cruelty and whims of brutal overseers, and they were flogged. But corporal punishment—usually by means of the birch—was a widespread phenomenon throughout all levels of British society and had become a commonly accepted form of social discipline. In convict Australia, the wonder is not that so much flogging occurred, but that so little actually took place. A statistical breakdown of punishment in Van Diemen's Land, for example, shows that most convicts experienced only one flogging during their sentences.[4] Furthermore, a recent analysis of convict society in New South Wales demonstrates that convicts and masters accepted flogging as one of the normal occurrences of life, just as it was in England, and that convicts did not appear to seethe with resentment and a desire for revenge when their masters resorted to the magistrate and the lash in the face of workers' recalcitrance.[5] There was an important protection for the convicts built into the system in Australia in that, from the time of Governor King, it was illegal for a master to order a flogging for his own convict servants. Only a magistrate could order a man flogged and, by Macquarie's time, the maximum number of lashes such a magistrate could order for the unsatisfactory performance of work had been reduced to fifty, and the usual sentence was twenty-five.

Rewards were also an inherent part of the system. At the end of a sentence of transportation, the regulations specified that ex-convicts were to receive a grant of land, together with stock, seed, and provisions for two years, to enable them to establish themselves as peasant farmers. The grants increased in size according to the number of a convict's dependants, who were also supported from 'the stores'. Most British convicts came from the ranks of the semi-professional and professional criminal milieu, known to contemporaries as 'the criminal classes', and the possibility of their becoming landowners was absolutely beyond their reach.[6] Moreover, in the British Isles,

THE CAT.

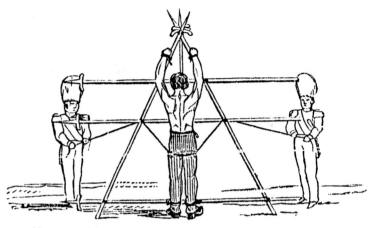

THE HALBERTS.

THE LADDER.

ownership of land carried with it connotations of wealth and social respectability. Many observers were scandalised that the convict system in Australia seemed positively to reward crime rather than to punish it and, by the end of Macquarie's period as governor of New South Wales, it had become an article of faith in official circles in Britain that the governor had erred on the side of leniency, thereby helping to rid a sentence of transportation to Australia of all its terrors. During the various parliamentary inquiries into the criminal justice system from 1812 to 1838, British magistrates and judges continually complained that some felons requested a sentence of transportation to

When the triangles were unavailable, flogging was carried out on whatever apparatus was obtainable. (Figures taken from *Illustrated London News*, 1 August 1846)

Australia or asked the court for advice concerning what crimes they needed to commit to obtain such a sentence. Leniency of treatment in Australia, it was felt, actually undermined the efficacy of British criminal law.

This view was supported by the exclusives in New South Wales, who resented Macquarie's favouring of the wealthy emancipists with social acceptance and appointments. The criticism derived from an economic and social outlook that was very different from that of the governor. The exclusives, under the leadership of John Macarthur, had developed a vision of the future of the country as a gigantic sheep farm involving large proprietors with scores of obedient and submissive shepherds and labourers working for them. Macquarie's implementation of British policies of making land grants to the lower levels of colonial society and to the native-born, undermined this vision because it was designed to make men independent and self-sufficient, whereas the exclusives wanted wage-dependent labourers.

The Bigge inquiry

In the Colonial Office, the secretary of state, Lord Bathurst, had begun to fear that New South Wales no longer fulfilled its role as a convict colony effectively. Terror had to be restored to a sentence of transportation, and this meant a change in policy. John Thomas Bigge was appointed to conduct an investigation into the state and condition of New South Wales, and to make recommendations as to the future pattern of its development. He was instructed to keep in mind that the primary function of the Australian settlements was the penal one, and that their growth as colonies must remain a secondary consideration.

Macquarie had incurred the ire of the British authorities because of his increasing expenditures in New South Wales. The government ordered retrenchment, but this unfortunately coincided with a rapid increase in Macquarie's expenditures brought about by circumstances quite beyond the governor's control.

To begin with, the end of the war with Napoleon in 1815 marked the onset of a large increase in the number of convicts sent to New South Wales. Between 1814 and 1821, 19 000 felons arrived, at the rate of about 2500 a year. They had to be housed, they had to be fed, they had to be clothed, and they had to be provided with work. During these years, however, agriculture in New South Wales experienced a run of continuous bad seasons, with caterpillar plagues and severe flooding

Lachlan Macquarie. (Australian History Museum, Macquarie University)

along the Hawkesbury River. Conditions became so bad for the farmers that they could no longer afford the upkeep of their assigned convict labourers and servants, and returned them to the care of the colonial government. Macquarie could not force settlers to take convict labourers, and so the colonial government had to carry the additional costs involved and find some sort of work for all these idle hands who had become 'government men' by default. Macquarie decided to embark upon a program of public works, which would employ the convicts and provide useful infrastructure for the growing colony. Public buildings such as barracks for soldiers, churches for the religiously minded, court buildings, a female factory for women convicts, an orphans' school, wharves, roads, and the creation of new towns at Windsor, Liverpool, Richmond, Pitt Town, Wilberforce, Penrith, Emu Plains, and Port Macquarie to name only some, were the product of this decision. His projects provided Australia with its first paved streets, fountains, and a lighthouse on the southern side of the entrance to Port Jackson at South Head. He used the convict architect Francis Greenway to design many of these structures, and they were edifices that combined utility and ornamentation in the most attractive way.

The Colonial Office and the Treasury were horrified at Macquarie's inability to curb his expenditure, and they listened to the whispers of the exclusives who proclaimed that the buildings were extravagances that kept convict labourers working for the government when they could have been more fruitfully employed in working on the properties of the exclusives. By mendaciously overlooking the fact that they had themselves returned their convict labourers to government service, they made the dispatch of Commissioner Bigge inevitable.

Bigge outranked Macquarie, and the commissioner and the governor quickly fell out. Within a month of arriving, Bigge had overruled the governor's appointment of the former convict Dr William Redfern to the magistracy, and it was not long before he had demonstrated that his sympathies clearly lay with the exclusives. He supported with enthusiasm John Macarthur's view that the future of the colony should be with the production of wool for British manufacturers, and recommended that land policy in New South Wales should change in favour of large proprietors with capital who would invest it in producing wool. He believed that the convicts, former convicts, and the native-born should be employed as shepherds in the rural districts of New South Wales. There, in the loneliness of the bush, they would have hard labour and the leisure to contemplate the evil of their ways, and this would be conducive to reform. They would no longer be affected by the proximity of evil companions and the temptations to crime afforded by working in gangs in urban centres, as had been the case under Macquarie's system. The new system would amply repay Britain in a very few years with such abundant supplies of fine wool at such a cheap price as to give British wool manufacturers a virtual monopoly in the market place. The convict system would become cheaper, and the sentence of transportation would regain its salutary terror.

Bigge spent seventeen months in Australia collecting evidence, before returning to Britain in February 1821. There he produced three voluminous reports between 1822 and 1823, and these mark the British government's acceptance of his general recommendation that a change of direction was necessary in Australia, and that encouraging ex-convicts and the lower orders to become small farmers should cease. Nor should official appointments be made available to such unworthy recipients. It was symptomatic of the commissioner's social outlook that he never referred to the former prisoners as 'free men' but always as 'convicts'. His attitude seemed to be 'once a convict always a convict', and the view that a convict past implied permanent moral inferiority pervaded his reports. Bigge reinforced existing British prejudices about the tainted population of Australia and refused to recommend either trial by jury or any form of elective legislature for such a suspect population.

Macquarie's recall

Macquarie returned to England in February 1822, three months after his replacement, Sir Thomas Brisbane, had arrived at Sydney Cove. Macquarie went with the warm affection of the emancipists and the native-born who appreciated all that he had tried to do for them. He also went as a failure, as a man who had stayed too long and outlived his usefulness. Bigge's reports attacked Macquarie for being too lenient and a poor administrator; and the man who is known to history as the father of Australia became another victim of Colonial Office disloyalty and the vicious enmity of the exclusives. Very few of the governors before Macquarie, or those for three decades after him, left New South Wales with their reputations intact, and the Colonial Office developed an appalling record of failing to support its own appointees once they were in the colony and embroiled in the conflict between the colonial factions. Macquarie died broken-hearted in July 1824 after fruitlessly trying to defend himself against the calumnies of the

Bigge reports. His passing was greatly regretted by the emancipists and native-born in New South Wales, who realised that an era had ended, and that they stood on the threshold of a new direction that would eventually alter the colony out of all recognition.

New South Wales in transition

Changes in direction, however, do not appear overnight, and the rest of the 1820s was a long transitional period as British policies moved inexorably to implement Bigge's recommendations and to produce a type of plantation economy in New South Wales. Brisbane was instructed to limit land grants to emancipists according to the means they possessed of doing justice—without support from the stores—to a grant of land. The next governor, General Ralph Darling, received instructions that made no mention of land grants to ex-convicts. Thenceforth, land would be issued to private persons in direct proportion to the amount of capital they had to invest. Moreover, an absolute minimum land grant size of 320 acres (129.6 hectares) was introduced—to qualify for which the prospective grantee needed to possess £250 of capital. This effectively placed the ownership of land beyond the reach of ordinary emancipists and the lower orders. A fixed scale of grants to capital came into effect that went up to 2560 acres (1037 hectares) for £3000 of capital.

On the surface, therefore, a clear social and political policy began to emerge during the 1820s—a policy that encouraged the perpetuation in New South Wales of traditional English estimations of the inherent value in land ownership, accompanied by an apparently deliberate attempt to create artificially a colonial equivalent of the British landed gentry. At the same time, and not unconnected with this re-evaluation, the British government also resolved to extend privileges to the growing free population in the settlement by establishing a Legislative Council to be appointed by the governor to advise him. The settlements in Van Diemen's

Land became a separate colony, and civil judges replaced military judges in the colonies' law courts—although trial by jury continued to be withheld from such morally tainted populations.

The convict portion of the population was growing rapidly. Between 1821 and 1830, 21 780 felons had been transported to New South Wales and an additional 10 000 to Van Diemen's Land. Between half and two-thirds of the convicts were habitual offenders who had already been punished for crimes in Britain, where conditions of life for those trapped at the lower levels of society were harsh and savage. Without an adequate police force, or centralised keeping of criminal records, it was common for criminals to be tried under different names in different magisterial districts. It was no more than luck when a prisoner in the dock was recognised as a former offender before the courts and dealt with accordingly. Yet so widespread was crime that the majority of convicts transported to Australia fell into this category of repeat offenders.

The growing population of emancipists and their supporters were soon to enjoy the leadership of an inspirational native-born Australian, William Charles Wentworth, and the outlet of their very own newspaper, partly owned by Wentworth, the *Australian*. They were to show, as the decade unfolded, an awareness and a pride in their contribution to their new home. They refused to become the submissive serfs that the exclusives desired, and were responsible for the emergence of a concept destined to exercise remarkable influence in Australian social and political life from then on—the idea that every White man in Australia was entitled to a 'fair go'. Birth or station in life did not affect this most basic of human entitlements. Secretaries of state, governors, and all those in positions of authority in the colonies could talk all they liked about the privileges afforded by wealth and status, but the colonists began to believe that they too had a privilege in this new land—the right to a 'fair go'. This belief became intertwined with a further conviction that the land of Australia rightfully belonged to the native-born and to the convicts who had pioneered it, and that they should enjoy the fruits of it over and above the free immigrants with capital. W.C. Wentworth articulated this view in the *Australian* in 1826:[7]

> Every young man in the Colony ought to be able to look forward with certainty to the prospect of having his own farm; of being able to settle upon it, as soon as he arrives at years of maturity. He can, on leaving his parental roof, commence in the world with much less capital, and yet with a greater prospect of success than the emigrants.

In this, Wentworth was reinforcing an assertion he had made earlier in the month when he published an 'Address of welcome to Governor Darling' and drew the governor's attention to the resentment felt by the native-born when they saw grants of land 'which they consider their own as it were by natural inheritance' being lavishly bestowed upon strangers with money.[8]

The name of the new newspaper was quite significant because, until this time, the term 'Australian' had been used to denote Aborigines, whereas the locally born White population described themselves as 'the native-born'. Wentworth appropriated the term 'Australian' for the native-born and, by the end of the decade, the term had moved into common usage to refer almost exclusively to the locally born White population.

A rising social consciousness

The fact was that Wentworth reflected a growing self-respect among the lower levels of colonial society. One of the first manifestations of this rising consciousness occurred in 1821, when the emancipists and lower orders of New South Wales petitioned the British government to grant them the right of trial by jury, as well as a parcel of other reforms designed to give them equal access with the exclusives to the law courts of the colony. This entangled the social struggle with the wider constitutional issues and, for the next three decades, ensured a divisiveness and a high level of venom whenever constitutional change was discussed. Trial by jury was granted in 1823, but emancipists were excluded from jury service until 1828. The political conflict between exclusives and emancipists also bedevilled the campaign for an elective legislature for New South Wales and greatly affected colonial attitudes towards the question of what restrictions ought be embodied in the franchise that both parties recognised would have to be granted ultimately.

Wentworth and his partner, Dr Robert Wardell, had provided this rising emancipist consciousness with a focus and an outlet in 1824 when they established the first free newspaper in the settlement, the *Australian*. Governor Sir Thomas Brisbane permitted the newspaper to remain in existence as an interesting experiment, and he also removed all restriction from the official *Sydney Gazette* to enable it to compete on equal terms with its new rival. When news of this reached Lord Bathurst in the Colonial

William Charles Wentworth. (Australian History Museum, Macquarie University)

Office, he expressed concern that a free press in a convict colony might cause considerable trouble and disruption, but Brisbane replied that, on balance, the unrestricted press did more good than harm, and he permitted them to continue untramelled. In time, Brisbane's successor Ralph Darling would find good cause to regret this liberality.

Governor Darling

All this, however, lay in the womb of time when Darling first took office in New South Wales in December 1825. For a period he enjoyed a honeymoon with both emancipist and exclusive factions and wrote to reassure the Colonial Office that the free newspapers of New South Wales—now including the *Monitor*, owned and edited by Edward Smith Hall—presented no threat to public order. In less than a year Darling began to have second thoughts. The newspapers, particularly the *Monitor* and the *Australian* took every opportunity to attack the exclusives and to hold them up to ridicule. Hall described the large landowners of the colony as cruel monsters whose activities as magistrates had evoked outrage and disgust throughout the world. Darling himself did not escape the unpleasant attentions of the press. Personal relations between Darling and the editors worsened, and the tirade of abuse levelled against government officials and the exclusives served only to push the governor into sympathy with the exclusive faction. This became particularly obvious when Darling came under attack for inhumanity and undue severity in his treatment of two soldiers of the 57th Regiment, Joseph Sudds and Patrick Thompson.

When Sudds and Thompson committed a theft in 1826—so that they might become convicts and stay in the colony rather than leave when their regiment was rotated out in the usual way—Darling resolved to make an example of them to deter others from what was becoming a disturbingly common pattern of behaviour. He transferred their trial from the civil court to a military court which sentenced the men to be publicly disgraced by being drummed out of their regiment, and thereafter worked in chains. At a special regimental parade the men were ceremonially stripped of their uniforms and forced to don the yellow clothing issued to convicts. Iron collars were fastened around their necks, and these were joined by chains to irons around their ankles and waists. They were then drummed out of the regiment to the tune of the *Rogue's March*. Although severe, the punishment was clearly intended to be symbolic and was designed to frighten other soldiers who had similar ambitions. But Sudds died a few days later, and the symbolic punishment of military defaulters became, for some in the colony, a different sort of symbol altogether. The *Australian* and the *Monitor* presented the incident as a martyrdom, inflicted by those who believed that the only way to deal with the lower orders was by severity and harshness. That the authorities had received no warning that Sudds was a sick man tended to be ignored, and the governor was maligned by Wentworth especially as a cold-hearted monster who might well find himself facing a charge of murder.

Land policy

While the attacks on Darling came to a head over the case of Sudds and Thompson, there is little doubt that the emancipists and their supporters would have attacked him anyway because of his implementation of the new policies flowing from the Bigge reports. The aspect that most displeased the emancipist faction was the policy restricting grants of land to those possessing large amounts of capital. Emancipist resentment of this alteration in priorities surfaced earlier in 1825 with the arrival in New South Wales of representatives of the Australian Agricultural Company.

The Australian Agricultural Company and the Van Diemen's Land Company were formed as a direct result of the Bigge reports. When the Colonial Office took up Bigge's recommendations that land be granted in accordance with the amount of capital an investor possessed, when it also placed a ceiling of 10 000 acres (4000 hectares) on the size of a grant to an individual (but put no restriction on the size of a grant to a corporation), and when it offered cheap convict labour to work the new properties, the stage was set for the arrival of large-scale capitalists in New South Wales. These two companies were the largest of a plethora of similar joint-stock companies floated in Britain from 1824 onwards, to take advantage of investment opportunities in Australia.

It was clearly the British government's intention to price land in Australia out of the reach of the lower orders, and the huge grants given to these two companies—of up to a million acres (400 000 hectares)—inflamed the emancipists. Darling just happened to be in office when the new policies began to bite in New South Wales, but whoever had been the governor at the time would have come under heavy attack. The Sudds and Thompson case, therefore, provided no more than a pretext to legitimise the attacks on Darling launched by Wentworth and Hall on behalf of the emancipist faction in New South Wales.

Darling and the press

The gulf between emancipists and the native-born on one side, and the exclusives on the other, had never seemed greater. The increasing identification of the lower orders with the country and their sense of possessing a distinct local identity separate from the John Bullism of the immigrant gentry emerged when the immigrant editor of the *Monitor* inadvisedly described the native-born as 'Australians', an expression hitherto used to describe Aborigines. They had become, he said:[9]

> . . . a poor grovelling race, who *cannot* be *inflamed* because they no longer think nor feel like Englishmen; their spirit is gone— the scourge, and the fetters, and the dungeon, and the Australian inquisition, have reduced them to a level with the negro—they are no longer *Britons* but *Australians*.

Four days later, the *Sydney Gazette*, edited by Robert Howe, the son of a convict and the husband of a currency lass, responded in rebuttal of this charge. It referred at length to the honesty, the industry, the sobriety, and the proverbial morality of the native-born; and Howe ended his peroration with the resounding statement:[10]

> We regret to see those violent, and ungrateful, and false attacks

upon the rising generation of a Country, whose posterity will
inevitably be the possessors of one of the most potent empires
that ever flourished. ADVANCE AUSTRALIA.

Edward Smith Hall soon made his peace with the native-born
and became something of a folk hero to the emancipist faction when
Darling brought a libel action against him and he ended up in jail.
Indeed, the *Monitor* and the *Australian* took the lead in attacking
Ralph Darling during 1827 and thereafter—on the grounds that his
cruelty provided proof of the defective nature of autocratic government
and demonstrated the necessity of trial by jury and a Legislative
Assembly as curbs on a governor's power. Darling used the law against
A.E. Hayes, the new editor and proprietor of the *Australian*, and
succeeded in having him jailed for libel following an attack upon the
governor in which Hayes had stated that Darling was so ignorant of
the law, and so ready to disregard it, that he was not a fit person to
rule over any British colony. To the governor's chagrin, but to the
delight of their supporters, both men continued to publish their
newspapers from prison and subjected every action of Darling to
close inspection. Darling's close identification with the exclusives
and his isolation from the wider colonial community, did not go
unremarked in Britain and, in March 1831, he received notification
that he was to be relieved. He felt he had been shabbily treated by
a British government that had failed to support him in his campaign
against the newspapers.

On the other hand, the recall was greeted by scenes of unfeigned
delight among the emancipists, and their newspapers rejoiced at
the discomfiture and departure of a man they had come to regard
as a tyrant. W.C. Wentworth threw a large party to celebrate the
victory and, while the band played 'Over the hills and far away',
more than 4000 emancipists and supporters guzzled gin and beer,
and ate gargantuan quantities of roast mutton and roast beef on
the lawn of Wentworth's mansion, Vaucluse House. The guests
did not note that Wentworth was already beginning to display a
liking for the trappings of wealth and social position or that he

had more in common with the exclusive view of the world than their own. A time would come when the lower levels of colonial society would regard Wentworth as an inveterate enemy who remorselessly opposed their every attempt to secure political advances and a colonial democracy. Darling's recall marks the beginning of a period of transition as Wentworth slowly came to realise that he had more in common with the wealthy exclusives than he did with the now largely landless emancipists. It was not to be too long before the people's hero of 1831 became the proponent of a scheme to establish a hereditary aristocracy of large landowners in New South Wales who would together constitute a colonial 'House of Lords' and protect New South Wales from the unsettling and levelling tendencies of colonial democracy. In short, he would come to be reviled as a man who sought to deny a 'fair go' to those less well situated than himself.

Van Diemen's Land and Swan River

Between 1824 and 1836, Van Diemen's Land was administered by Lieutenant-Governor Sir George Arthur, who presided over an administration that became renowned for severity and close supervision. Arthur shared the military background of Ralph Darling, and implemented policies that were just as unpopular as those of Darling, but the small size of the island colony permitted Arthur to take personal control of every aspect of administration, in a way Darling was unable to do in New South Wales. The outcome of these quite fortuitous circumstances was that Arthur succeeded where Darling failed. Arthur drove the hostile newspaper out of business by publishing an official newspaper in opposition. He established a convict system that became the envy of New South Wales' officials because of his personal control over each and every step in a convict's passage through the system. Good conduct brought graduated relaxation of discipline, but poor conduct resulted in a descent through ever harsher levels of punishment until the unfortunate felon ended up in the hell of the colonies of secondary punishment at Macquarie Harbour and, later on, at Port Arthur. These were not typical of the treatment accorded most convicts and only a small percentage of prisoners ever served time there. Nevertheless, they became bywords for horror and brutality, and Arthur believed that their existence provided an incentive to convicts to behave.

In 1829, the first free colony in Australia was founded at Swan River in Western Australia, although its genesis lay in the historical rivalry between France and Britain. The governor of the new colony, Captain James Stirling RN, had visited the Swan River for a brief three-week period in 1826, and had been agitating for a settlement to forestall the French—with himself as governor—ever since. Between 1826 and 1829, the British government vacillated over the expense of any new colony in Australia. When Stirling suggested a colony financed by private entrepreneurs in a joint-stock company like the Australian Agricultural Company or the Van Diemen's Land Company, the Colonial Office became more interested. The Swan River Association, headed by Thomas Peel, the cousin of the home secretary, requested a land grant of four million acres (1 620 000 hectares) in return for establishing the new colony and sending out settlers. The British government baulked at handing over such an enormous area to private proprietors, and the scheme apparently languished. Thomas Peel went on alone, with behind-the-scenes support from the ex-convict money-lender Solomon Levey.

In the meantime, support for the new colony among those in British society in possession of a modest amount of capital continued to grow. In January 1829 the administration published a set of regulations for would-be settlers which spelt out very clearly the government's policy towards the new venture. It was to be an agricultural colony with no convicts or paupers, financed by a wide range of middle-class investors. The *Times* pointed out the implications embodied in the regulations and the limited involvement of the British government in the scheme:[11]

It is obvious from the terms held out to the colonists, that none but men of some capital are wished for by the King's government as undertakers of the projected enterprise. The state is to be at no expense whatever. The colonist is to support himself and family throughout the voyage and after the disembarkation, and to protect from want, at his own proper charge, any labourer or servants whom he may take out from England.

Land in the new colony was to be granted free of charge in direct proportion to the amount of capital or property a settler invested. All items of property were considered appropriate for valuation as investment capital, whether or not they were useful for agricultural pursuits, and the records of the colonial secretary's office in Western Australia show that some settlers absurdly overvalued their possessions for land grant purposes, and some labourers likewise. One gentleman valued two sporting rifles at £600, and labourers attempted to include the value of their clothing and any personal goods they brought with them. One man claimed a wheelbarrow wheel as a capital investment; another attempted to value a rabbit as livestock. The regulations provided for a land grant in the ratio of one acre (0.4 hectares) for one shilling and sixpence worth of capital. This was extremely generous and, as a result, many large and uneconomic grants were made to individuals who proved unable to work them, whereas others who might have made the land productive were forced to take inferior grants without adequate water or access to market. The larger investors received first choice, and those unfortunate enough to have come to the colony as workers found themselves in danger of starving to death.

The plantation society that had become characteristic of the eastern convict colonies was reproduced in the Swan River colony— the only difference being that in Western Australia convicts had been replaced at the bottom of society by indentured labourers and their families. Social relations, however, were similar in all the colonies. Within a year of settlement, Governor Stirling had established a magistracy and a body of constables to control the labourers and to protect the masters in their rights and property. The situation of labourers in Western Australia was akin to that of convicts working on assignment in New South Wales and Van Diemen's Land, and their working hours and conditions were established by law. Workers were forbidden to leave their masters' premises without permission and could not work for another master in their own time without first obtaining the consent of the master to whom they were indentured. In return they received a limited and insufficient ration of food which did not include vegetables. Scurvy was widespread during the early years. Nor did the master class live up to its side of the indentures. By the middle of 1830, Thomas Peel faced a catastrophe. Peel's management of his and Levey's land grant and his failure to provide adequate sustenance for the hundreds of people he had brought out from England as indentured labour, resulted in the deaths of twenty-eight people, mostly of dysentery and scurvy, and many more of the 450 people under Peel's control were sick with the same conditions. The courts of the new colony continued to enforce the indenture contracts, and many of the labourers fled from Western Australia to seek their fortunes in New South Wales and Van Diemen's Land.[12]

Australia all over

By the end of Darling's period in New South Wales, Britain had made good its claim to the entire continent of Australia. In 1829 a new colony of a million square miles (1.6 million square kilometres) in Western Australia had marked the final stage of acquisition, and Darling, as governor of New South Wales, had become the most senior representative of the crown in Australia. James Stirling and George Arthur were of equal status as lieutenant-governors, and all three men possessed extensive powers. They were to be the last of Australia's autocrats, for the march of events in Britain had finally produced a change of government and the Whigs, after spending decades in opposition, had returned to power. The unpopular and conservative Darling was replaced by a liberal in Major-General Richard Bourke, and the system of land alienation in all three Australian colonies was to be fundamentally recast. Great changes were afoot. Commissioner Bigge had produced the first major reassessment a decade earlier, and he at least had possessed the advantage of time actually spent in Australia. The new voice came appropriately perhaps from Newgate Prison, and from an individual who was destined never at any time in his life to set foot on Australian soil. Nevertheless, Edward Gibbon Wakefield was to bring about a major change in British colonial practice, and to be directly responsible for the stimulus that caused the foundation of another free colony in Australia—a colony that was destined to leave the stagnating and introverted settlement of Western Australia far behind. Wakefield's contribution to Australian development lay in the area of ideas. His opinions reflected the concerns of his contemporaries, and he articulated them in a way that was both stimulating and attractive. His views on the social and economic conditions in England, and the way in which a revised system of colonisation could benefit both mother country and the colonies, were to prove enormously influential in the decades to come.

Wakefield

Edward Gibbon Wakefield was an adventurer. He came from a respectable Quaker family and was related to the prison reformer Elizabeth Fry. Wakefield's visit to prison was the result of his efforts to abduct and marry a teenage schoolgirl and thereby gain access to her money and the political connections of her family. The kidnapping was carried out, but the runaway couple was run to ground in France shortly thereafter by the girl's infuriated relatives. A special Act of Parliament annulled the marriage, and Wakefield found himself sentenced to three years' jail for abduction. British prisons at this time—for those who had money—were places of ease and comparative comfort, and Wakefield read widely. As a result of his reading he developed an interest in Australia and in the possible future open to those of his fellow convicts who were to be transported there. He became increasingly engrossed by the subject and developed the basic corpus of ideas which were to underlie his subsequent theories of colonisation. In 1829, the *Morning Chronicle* newspaper published a series of letters that purported to be from a settler in New South Wales. They were fictions produced by Wakefield to trial his theories, and were later published under the title *A Letter from Sydney the principal town of Australasia.* Here, and in his later publications, Wakefield set out his analysis of the problems facing England and his proposals for solving them.

According to Wakefield, Britain suffered from a super-abundance of capital that kept interest rates too low for those who wanted to live on investment income, and an oversupply of labourers that kept wages at or below subsistence level and encouraged radicalism among the lower orders. On the other hand, the colonies were crying out for investment capital and for labourers to work the large landholdings that men of capital possessed. What was needed was a method of shifting the capital and labour to the Australian colonies where they would be gainfully employed. English investors would earn a safe return, and the labourers would enjoy immeasurably better living standards and a surety of employment.

In New South Wales, Wakefield claimed incorrectly, too much land had been granted and it was too easy for workers to obtain land and then compete with their former employers for a shrinking pool of labour. In fact, few labourers could have afforded or accumulated the capital necessary to qualify for a minimum grant of land, but Wakefield was never one to allow inconvenient facts to interfere with his flights of fancy. As men and capital migrated into New South Wales during the 1820s, the demand for labour soon outstripped the supply of convicts. The shortage of labour in New South Wales towards the end of the decade therefore was caused by the demands of the very immigrant capitalists lured to the colony with the promise of free land and cheap labour, and not by workers becoming landowners too easily. Wakefield's analysis was fundamentally wrong.

In *A Letter from Sydney*, Wakefield argued that the current system of land disposal was wasteful, and he proposed a new systematic method of land purchase, the proceeds of which were to be used to pay the passages of labourers from England. Thus the more land sold, the more labourers would flow into the colony. Land would gain an intrinsic value in Australia that it had not hitherto possessed, being considered valuable only insofar as it could be exploited. By manipulating the purchase price, the authorities could ensure a 'sufficient price' whereby land was always priced beyond the reach of immigrant workers who would therefore be forced to work for the landowners until they had saved sufficient to purchase land for themselves. Land in the colonies would become what it already was in Britain, a measure of social and economic status, and the important social distinctions between owners of property and the rest of society that were inherent in British society would be reproduced in the Australian colonies. The dangerous egalitarianism of colonial life would be corrected and workers would again become imbued with that traditional subservience and respect which they showed to their betters back home. British investment would flow into these new opportunities in Australia, and Britain would find itself relieved of its excess of capital and workers, whereas New South Wales would gain desperately needed supplies of both.

Wakefield's ideas influenced British policies and colonisation procedures throughout Australia and New Zealand during the 1830s and 1840s. This was not so much a result of the imperial government's becoming an enthusiastic convert to Wakefieldian ideology, as it was a reflection of the way in which Wakefield's theories coincidentally happened to approximate the general *ad hoc* movement of British policy in the direction of selling land in the colonies to produce a useful revenue. In Australia, land had been sold from Darling's time onwards, but Wakefield provided British governments with a vocabulary and a system to justify the hesitant move in the direction of land sales during the 1820s. By 1831, an improved system of land alienation and a new governor in New South Wales heralded the opening of an era of innovation and development throughout the Australian colonies.

4

Agrarian Ideology
vs Pastoral Reality

Edward Gibbon Wakefield's proposals received a partial application by the Colonial Office in the Ripon Regulations of 1831, which provided for the sale by auction of Crown lands in New South Wales and Van Diemen's Land, and stipulated that part of the money thus produced should create a fund with which to defray the costs of carrying free British emigrants to the colonies. The new system was intended to rationalise British land and emigration policies in Australia, and it represented an important change of emphasis in British policy, as an interlocking system of land sales and emigration had not hitherto been tried. The Ripon Regulations made waste lands (unused by Europeans) or Crown lands in Australia available for purchase with a minimum reserve price of five shillings an acre. Revenue thus gained was earmarked to subsidise free pauper emigration to Australia.

Revising the land system

The 1820s had been a decade of great pastoral expansion in Australia, and colonial exports of wool to the mother country had become increasingly consequential. In 1821, the year the first commercial export of wool was sent to England, the clip amounted to only 1 754 000 pounds weight (79 632 kilograms). In 1830, 2 000 000 pounds (900 000 kilograms) of wool were sent to the United Kingdom, and exports rose steadily—so that, by 1850, Australia was sending an annual wool clip of just under 40 000 000 pounds (18 000 000 kilograms) to Britain. At that time, this accounted for more than half of the country's entire import of wool.

It is against this background that British attempts to revise the land system in Australia should be viewed. In some respects, British policies seemed out of touch with the economic realities in Australia between 1831 and 1855, and there appeared to be an unrealistic preoccupation with agricultural development—despite the obvious and increasing importance of wool. The settlements of Western Australia and South Australia were both projected as agricultural colonies, and much of the official and the private propaganda encouraging the lower classes to emigrate to Australia stressed the agricultural rather than the pastoral potential of the Australian colonies.[1]

Domestic conditions in Britain undoubtedly help to explain why Englishmen tended to associate the future of Australia so perversely and resolutely with cultivation. What could lower-class emigrants do in Australia—where there was little industry to offer factory jobs—but farm on their own account? Britain had little experience with a pastoral model like Australia's, and the possibilities of jobs in the wool industry did not impinge on the consciousness of most commentators, who also reacted against the horrors of industrialisation by idealising and romanticising the way of life lived in the rural districts of pre-industrial England. The ideology of yearning to return to a golden age of individual self-sufficiency based on farming could no longer be achieved in the British Isles, but it might still be attainable in the Australian colonies. The cult of virgin lands provided Britain with a psychological and emotional frontier of its own to match the attractions of the American west.

Moreover, as a corollary to the feeling that cultivation represented a superior way of life, many Englishmen believed that pastoral occupations—generally termed 'squatting' in Australia—led inexorably to moral degeneration, especially when the labour force was comprised of convicts and former convicts. The widespread dispersal of a morally corrupt population across the Australian bush was a cause for much concern, and the slaughter of Aborigines on outback sheep stations lent weight to such views. Throughout the 1830s and 1840s Wakefield, and Colonial Office functionaries under the influence of his ideas, continued to reiterate the warning that if Australian colonists turned their energies to pastoral rather than agricultural pursuits, the inevitable result would be the establishment within a few generations of 'a race approaching to barbarism'.[2]

The Ripon Regulations

Land policy, drawn up in London in such a climate of opinion, often proved hopelessly out of touch with colonial realities in Australia. The Ripon Regulations were expressly designed to concentrate settlement into compact agricultural communities. However, as early as 1831—the year of their implementation—Governor Darling pointed out to the Colonial Office that it was already impossible to prevent settlers from sending their sheep and cattle beyond the formal boundaries of the settled districts. By 1835, the problem of regulating the massive expansion of the pastoral industry faced Governor Richard Bourke and could no longer be delayed. It had already become obvious that pastoral expansion into the interior of New South Wales was both inevitable and necessary if the colony was to continue to prosper. The Ripon Regulations certainly succeeded in providing a revenue, just as Wakefield had predicted, but they failed as a mechanism for concentrating population.

The potential for massive profit in moving flocks of sheep onto Crown lands that cost the owner of the sheep nothing, and therefore tied up no capital, proved to be too alluring. In 1835 Bourke estimated that more than one million sheep were engaged in unauthorised grazing on crown lands in New South Wales. The flock owners simply moved their sheep to a vacant area of

Crown land and 'squatted' on it by allowing their sheep to indulge in free-range grazing. Already such squatters were hundreds of kilometres beyond the boundaries of formal settlement, and Bourke recognised the impossibility of stemming this flow of men and animals. He could, however, attempt to come to terms with it, and regulate and supervise what he could not halt. Failure to do so would have amounted to an abdication of the Crown's authority over all the lands beyond the official boundaries.

Conditions in the frontier districts demanded that the governor act quickly to establish government authority. The stock and property of the squatters were under threat from the depredations of lawless vagabonds and bushrangers who infested the pastoral districts and harassed the flocks of the larger sheep men. The inability of the colonial government to ensure the protection of the squatters from bushrangers and Aborigines led to a resort to vigilante violence on the frontier, and the *Sydney Gazette* drew attention to the increasing lawlessness:[3]

> In every part of the country squatters without any reasonable means of maintaining themselves by honesty, have formed stations, and evidently pursued a predatory warfare against the flocks and herds in the vicinity.

Bourke's Act

In 1836, the Legislative Council of New South Wales passed Bourke's Act to restrain and regulate the occupation of crown lands. Commissioners of Crown lands, who were also stipendiary magistrates, were appointed. Their job was to protect Crown lands from unauthorised occupation, to enforce the rule of law, to keep the peace between settlers and Aborigines, and to keep track of ticket-of-leave convicts in the frontier districts. In addition, the Act provided that any respectable colonist beyond the formal limits of settlement could legally graze his stock over as much land as he pleased upon payment of a £10 annual licence fee. The commissioners were to be assisted by a small force of police, and were to arbitrate between pastoralists who disagreed over rights to a particular run, and to remove unlicensed intruders on Crown lands. As a result of this Act, respectable persons could now legally occupy Crown lands, and the principal settlers of the colony quickly took advantage of the situation and invested considerable capital in squatting.

It is important to note that the decision taken by Bourke ran counter to official British policy on Crown lands in Australia, but the imperial government approved the device the following year. The explanation for this inconsistency lies in a quirk of British law that maintains that possession of a tract or piece of land for a prolonged period of time eventually confers ownership on the possessor. Known as 'possessory title', this maxim placed at risk Crown ownership of land in the squatting districts. Bourke's Act provided security and a measure of protection for pastoralists if they took out a licence, but the very taking of the licence effectively marked their recognition of the Crown's right to issue the licence, and therefore of the Crown's ownership of the Crown lands. It was an urgent necessity for Bourke to obtain such an acknowledgment, but it highlights a great contradiction between policy and practice in the area of control of Crown lands in Australia. At the very time when a new colony designed specifically to implement Wakefield's vision of a concentrated agricultural utopia was being founded in South Australia, the British authorities approved a colonial Act that gave both encouragement and legal sanction to squatters to occupy thousands of hectares of land—right up to the borders of the new colony—in clear violation of policy and prevailing ideology.

The Ripon Regulations also had important knock-on effects in the smaller colonies of Van Diemen's Land and Western Australia. In the island colony, the amount of usable Crown land that remained ungranted by 1831 was quite small. Thus the revenue potential of the new system for Van Diemen's Land was nowhere near as great as for the mother colony of New South Wales. The import of this situation was that the island colony did not possess the means to pay its own way when the British authorities began to cut back on expenditure of British revenues on the convict system and colonial administration, and to levy those costs against local revenues raised in each colony. But the impact on Western Australia was even more damaging. The application of the Ripon Regulations to the fledgling colony produced economic collapse and disaster. Under the regulations, Crown land was to be sold at auction for a minimum reserve price of 5 shillings an acre, and the revenue was used to pay the passages of labourers to work the properties. In Western Australia, however, the original land grants had been so large, and the population so small, that land on the private market was selling for a fraction of the new set price. Consequently, very little new land was sold, very little revenue was raised, and therefore no new labourers could be brought out to the colony. Without labour the colony could not develop, and without development the land price remained obdurately below the set price. When, in 1842, the official reserve price for land in the Australian colonies was raised to £1 an acre, the gap between the price of land on the official and the private markets yawned as widely as ever. The colonists, unable to bring labour into the colony from England, decided that the only way they could break out of this impasse was to follow the successful pattern set by New South Wales and, in 1847, they set aside their scruples and petitioned the British government to make Western Australia a convict colony.

Educating the rising generation

In New South Wales, the liberal Richard Bourke turned his attention to the question of educating the native-born. What sort of education would be best suited to the progeny of convicts, former convicts, and lower-class free immigrants? The sons of the exclusives usually were sent home to England to be educated as befitted the next generation of the ruling class, and many sent their daughters as well. Could a system of education be devised that would counteract the tainted bloodlines of the colony and the baleful influence of convictism? British education theorist Dr Thomas Arnold, the headmaster of Rugby School, had no illusions that education might become a social corrective for inherited criminality:[4]

> If they will colonise with convicts, I am satisfied that the stain should last, not only for one whole life, but for more than one generation; that no convict or convict's child should ever be a free citizen; and that, even in the third generation, the offspring should be excluded from all offices of honour or authority in the colony.

In 1835, the secretary of state for the Colonies, Lord Glenelg, wrote to Richard Bourke of his belief that 'in no part of the World, is the general Education of the People a more sacred and necessary duty of the Government than in New South Wales'.[5] This prejudice against the children of the colony arose from British perceptions that, in colonising with criminals, the mother country had mortgaged the long-term future of Australia. Education at government expense was to be encouraged for colonial children at a time when such expenditures were not acceptable in Britain itself. The depth of British concern can be gauged from governmental involvement in an age of educational laissez-faire.

Bourke attempted to introduce a secular form of education into New South Wales modelled on the Irish National System. Briefly, the government would bear the costs of providing a non-denominational Christian education which stressed moral training in Christian ethics and, at the same time, opportunities would be provided for instructors of the different Christian sects in the colony to impart their own sectarian teaching to the children of their particular flock. All denominations were to be afforded equal access to the children of their persuasion but, aside from this, the children were to receive a common education.

To his surprise and alarm Bourke found that this reasonable and tolerant attempt to highlight the common ground between the various religious groups in the colony led to an outbreak of sectarian prejudice from the Anglican and Presbyterian clergy directed at the equal treatment afforded to the Roman Catholics. Christian charity was the one thing apparently lacking in this bruising confrontation between conflicting religious denominations in New South Wales. Bourke's proposed rationalisation of education into a single non-denominational system collapsed in the face of the intemperate ranting bigotry of the Anglican leader, Bishop Broughton, and the Presbyterian leader, the Reverend John Dunmore Lang, who cooperated together against Bourke in a 'No-Popery' campaign. Bourke found himself reduced to the inefficient, expensive, and unwieldy stratagem of subsidising the schools of all the denominations irrespective of their enrolments and effectiveness.

Settling South Australia

Cumbersome expedients seem to have been characteristic of British policy in Australia during the 1830s, and the settlement of South Australia in 1836 proved no exception. Established by an Act of the Imperial Parliament two years earlier, and designed as a test case for Wakefieldian colonisation theories, the new colony possessed one of the clumsiest administrative setups ever foisted upon a new settlement. The British government and a joint-stock company known as the South Australian Company—comprising investors anxious to test Wakefield's colonisation blueprint—agreed, after a series of compromises, to establish a new colony in that part of New South Wales that is now known as South Australia. The outcome of their negotiations was a strange hybrid of a colony. It was to be a Crown colony with a governor appointed by the British government, but the South Australian Association was to appoint a board of commissioners to supervise the sale of land and to control the land fund. This board would be represented in the colony by a resident commissioner who would accompany the first governor to the colony in 1836 and divide the administration with him.

The first governor, Hindmarsh, and the first commissioner, Fisher, failed to agree on nearly everything, and each disagreement was treated as a trial of strength. Government was impossible and administration degenerated into a series of childish altercations while migrants flooded into the colony, land speculation flourished, and farming languished. The colony, which was to receive no convicts, rode on the back of a wave of capital importation, as each wave of immigrants indulged in an orgy of land-buying from settlers in the previous wave. Metropolitan land values in the capital, Adelaide, soared. However, in four years, only 443 acres (179 hectares) of farm land actually came into production. In the years 1838 and 1839 for example, exports from the colony earned £22 500 while colonists splurged £505 200 on the purchase of imported goods. Such a situation could not continue indefinitely.

A new governor, George Gawler, was dispatched to South Australia, and he combined the functions of resident commissioner with his vice-regal position in an obvious attempt to overcome the administrative imbroglio. Gawler found the colony in a sorry state when he arrived:[6]

> Scarcely any settlers in the country, no tillage, very little sheep and cattle pasturing, and then only by a few enterprising individuals risking their chance as squatters. The population shut up in Adelaide existing principally upon the unhealthy and uncertain profits of land jobbing; capital flowing out for the necessities of life to Sydney and Van Diemen's Land almost as fast as it was brought in by passengers from England.

The governor's method of dealing with this situation was to spend money lavishly on public works to provide employment for the labourers and to reorganise the survey office in an effort to hasten its activities and get would-be farmers away from the temptations of land speculation in Adelaide and on to their farms. To finance this program of recovery, Gawler drew bills on the South

Australian Commissioners in London. The bills were dishonoured and, ultimately, the British government ended the Wakefield experiment, took over the bankrupt colony's debts, and sent in an efficient administrator in Sir George Grey with firm instructions to reform and retrench. Grey's arrival coincided with a severe colonial recession, the effects of which were felt throughout Australia, and he ruthlessly cut back on public works, forcing the labourers to leave for other colonies or to go out into the bush looking for work on the farms now at last beginning to come into production. Convict and former convict stockmen from New South Wales established an overland stock route to the new colony, and taught the inexperienced settlers the techniques of survival in Australian conditions. Sheep flocks increased, a large migration of religious refugees from Germany occurred, wheat began to be exported to the other colonies and, in 1846, copper mines were discovered which boosted the colony's export earnings. Slowly South Australia dragged itself from the debit to the credit side of the ledger, and it formed an important part of a thriving intercolonial trading network which included New South Wales, New Zealand, and Van Diemen's Land as the 1840s progressed.

Port Phillip: a sub-imperial expansion

At the same time as the South Australian colony was being founded from England, the colony of Van Diemen's Land engaged in a venture of sub-imperial expansion in its own right. Originally settled from the colony of New South Wales, Van Diemen's Land's expansion into the Port Phillip district of southern New South Wales during the 1830s demonstrates the dynamic and expansionary forces engendered in the environment of colonies of settlement. New Zealand also felt the effects of energetic sub-imperialism from New South Wales, as private entrepreneurs such as W.C. Wentworth and bible-toting missionaries such as the Reverend Samuel Marsden turned their attention to that green and fertile land. In both cases, the expansionary stimulus was economic, and informal settlement took place in advance of formal recognition from the mother country.

In New South Wales, reports from exploring expeditions had aroused considerable interest in the grazing potential of the colony's southern region. By the early 1830s, a few overlanders from further north were pushing into the Port Phillip area in search of squatting territory. But the main impetus for settlement of the area came from a group of businessmen in Van Diemen's Land who found themselves restricted by the unavailability of further grazing land, and by government attempts to make them purchase their holdings after the implementation of the Ripon Regulations. They came together in the Port Phillip Bay Association and determined to move their flocks across to the mainland where pastoralism could be pursued without the interference of the Ripon Regulations. John Batman, as the representative of the group, negotiated a series of treaties and land cessions from the Port Phillip Aborigines, which threw into question the whole subject of land ownership in Australia. Did it rightfully belong to the Aborigines, or was it, as the lawyers maintained, the property of the Crown?

Batman's 'Treaties'

For a small collection of mirrors, tomahawks, shirts and several hundredweight of flour, Batman claimed to have purchased extensive areas of land from the Aborigines on behalf of the association. These proceedings caused considerable alarm to the authorities both in Sydney and in Britain. Governor Bourke issued a proclamation in which he stated that Batman and the other squatters in the Port Phillip Bay region were illegally trespassing on Crown lands. In Britain, the secretary of state, Lord Glenelg, rejected out of hand the view that Aborigines possessed any right to dispose of their land:[7]

It is indeed enough to observe, that such a concession would

John Batman signs the treaty with the Aborigines of the Geelong district. (Australian History Museum, Macquarie University)

> subvert the foundation on which all Proprietary Rights in New South Wales at present rest, and defeat a large part of the most important Regulations of the local Government.

Any recognition extended to Batman's treaties could have had catastrophic effects on the administration of land policy throughout Australia. It would have amounted to an admission by the British authorities that land in Australia was not the property of the Crown but belonged to the natives. It would thus have constituted an admission that, since 1788, the British had been freely disposing of an estate that did not belong to them. For these reasons there was no question of the treaties' being accepted. The implications were too overwhelming to contemplate.

Settlers flowed into the newly opened district and, in 1836, London agreed to recognise the inevitable and acceded to requests to allow a formal status to the embryo colony. The site for the principal city was chosen and named 'Melbourne' in honour of Viscount Melbourne, the British prime minister at the time. Captain William Lonsdale was appointed magistrate to superintend the tiny settlement. In 1839 Charles La Trobe became resident superintendent of the Port Phillip district—a role he fulfilled until 1850 when the position was transformed and he became the first lieutenant-governor of the new colony of Victoria, as the Port Phillip district then became.

The pastoral boom

All this expansionary activity took place as a consequence of the pastoral boom that lasted throughout the 1830s. Colonists and their flocks established a presence at this time that dramatically expanded the area of effective settlement, and consequently placed enormous strains on the administration of New South Wales. Settlement expanded northwards from Sydney into what was to become the colony of Queensland, as well as into central New South Wales, and all Bourke that could do was to attempt to license the squatters. He was forced to recognise that he was powerless to prevent pastoral expansion so long as a sure market and limitless supplies of capital were to be found in Britain. In many ways, this inability to control events was characteristic of the British authorities from the 1830s onwards. They consistently accepted, albeit with reluctance, that the inhabitants of New South Wales (and to a lesser extent those of the smaller colonies) could no longer be coerced into settlement patterns that they did not desire— no matter how favourably these might recommend themselves to British armchair-theorists back home. The pastoral boom showed this to be so, and the gold rushes proved it beyond doubt.

Convicts reconsidered

As the tide of free immigration flowed into Australia after 1831, and as it became apparent that the revenue from sales of Crown lands was proving to be far greater than anything the British authorities had anticipated, the realisation began to dawn that convicts were no longer the only human resource available for

colonial development. Between 1831 and 1841, 96 606 free
emigrants travelled from Britain to the Australian colonies, and
this caused observers both in Britain and in Australia to question
the continuance of convict transportation.[8] Convict Australia's
tainted bloodlines were already the cause of considerable concern
and, even in Australia, some exclusives such as James Macarthur,
to say nothing of Governor Richard Bourke himself, felt that free
immigration provided a sounder basis for social growth and moral
improvement of the population.

Meanwhile, agitation in Britain against the system of convict
transportation and assignment had increased dramatically. Much
of the opposition was mutually contradictory, but there was so
much of it that change could no longer be avoided. Some believed
that assignment and slavery were too similar, and that this made a
mockery of Britain's decision, in 1834, to abolish Black slavery if
it still permitted White slavery to continue. Others felt that
assignment failed to deter crime in Britain because life for convicts
in Australia was a life of ease and comfort with a better climate in
a land of opportunity. Other opponents were followers of
Wakefield, and they expressed concern that the continuation of
assignment in New South Wales and Van Diemen's Land gave
those colonies an unfair advantage in attracting migrants and capital
over the non-convict South Australia. They all shared an
indignation at the continuation of a morally corrupt system of
punishment, and an ignorance and unconcern of colonists'
opinions on the question. The high moral ground became very
crowded and, in 1837, opponents of transportation and assignment
succeeded in securing the appointment of a parliamentary select
committee under the chairmanship of Wakefield's disciple, Sir
William Molesworth, to inquire into the convict system. The
committee was made up of known opponents of the status quo,
and condemnation of existing penal institutions and practices was
certain. In 1838, the select committee recommended that
transportation to the settled districts of New South Wales and

Van Diemen's Land should be abandoned as soon as possible, and that the system of assignment be abolished forthwith.

In 1840, the British government abolished assignment throughout the Australian colonies, halted transportation to New South Wales altogether, and directed the entire stream of transported felons to Van Diemen's Land and its dependency, Norfolk Island. A new probation system was introduced that was designed to ensure equality of punishment by gathering all convicts into a number of probation stations where they worked for the government in gangs. Treatment was to be uniform and harsh, but convicts could gain a steadily increasing degree of freedom by good behaviour, until they were released into the workforce as wage labourers.

Gipps and the conversion to a free colony

The implementation of this new policy and the superintendence of New South Wales during its progress from penal settlement to free colony fell to the care of Sir George Gipps. Gipps arrived as governor of New South Wales in 1838 with an established reputation both as a soldier and as an administrator. His time in the colony coincided with a period of economic recession, pastoral expansion, the establishment of a partially elected Legislative Council, and a bout of political agitation that would have overwhelmed most men. He acted with courage and integrity in an impossible situation, and returned to England eight years later with his health shattered after having been abandoned by the Colonial Office in his dispute with the squatters over land tenure. In fact, in the eight years that Gipps spent in New South Wales, he found himself expected to play the role of referee between the landed gentry and the squatters on the one hand, and a growing party of land-hungry urban radicals on the other. The continuing dispute among colonists over land ownership which had begun in Darling's time continued to bedevil Gipps' period in the colony, as did the town versus country antipathies that can also be discerned here.

In 1842, the secretary of state for the Colonies, Lord Stanley, introduced a Bill into the House of Commons for the better government of New South Wales. The Bill expanded the Legislative Council to 36 members, two-thirds of whom were to be elected by the owners of property in the colony from among their own ranks. The new Legislative Council was empowered to make laws for the colony—subject to approval in Britain—but it was expressly forbidden from appropriating the land revenues or altering the Civil List from which official salaries were paid. The straight property qualifications for members of the Legislative Council, and for voters, heralded the end of open conflict between emancipists and exclusives, and it had become obvious that, with the cessation of transportation, the emancipists, in a comparatively short time, would be swamped under the flood of free immigrants.[9]

Gipps and the Legislative Council

The maintenance of British control over land policy infuriated the squatters who dominated the legislature. Conflict between Gipps and the Legislative Council became endemic as the pastoral interests openly attempted to force the executive officers of the Crown into a position of financial dependence. The reserved Civil List rendered this impossible, and therefore became an issue of contention when colonists claimed that it amounted to taxation without representation.[10] It was over the land issue, however, that the dispute between Gipps and the Legislative Council came most sharply into focus.

When Sir George Gipps arrived in New South Wales in February 1838, the squatting boom was in full swing. Prices for Australian wool had begun to fall but were still buoyant, and the boom was fuelled by a constant flow of investment capital from Britain to New South Wales. This marked the weak link in the pastoral economy, for the boom depended on a continuing inflow of new capital, and a series of events between 1838 and 1842 jeopardised this flow. There was a financial crisis in England, a drought in New South Wales, a slump in wool prices, and a labour shortage. As investment capital ceased to enter Australia in significant quantities, the precarious foundations of the preceding boom were fully exposed.

Squatters relied on the income earned from their wool clip for the payment of debt to merchants and suppliers who extended credit to the pastoralists on the expectation of payment from the wool cheque. Wool met the running costs, but the real profit came from the sale of the lambs. The increase in sheep (which were the capital of the enterprise) represented a capital accumulation. When sheep were sold, there was money to pay interest, to pay dividends to investors in Britain, or to pay returns on the original capital borrowed to buy the sheep and establish the station in the first place. The value of the entire enterprise was closely associated with the price of sheep, and while that stayed high, with would-be squatters arriving with capital to invest, thousands of sheep were required and profits were large. But when demand ceased fairly abruptly after 1841, the high price for sheep could no longer be sustained and the bubble burst. Wool prices fell at the same time, and many squatters faced ruin. This economic situation gave an added stridency to the constitutional demands of the squatters in the Legislative Council during the 1840s, especially when Gipps attempted to rationalise the administration of Crown lands.

Gipps and the squatters

The licence system instituted by Bourke was not working. It did force squatters to acknowledge the rights of the Crown, but it also allowed a comparatively small number of men to control thousands of square kilometres of land for a comparatively trivial payment. The squatters claimed that these vast tracts of land had lain idle for centuries before they had arrived, and that by hard work and risk-taking they had rendered them productive. It was their effort and capital that had developed the colony, it was their vision that had opened up huge areas of inland Australia, and it was they who were denied any security of tenure by the Crown's claim to ownership of the land. They argued that they were the economic mainstay of Australia, they provided the exports and the jobs for labourers, and they resented Gipps' proposals to levy financial burdens upon them at a time when their very survival was in question.

Gipps' attempts to rationalise and regulate the squatting industry caused him the greatest trouble of his turbulent years in New South Wales. In April 1844, he published two sets of regulations covering the occupation and the purchase of runs by the squatters. These were designed to force the pastoralists to contribute to the land fund of the colony, and to make it possible for some security of tenure to be given to them. On the other hand, Gipps was attempting to ensure that the squatters did not lock up millions of hectares of land and deny it forever to future settlers. By combining a licence system with a system of compulsory periodic purchase of a small portion of each station licensed, Gipps attempted to give squatters an incentive to improve their runs and to build homesteads on the freehold portion of the station. Unfortunately, Gipps was attempting to extract large sums of money from squatters who had become used to paying next to nothing, and he was trying to do this at a time when they had not recovered from a severe depression in which many pastoralists had been ruined. It is not surprising, therefore, that the proposed regulations aroused a storm of protest from the squatters and their supporters in the Legislative Council. After all, men such as W.C. Wentworth and Benjamin Boyd would have faced payouts of several hundred pounds every year for licences and many thousands of pounds every eight years for compulsory purchases—when previously they had paid virtually nothing.

The squatters clamoured that they faced bankruptcy and ruin, and many undoubtedly did. But Gipps had failed adequately to appreciate the centrality of the pastoralists to the colonial economy of New South Wales. Quite simply, the squatters were crucial to the survival of the urban merchants and financial interests who had extended them credit during the halcyon years of the boom. If the squatters went into wholesale bankruptcy, these debts would not be recovered, and the providers of credit would also be ruined. The linked indebtedness meant that if pastoralists went to the wall the urban merchants and bankers went with them. For these reasons, the city interests opposed Gipps' regulations and fully supported the squatters in their campaign against the governor.

Moreover, Gipps' political naivety was such that he was surprised to find that the labouring classes in the towns and in Sydney showed similar support for the pastoralists. The reasons for this strange and short-lived alliance between urban radicals and conservative pastoralists lay in one of the anomalies of the economic depression—whereby labourers in the city experienced widespread unemployment and hardship at the same time as the squatters faced an acute labour shortage. When Gipps announced that one of his aims with the new regulations was to produce a revenue with which to resume the shipment of assisted immigrants from the British Isles, he outraged working-class urban dwellers who had experienced such devastating unemployment. They refused to move into the pastoral districts because of the poor reputation of squatters as employers who mistreated and victimised their workforce, and preferred to remain in familiar urban environments subsisting on charity. At the height of the depression, several hundreds of them actually emigrated to Chile rather than take up positions offered by the squatters. Nevertheless, urban workers found themselves supporting the pastoralists against the governor because they regarded any intake of new migrants as a threat to their living standards and wage levels.

The final nail in the coffin for Gipps' regulations came from

British wool manufacturers. They lobbied the British authorities and pointed out that Gipps' restructuring of the land system in New South Wales had more than just colonial significance. It could seriously disrupt the flow of wool exports to British industries that had become completely dependent on Australian supplies. One immediate consequence of any stoppage in supplies would be widespread unemployment throughout the industry. Gipps' tinkering with the land system in Australia could, therefore, produce embarrassing political fallout in Britain.

Given the torrent of opposition he aroused, Gipps soon found himself abandoned by the Colonial Office. Successive secretaries of state distanced themselves from their loyal servant until, in 1847, the third Earl Grey passed an Order-in-Council which granted the squatters everything they had demanded in the form of 14-year leases in the pastoral districts plus pre-emptive rights of purchase should the government decide to put the run up for sale. Gipps' regulations were never put into effect, and he left New South Wales in dishonour and disgrace.

The discovery of gold

Isolated finds of gold had been reported in New South Wales from the 1820s onwards, but the colonial authorities suppressed the news. The unsettling effects of a gold rush in a convict colony were too awesome to contemplate. There was also the question of legal ownership of gold or any minerals found on Crown land or even on freehold land. One of the great differences between the land systems of the United States of America and the Australian colonies lay in the fact that in America ownership of land automatically brought with it ownership of all minerals found on or under the surface of that land. British colonies, however, maintained the British system which held that minerals always remained the property of the Crown, even when found on private land. When Edward Hammond Hargraves set off a gold rush in 1851—to the Bathurst district of New South Wales where he claimed to have unearthed some small although promising nuggets of gold—the rush overwhelmed the Crown. By the time that the colonial authorities realised they faced a crisis, it was too late for them to do anything about it. Hundreds were already digging on the field named 'Ophir' by Hargraves (after the field in California of the same name), and thousands more were on their way.

The new colony of Victoria, formed from the Port Phillip district of New South Wales in 1850, faced the alarming prospect of losing the bulk of its population as men streamed north towards Bathurst. To counteract this population loss, the Victorian government resolved to offer rewards for the first payable gold fields discovered in the colony. Very soon, the fabulously wealthy alluvial fields at Ballarat and Bendigo had turned Victoria into a magnet for gold-seekers—who came in their hundreds of thousands from all over the world. In 1851 the population of Victoria stood at approximately 80 000, and a decade later it numbered more than 500 000.

The authorities in both New South Wales and Victoria resolved to license the gold diggers. The possession of a miner's licence permitted a digger to keep whatever gold he found on his own claim. In return for the licence fee, the Crown waived its rights of ownership over the gold. But failure to possess a licence meant that the digger was effectively stealing Crown property and was liable to suffer criminal proceedings at law. The licence system caused great outrage among the miners. The problem was that the licence had to be purchased in advance, it cost £1/10s per month, and it had to be paid irrespective of the digger's success or failure in his search for gold. Miners who struck it rich experienced no difficulty in paying the licence fee, but it became a definite cause of resentment among the majority who enjoyed only moderate or no success. Moreover, the licence system on the Victorian diggings was rendered even more explosive by the excessively low calibre of the police employed to enforce the law. They became notorious

Licence Inspection 1852–53, by
S.T. Gill. (Australian History
Museum, Macquarie University)

for their brutality and corruption and, before long, were the most detested people on the diggings.

The huge influx of population caused enormous administrative difficulties for the fledgling Victorian government. Most of the police and civil servants decamped for the diggings. Those few who remained were unable to cope with the situation. Crews abandoned ship in Port Phillip Bay and headed inland to the gold fields, husbands and fathers deserted their families in favour of the diggings, employers found it virtually impossible to get workmen, and the squatters lost the bulk of their labour force. The effects on the wool industry did not produce the catastrophe squatters expected—because the sheep were shorn in the shearing season, and there were just enough men to look after the flocks between shearings. Moreover, the large gold-field populations proved eager purchasers of mutton and agricultural produce, so that many small agriculturalists found that they could make a good living out of the gold diggings, if not by gold digging.

Life on the gold fields was very hard. Many men worked ten metres below ground, often up to their waists in water at the bottom of shafts that were poorly shored up and that occasionally collapsed, killing those below. Nationalities tended to congregate together, and certain areas became the unofficial territory of the Irish, the Americans, the French, and the Germans. Periodic brawls would break out as the men from different Irish counties fought one another, or the Irish turned in a group on the Van Diemonians. Corrupt law-enforcement officers made regular licence hunts, for the law insisted that a miner must carry his licence at all times, and produce it on demand from a duly authorised officer of the law. The licences were made of paper, and carrying them at all times presented a difficulty to men who were working underground in water. Diggers were often called to the surface of their shafts many times a day to satisfy police demands. Again, men would sometimes accumulate a load of gravel on their claim, and then carry it quite long distances to wash for gold in the nearest creek or river; and the police took a special delight in stopping such heavily laden miners and demanding that they produce their licences. Failure to produce the licence—no matter what the excuse—led to miners, even those who owned a licence, being hauled off, chained to a nearby log, and then fined by the resident commissioner.

Rising tensions

By 1854, the days of alluvial mining by individuals, or by a small group of friends working in partnership, were clearly numbered. There was an ominous switch to deep-lead mining with crushing plants and machinery requiring heavy capitalisation. The miners' realisation of this inevitable tide of change gave an added urgency to their efforts and helped produce a volatile situation. In November 1854, a series of public meetings took place, and the miners formed the Ballarat Reform League, to seek a change in the licensing system and the vote for every man. A domestic issue—relating to the alleged corruption of a local magistrate who was suspected of accepting a bribe in a murder trial—helped to fuel the diggers' anger.

On Friday 1 December the miners—under the leadership of an Irish immigrant, Peter Lalor—erected a rough palisade of logs and withdrew behind it to defy the police and the army. It was a symbolic action rather than a serious rebellion and, by Saturday night, most of the diggers had quietly faded away and returned to their claims. Many were alienated by the increasingly Irish nature of the affair, and others were aware of the stockaders' great shortage of arms and ammunition. Early on the morning of Sunday 3 December more than 400 police and soldiers rushed the 120 or so miners still within the stockade and, after ten minutes of vicious hand-to-hand fighting, it was all over. The stockade was destroyed and the rebel flag of the Southern Cross was hauled down and trampled into the dust by the soldiers. The affair was largely confined to immigrants and foreigners. Not one of the leaders or casualties was a native-born settler. The leaders in the days before the attack were Irish, American, German, Italian, and Canadian; and the casualties were overwhelmingly Irish. It appears that the Irish domination of the movement was so great that many diggers refused to become involved.[11]

In the trials that followed the Eureka Rebellion, as this little fracas became grandiloquently entitled, juries refused to find any of the miners guilty, and the authorities wisely decided to let the matter drop. The Eureka Stockade did, however, bring to light one interesting facet of the developing national character—it showed clearly that native-born Australians would not take up arms for their political beliefs. The large exodus of men from the stockade before the events of Sunday morning indicates a propensity to sympathise with the demand for a 'fair go' from the authorities, but also a healthy regard for their own skins. Events in the next decades were to show that colonists would take up arms to enhance their own individual welfare, but they would not do so in significant numbers for any political or social cause.

Responsible government

Gold placed the financial viability of both Victoria and New South Wales beyond dispute, and removed any remaining excuse for Britain to withhold self-government from her Australian colonies. In all the colonies, with the exception of Western Australia, the general direction of political development followed a similar pattern. The colonial legislatures during the 1850s eventually produced constitutions calling for bicameral systems comprising lower houses (of 'Legislative Assembly') and upper chambers of review (called 'Legislative Councils'). The squatters sought to entrench themselves in power in the colonial Legislative Councils by a variety of devices. In New South Wales, W.C. Wentworth proposed the establishment of an hereditary aristocracy of pastoralists who would become a colonial 'House of Lords'. This self-serving piece of nonsense was laughed to scorn by a colonial populace from whom Wentworth had become increasingly estranged. Derided as a 'Bunyip Aristocracy', the proposal was ridiculed out of existence. Nevertheless, the squatters did succeed in securing a nominated Legislative Council in New South Wales, in which they hoped to withstand the attacks of the urban liberals and radical democrats in the Legislative Assembly. In Victoria, Tasmania (as Van Diemen's Land became) and South Australia, the pastoral élites managed to entrench themselves in the Legislative Councils by means of restricted property franchises. By 1861, all the Australian colonies, except Western Australia, possessed bicameral legislatures with universal manhood suffrage for the Legislative Assemblies, and Legislative Councils with various sorts of restriction based on possession of property, making the upper houses the exclusive preserve of the rich.

5

The Long Boom

The colony of Victoria had been cut from the southern portion of New South Wales in 1850 and, before the end of the decade, a further surgical excision from the mother colony resulted in the formation of Queensland to the north. The British had attempted to renew transportation of convicts to New South Wales in the late 1840s. Anti-transportation sentiment grew in the major cities of Melbourne and Sydney, and the British had flirted with the idea of forming a new convict colony in northern New South Wales. The northern squatters were not averse to this plan, but the population of Brisbane, the major town in the north, was resolutely opposed to any renewal of transportation to the region. Even the bait of independence from far-off Sydney proved insufficient to alter this resolution against convictism.

The area had been opened up originally in the 1820s as a penal station for recalcitrant convicts, and had remained a penal settlement until 1839, when the number of convicts declined and the colonial authorities decided to permit free settlement. Brisbane developed as an urban service centre for squatters operating to its west and south. From 1843 the locals had elected representatives to the Legislative Council in Sydney, but the distance from the seat of government and the belief that local problems could best be solved by a local legislature, had led to the growth of separatist sentiment. In 1859 the new colony of Queensland was formally established with its own bicameral legislature and responsible government on the same model as that granted to the other colonies. It was quite a concession, since the White population numbered barely 20 000.

Squatters and large landowners dominated the economy, and a shortage of labour in the area in 1863 resulted in the importation of indentured Pacific Islanders to work on the sugar plantations of the colony. Europeans were believed to be unsuited for hard physical work in a tropical climate, and the trade in South Sea 'Kanakas', as they were called, became a brisk one. In the next five years almost two thousand Kanakas were introduced into Queensland. The trade was a brutal variant of slavery, and many Kanakas became the victims of kidnapping by unscrupulous ships' captains who found that they could turn a handsome profit by trafficking in human beings. After protests from urban workers who feared a lowering of wages and living standards, and from humanitarians who were horrified at a renewal of the slave trade, the Queensland legislature passed an Act in 1868 to set minimum standards on the ships and to ensure that Kanakas were paid at least £6 a year and repatriated at the end of their contracts. Reliance on South Sea Islanders as a tropical workforce began very early in Queensland's history and continued for the rest of the nineteenth century, eventually becoming one of the major hurdles to be surmounted on the road to federation.

Land policy revisited

Meanwhile, in the other colonies, a new variation on an old theme had begun to cause considerable concern. From the 1830s onwards, emigration propaganda in Britain had stressed the possibilities of labouring men possessing their own land in Australia. Even when the bulk of the immigrants came from the ranks of the urban and industrial proletariat, the lure of land proved most attractive. Land, after all, meant that a person had made something of himself in

Britain, and constituted an important measure of economic and social advancement. Thus, the unwillingness of the workers to travel out into the bush and work for squatters did not mean that they were not anxious to be proprietors of their own small farms and properties. The problem was, that the pastoral interests seemed to have locked up the lands of the colony following the Order-in-Council of 1847 and, throughout the 1850s, urban radicals and labourers found common cause in repeated attempts to make it possible for those without land to obtain some.

From 1856 onwards, the new Legislative Assemblies found themselves repeatedly petitioned by requests that the Crown lands be thrown open to settlement. Indeed, one of the great stimulants to electoral reform and the introduction of universal manhood suffrage in all the colonies stemmed from the realisation by liberals and radicals that the pastoralists' grip on the lands of Australia could be broken only by reducing their predominance and control over local politics. By 1859, political reform in New South Wales had ensured that Charles Cowper, Henry Parkes, and John Robertson formed a liberal government with a majority in the Legislative Assembly. Robertson, as secretary for Lands, pledged to supervise the establishment of an agricultural paradise of small yeoman farmers by unlocking the Crown lands and making them available for selection by small holders.

Robertson's Land Bills

Robertson was both a landowner and a squatter, and his Bills were, in fact, quite moderate. He proposed to make the Crown lands available for selection, but not indiscriminately and not without safeguards. The amount of land an individual could select varied from a minimum of 40 acres (16.2 hectares) to a maximum of 320 acres (129.6 hectares), at a price of £1 an acre. The selector was free to select his land anywhere in the rural districts, irrespective of whether or not it was currently part of a squatter's run. But the

John Robertson, the father of free selection. (Australian History Museum, Macquarie University)

land did not come *gratis*, it had to be paid for at the rate of four shillings an acre on the day that the selection was officially registered, and the balance over the next three years. Land was not, therefore, to be freely available to every urban worker who wanted it, but only to those who had accumulated a substantial capital investment. Only workers and tradesmen who could accumulate the necessary capital were to be rewarded by an opportunity to become owners of land. There was no place for the impoverished in Robertson's paradise, and the plan was soundly based on the middle-class values of self-help and individualism.

Nevertheless, despite the innate conservatism of the proposals, the squatter-dominated Legislative Council obdurately refused to pass Robertson's Bills, and the premier, Charles Cowper, approached the governor, Sir John Young, and requested that he be permitted to break the impasse by nominating sufficient new members to the upper house to ensure that the legislation had a majority. The governor agreed, but the conservative members boycotted the sitting—thereby denying the reformers a quorum and delaying passage of the Bills. Eventually, the pastoral interests reluctantly gave in and passed the legislation. The Bills were basically conservative and could not be seen as an attempt to redistribute the property of the rich to the lowest members of colonial society. Besides, Cowper had demonstrated the essential weakness of a nominated upper house—it could always be swamped by additional nominees if it proved too recalcitrant. More radical measures might well follow if the pastoralists insisted on thwarting the lower chamber of the legislature and, in the final analysis, Robertson was one of them and could be relied upon to protect their property rights. In Victoria, on the other hand, the Legislative Council was elected on a very restrictive franchise, and proved far more effective an opponent to liberal governments for the very reason that its franchise could not be altered without its consent.

In the event, Robertson managed to pilot his Bills through the Legislative Council at the end of 1861, and the new Acts received an enthusiastic welcome by liberals in Sydney. The liberal newspaper the *Empire* maintained that New South Wales stood on the threshold of a new era in which opportunities would abound for both pastoralists and for small farmers. The increasing population would provide ever-growing markets for both groups, and the country seemed set to become a society of property owners.[1] It was this conservative stress on property and the rights of property owners that led the arch-conservative *Sydney Morning Herald* to grant a measure of reluctant acquiescence to the legislation. Doubtless the poor and landless labourers of Sydney were anxious to obtain access to the land, but these enactments did not permit that. Land was freely available for selection, but only to those who already possessed capital, and herein lay the safeguard. There would be no confiscatory attacks on property under the terms of this legislation.[2]

Robertson's free-selection legislation provided something of a model for similar enactments in other colonies, but they all shared the principle of the right to select land held under lease by pastoralists. In 1862 the liberal government of Charles Duffy introduced selection after survey in Victoria—with a maximum selection of 640 acres (259.2 hectares) later reduced to 320 acres (129.6 hectares) in 1869. In Queensland and South Australia similar legislation was passed at the end of the 1860s defining agricultural areas where selection could occur and emphasising occupation of the land selected not just its alienation.

Free selection

The Acts in Queensland and South Australia stressed actual occupation of the land because of the speculation and dubious behaviour indulged in by both squatters and selectors in New South Wales and Victoria. The legislation actually made it possible for squatters to protect their runs by careful selection of prime sections of them. A squatter could select land in his own name, in the names of family members and friends, in the names of willing employees, and in the names of non-existent people. Such subterfuges became known as 'dummying', and Robertson's original legislation made it possible because the Act had assumed that only genuine selectors would make use of its provisions and had therefore not insisted that the selector actually occupy his holding. By careful selection of waterholes, and river and creek frontages, squatters could render useless most of the rest of their runs. This process of picking the eyes out of a run became known as 'peacocking'. The pastoralists were not alone in their misuse of the legislation, and free selectors and 'land sharks' could also indulge in peacocking and then hold a squatter to ransom by cutting off his access to water for his stock. As time went by, squatters also complained about the depredations on their flocks and herds inflicted by impoverished free selectors. Much of the rural poverty and misery so widespread in New South Wales and Victoria in the second half of the nineteenth century stems from selectors attempting to wrest a living from land manifestly unsuited to small-scale farming in a climate heavily influenced by the El Niño cycles of long periods without significant rain. The properties were too small to be viable in the long run, and condemned the majority of selectors to inevitable ruin.

Nevertheless, it would be hard to overestimate the importance placed on the acquisition of their own piece of land by both urban and rural workers. The free selection Acts were amended to establish the principle that the selection must be occupied by the selector in

Selectors' children in front of typical slab hut. (Taken from Jack Cato, *The Story of the Camera in Australia*, Melbourne, 1955)

an effort to eradicate the avaricious speculation unleashed by the original legislation. Even a small holding of forty acres was beyond the reach of many of the unskilled workers and unsuccessful gold miners, yet their desperation to own land was clearly demonstrated in 1863–65, when more than two thousand of them volunteered to serve in New Zealand in the Maori Wars on the promise of free land grants upon confiscated Maori land when hostilities were concluded. Native-born Australians would not risk their lives fighting for the political program of the Ballarat Reform League or the principles enshrined in the Eureka Stockade, but thousands of them enlisted to fight in New Zealand, lured by the hope of possessing land of their own in return for fighting and subsequent garrison duty as military settlers. The men who enlisted for New Zealand signed up for three years of military duty and, in return, were promised town lots and farms ranging from 50 acres (20.25 hectares) for privates to 400 acres (81 hectares) for officers of field rank.[3]

The results of free selection legislation throughout the Australian colonies have been the subject of some debate. The traditional view is that free selection was not successful in human or in economic terms, and that it meant indescribable hardship and drudgery for those families who persisted on their holdings. Children came to be regarded as cheap 'hands' rather than as family, and great tensions existed between the heads of the families and their workforce of sons. The farms were too small to be divided among the sons and retain even marginal viability, so they were usually left to the eldest boy and the other sons either left the land or eked out an existence as rural labourers.

Women and children, like their menfolk, lived lives of backbreaking labour to wrest a precarious living from an unwilling soil. The women became breeders of cheap labour for their husbands, and large families were the norm. Many selectors' wives died in childbirth, and second and third marriages were not uncommon for the men. The only future for their daughters lay in following the same pattern as their mothers, and incubating the next generation of 'hands'. It was very difficult for selectors' families to break out of the poverty cycle while the family stayed on the farm—although, occasionally, some exceptional women like the suffragist Louisa Lawson would just walk off the property while their husbands were absent and take themselves and their children off to the city to start again.

Those smallholders who could not live up to their dreams of independence on their own properties often turned to petty crime to survive, and squatters' complaints of cattle duffing and sheep and horse stealing were endemic in the vicinity of selectors. A few found themselves sucked into a life of more violent crime, and the widespread admiration and support found among the smallholders for bushrangers such as Ben Hall, or Ned Kelly and his gang, caused alarm and anger to those in authority. Kelly and his followers were the product of failed farms, and they turned to predation when the authorities attempted to harass and intimidate them into leaving their selections. Shared hardship produced an 'us and them' mentality that shrewd men like Kelly were able to manipulate to their advantage. In general, conditions of life for most smallholders were such as to produce what one writer has described as a race of 'bush barbarians'.[4]

There were parts of Australia, however, where the reality was not so bleak. In South Australia and in Queensland, free selection cannot be dismissed as producing human and economic failure. By the end of the 1860s, South Australia already grew half of Australia's wheat—and exported wheat to the other colonies, as well as to Mauritius, South Africa, and Britain. In 1869 the surveyor-general, G.W. Goyder, named six agricultural areas describing the nature of the soil and the average annual rainfall for each one. Free selection began in those districts. A series of good rains in a wet El Niño cycle led Goyder's carefully calculated line of demarcation—between agricultural districts with sufficient rain to make cultivation viable, and pastoral districts with insufficient rain to make agriculture unviable—to be shifted northwards. Finally, in 1874, the whole colony was made available for free selection. The wet cycle of El Niño continued for a few more years, and selectors moved far beyond Goyder's line into pastoral districts where farming had never before existed. Eventually, between 1881 and 1884, the run of wet seasons broke and, in the following dry cycle, Goyder's judgment was thoroughly vindicated when the vast majority of farmers north of his line lost everything. Selection continued successfully to the south of Goyder's line.

In South Australia, free selection had ensured that almost two million additional acres (810 000 hectares) of land came into agricultural production. The colony reaped annual wheat harvests greater than those of New South Wales and Victoria combined, and a prosperous middle class of farmers had been successfully established by 1890. South Australia is the success story of attempts to establish small-scale agriculture in Australia. In Queensland, a success in the Darling Downs area could be assured, because the soil was volcanic and so rich that it could be farmed for years without the need for fertiliser. Mixed farming of wheat, maize, and vegetables was the norm, and when a good wheat crop was reaped—every three years or so—the rewards were lucrative. But, in social terms, the price was high, and selectors' families worked like slaves to force the land into a payable proposition.

Continuing Aboriginal troubles

With conditions of life so hard, it is no surprise to find that few Australians in the second half of the nineteenth century spared much time to consider the welfare of the Aborigines or what was being done to them. In the cities, the Blacks lived by prostitution and begging—constituting a degraded remnant of the local tribes. Destroyed by disease and alcohol, they eked out a precarious existence on the outskirts of the cities and, by their condition and way of life, went far towards reinforcing the prejudices of the Whites who had begun to think of them as a race predestined for extinction. In the inland districts, however, the situation was different. In parts of New South Wales and Victoria during the gold rushes, Aborigines had replaced Whites as shepherds and stockmen. Further north, Aborigines were even more important as cheap rural labour. The Queensland cattle industry came to rely heavily on Aboriginal stockmen who received rations or a mere pittance of the wages that would have been paid to them had they been White. Moreover, the warfare between Blacks and Whites over control of the land and access to women continued until well into the twentieth century in both Queensland and Western Australia. Blacks resisted the incoming Whites in both colonies, and the result was a series of murders and massacres conducted by the settlers until the back of native resistance was broken. Early pioneers such as the Jardines in northern Australia are reputed to have killed hundreds of Aborigines in establishing their stations. Once the men had been disposed of, the station owners and their employees took Black women whenever they wanted them—precipitating a repetitive spiral of violence beginning with Aboriginal reprisals that were followed by a further round of murders.[5]

Land also continued to be a major source of hostilities. The Whites—aided by a murderous Aboriginal police force of Blacks recruited from the pacified districts further south, and armed with breech-loading rifles—killed large numbers of Aborigines who speared stock or threatened to oppose the further spread of pastoralism. The squatters did not find the land empty, but occupied by a native race who were mercilessly disposed of when they resisted the invasion of their territory and their incorporation into a dependent system of peonage. In northern Australia the usual behaviour of the newly arrived White men on seeing an Aborigine was to shoot him and to force the females to become the concubines of the murderers. Aboriginal men and women were routinely kidnapped to work in the pearling industry in Western Australia, where attempts to escape resulted in floggings and branding to identify troublemakers. The unwillingness of traditional hunter–gatherers to work for the Whites 'proved' beyond doubt that Aborigines were lazy, incapable of improvement, and destined to die out as the inevitable result of contact between a superior civilisation and a primitive race of nomads.

In 1867 in New Zealand, at the conclusion of a bloody war between Maori and settlers aided by a British army, respect for the native people of the land had been freely and openly expressed in the colonial parliament where colonists described them as 'a remarkably noble and generous-hearted people'. This claim was greeted by cheers of approbation in the New Zealand House of Representatives.[6] A similar statement would have been treated with derision and as a sign of madness had it been made in any colonial legislature in Australia on behalf of Aborigines. Settlers in Australia admired the Maori people and despised Aborigines as being many grades below the New Zealanders in their aptitude for civilisation.

The Chinese

The alleged superiority of the Australian variant of British civilisation was also expressed at the expense of the Chinese who came in large numbers to Australia during the gold-rush years. By the middle of 1854 there were nearly four thousand Chinese diggers on the gold fields of Australia, most of them in Victoria. They were not usually individualists like the European diggers, but most worked as indentured labourers for Chinese capitalists back home. They lived simply and frugally and, because they had lower expectations than did most White miners, they were able to extract sufficient gold to make a profit after Whites found a field to have become unremunerative. Earlier in the previous decade, squatters had attempted to introduce coolies as pastoral workers, so White labourers already were suspicious and predisposed to see the Chinese as a threat to wage levels and living conditions. On the Bendigo gold field, Chinese miners were hated, not because of their alleged immorality or their wastage of water or their foreign culture, but because they lowered the level of wages and rendered the diggings less productive.[7]

The trickle of Chinese miners was to become a torrent. In 1855 the Victorian legislature passed an Act imposing a poll tax of £10 per head on every Chinese immigrant landed. Shipowners, however, soon discovered that they could avoid this imposition simply by landing their Chinese passengers at Robe in South Australia— whence they could travel overland into Victoria and avoid the new tax. By 1857 there were 23 623 Chinese on the Victorian gold fields and a growing sentiment throughout the colony that something would have to be done. At Buckland River in July of that year, miners attacked the Chinese and drove them from the diggings—becoming, in the process, thieves and ruffians as they stole Chinese possessions and maltreated Chinese miners.

Discontent and rationalisation now became focused on the habits of the Chinese as the economic fears of European workers

Contemporary cartoon depicting Chinese trekking to the gold fields. (Australian History Museum, Macquarie University)

had produced little reaction from the colonial legislatures. The trappings and language of racial prejudice became increasingly common as opponents of Chinese immigration appealed to the emotions of their fellow colonists. The Chinese were said to be immoral because they came without women and therefore engaged in unnatural vice or else attempted to debauch White women. Furthermore, they were heathens who indulged in strange rites in their joss houses, and even smoked opium—habits that had no place in a British colony. And finally, they sent their gold out of the colony back to China, and purchased only the necessities of life and so contributed little to the colonial economy.

Pressure from Victoria finally led South Australia to impose a poll tax of £10 on all Chinese arriving in the colony, to permit only one Chinese immigrant for every 10 tons burden on ships from Chinese ports, and to enforce a ratio of one Chinese passenger to every six European immigrants. This had the desired effect and, within a few months, the port of Robe had become almost deserted. In New South Wales, miners and urban working men sent petition after petition to the local legislature praying that something be done to curb the flood of Chinese into the mother colony. Here again, a major cause of the animus appears to have been economic, and many such petitions came from inner-city areas where there were no Chinese residents. It is noteworthy that the language of the petitions became increasingly prejudiced and hysterical as the proximity to large congregations of Chinese increased.

Eventually, the pot boiled over in New South Wales on the Lambing Flat gold field in 1861, when over a thousand miners marched into the Chinese encampment behind a brass band, and drove the Chinese out. They blamed the current insolvent condition of most alluvial miners on the fact that the Chinese swarmed like locusts on the gold fields and beat them to the prize. The Chinese tents were fired and all their possessions stolen, although no Chinese lost their lives as a result of the violence. The government responded after the event by sending soldiers to the field to restore order but, when some of the diggers' leaders were brought to trial, juries consistently and resolutely refused to find them guilty. Anti-Chinese sentiment was a widely shared phenomenon wherever itinerant miners travelled, and they travelled the length and breadth of the country.

By 1877, on the Palmer River gold field in Queensland, the same problem emerged, and here, as in the other colonies, it was the fear that European miners would be swamped under a sea of Chinese diggers that seemed to activate the hatred. At Palmer River there were 18 000 Chinese gold-seekers, and only 1500 Europeans. To make matters worse, the Chinese community dissolved into communal conflict when miners from Canton attacked and slaughtered more than fifty miners from Beijing with pick-handles, meat-cleavers, axes, and shovels. Bloody fighting continued for about four days until the native police force intervened and disarmed the combatants. When they returned to their camps, the Chinese discovered that, in their absence, the Europeans had robbed them of all the gold they had won. By then, most of the alluvial gold at Palmer River had been worked out, and the Chinese had little option but to return to China—although some elected to remain in Australia where they worked as market gardeners, cooks, station rouseabouts, and in furniture manufacturing. No Whites were ever charged with the theft of Chinese gold at Palmer River, and the concept of the 'fair go' manifestly did not apply to other races such as the Chinese or Aborigines. Colonists seemed to feel perfectly free to rob, attack, and exploit both peoples without a qualm of conscience. Aborigines could be raped and massacred, and Chinese could be beaten and robbed without violation of the creed of the 'fair go' which applied only to Whites—and as more and more women had perhaps begun to suspect, only to White males.

Colonial women

Women in nineteenth-century Australia were in many ways second-class citizens. The early years of settlement with the great preponderance of males among the convicts and emancipists, had produced a male-dominated society in which masculine values dominated. Power was exercised by men, and women were reduced to the level of moral influence and regeneration of their menfolk. Where equality between the sexes did exist, it was the equality of hardship on the small holdings of the selectors. But, in the eyes of the law of the various colonies, women were not equal to men. They could not vote or stand for parliament; once married they could not possess property in their own right (all they owned passing into the control of their husbands); and they were discriminated against in the divorce courts where men could obtain a divorce far more easily than could women. In New South Wales, divorced women were not entitled to a licence to sell intoxicating liquors, and females were not permitted to enter the professions or read for university degrees until almost the end of the nineteenth century.

Work opportunities and consequent social mobility were less available to women, and their chances of employment were extremely limited. In respectable circles, domestic service, dressmaking, and teaching or governessing were the only occupations open to females who did not want to risk losing their respectability. More menial possibilities included becoming maids, cooks, washerwomen, barmaids, sales assistants, dressmakers or tailoresses (as outworkers or in factories), nurses, waitresses and, of course, prostitutes. There was a chronic shortage of domestic servants in the houses of the well-to-do during the second half of the nineteenth century caused by the preference of the native-born girls for the independence of factory employment despite its low wages—in preference to the higher pay available to domestics working for the rich.

In the factories and in tailoring outwork, women received

Emma Miller, Queensland suffragist and labour reformer. (Taken from Ross McMullin, *The Light on the Hill: The Australian Labor Party 1891–1991*, Melbourne, 1991)

substantially less money than the men. For example, a male tailor earned 14 shillings for making a coat, whereas a female making an identical coat earned 2 shillings. Women generally received only a quarter of what men earned in the tailoring trade, although they made the identical articles. The combination of low wages, long hours, and poor conditions in the sweatshops of Melbourne sparked the tailoresses' strike of 1883, which led to improved conditions and the growth of militant unionism among the women factory workers. Nevertheless, as the lives of female labour leaders such as

Louisa Lawson and Emma Miller make plain, women ran into a great deal of prejudice from the trade union movement which tended to view working women in much the same way as it regarded Chinese workers—as threats to the jobs and living standards of men. It was to take nearly another century of struggle before the principle of equal pay for equal work was established as a right of all workers in the 1970s.

Women were also heavily involved in politics via the suffrage movement and the women's Christian temperance unions—wherein they fought to obtain the vote and to affect legislation on a wide range of social issues, particularly temperance. Prominent members of these campaigns included Rose Scott and Louisa Lawson in New South Wales, Emma Miller in Queensland, Vida Goldstein in Victoria, and Catherine Spence in South Australia. Louisa Lawson founded a journal, the *Dawn*, to concentrate on women's issues. However, despite all the agitation produced by such activist women, the constitutional crises of this period were not about women's role in colonial society but were concerned with the powers of the colonial upper houses, and whether supply could be refused to governments with working majorities in the lower houses.

Constitutional crises

The power of Legislative Councils to obstruct governments became the subject of considerable attention during the second half of the nineteenth century, especially in Victoria where the upper house could not be coerced by the threat of nominating additional members until it did the government's bidding. The first major bone of contention emerged in 1865 when the Victorian Legislative Assembly sought to introduce a measure of tariff protection for the manufacturers and businessmen who dominated the lower house. They had not reckoned on the fact that the pastoralists who controlled the upper house were free-trade enthusiasts who believed that protection could adversely affect their profits. The Legislative Council refused to accept the tariff proposals that the government, led by James McCulloch, had attached to the annual budget in an attempt to make it impossible for the provision to be overthrown. The upper house refused to pass the budget, and the treasurer announced that the government would soon run out of money to pay salaries and the wages of public servants. The governor, Sir Charles Darling, sided with the Legislative Assembly, and the Colonial Office withdrew him immediately from the colony for his failure to force concessions from the lower house. It would be the last time in Australian history that a vice-regal representative would side with the people's house in any constitutional crisis over supply.

In 1877, a similar conflict between the two houses of the legislature broke out over the issue of payment for members of parliament. The upper house opposed the whole idea of wages for service in parliament, on the grounds that it would encourage ruffians—it meant workers and unionists—and lower the tone of proceedings. Premier Graham Berry attached the measure to the Budget Bill, and again the Legislative Council baulked at passing an Appropriation Bill with additional extraneous political proposals grafted onto it. This time, the government sacked senior civil servants known to be sympathetic to the Council's position, and moved on to dismiss from their offices the judges of the county courts, police magistrates, coroners, and crown prosecutors. Berry then sailed for Britain in an attempt to convince the British government that the Victorian constitution had become essentially unworkable with an upper house hellbent on obstructing any progressive government. The British authorities stonewalled Berry, and eventually he was forced to return to Victoria where he was compelled to resign. The forces of conservatism had won another victory.

Colonists in arms: the Sudan

Throughout the constitutional crises, one constant feature was that Australian colonists would not take up arms to assert their political rights. At no time during the Berry imbroglio did a resort to force to resolve the dispute appear likely. Politics and politicians did not engage the emotions of colonists at that visceral level. But let the empire of which Australia formed such a small part come under attack, and colonists would then enlist to fight in a conflict thousands of kilometres away and of no relevance to them whatsoever.

Since 1883, British forces had been fighting in the Sudan against the followers of the Islamic leader known as the Mahdi. When the news of the death of General Gordon in Khartoum at the hands of the Mahdi's supporters reached Australia in February 1885, it caused an outbreak of imperial patriotism and an indignant call for revenge against the savages who could do away with so admired an exponent of Christian imperialism. The colony of New South Wales offered a contingent of troops to a surprised British government, which gratefully accepted the offer. On 3 March, a public holiday was proclaimed in New South Wales to enable people to farewell the troops as they marched through Sydney and embarked for the Sudan. Thousands of people lined the route of the march and gave the soldiers a riotously patriotic send-off. Victoria scrambled to match the offer of troops, but these were refused by Whitehall—whereupon the premier, James Service, assured England that so long as Victoria possessed a man, a shop, or a shilling, the mother country would never lack assistance.[8]

The New South Wales' contingent consisted of 532 infantry, a battery of artillery numbering 250, and an ambulance group of 36. Two hundred horses also embarked with the force. Some recruits came from the New South Wales' regiments, some from the police force, and some were colonists who had served in the British army. About half of the group were native-born Australians. By the time that they arrived in the Sudan the campaign was in its final stages, and the men saw little action. Three were wounded in fighting, and seven died from other causes. The rest took ship for home in May 1885 and reached Sydney late in June.

The strength of British ties

Britain enjoyed considerable support from Australians in the nineteenth and early twentieth centuries. Colonists seemed to see no conflict in being both Australian and British simultaneously. They could attack imperial functionaries for being obstructive and unhelpful in times of constitutional crisis. They could deplore the lack of activity shown by British officials in supporting colonial attempts to annex territories to the British Empire in the antipodes. And the lower levels of colonial Australia—especially those of Irish background—could delight in pricking and pillorying the pomposity of the English and their insufferable condescension towards things colonial. But these were superficialities and cannot be allowed to obscure the basic reality that Australians were inordinately proud of their British origins, that idolatry towards Queen Victoria and other British royals was embarrassingly profuse throughout all levels of colonial society, and that republicanism and the desire to make Australia free of all ties to England and the Crown was persistently rejected by the majority of the colonial populace. The anti-British republicanism of the Reverend John Dunmore Lang and the nationalistic republicanism of the *Bulletin* late in the nineteenth century represented only a tiny segment of colonial sentiment.

Nor did the pride of the native-born in being Australian involve any thought of the development of a new ethnic group that had become distinct from the original English and Irish stock. Colonists seemed more than capable of identifying with the countries from which their parents came in preference to the country of their birth. For example, William Charles Wentworth retired to live out his final days in England, and Ned Kelly gloried in the fact that he was an Irishman and swore to raise the green flag of Ireland in Australia once he had swept the police and troopers out of his path. Both men were Australian-born, yet their loyalties were to the wider Anglo-Saxon or Celtic cultures from which their forebears came. There appeared to be no apparent conflict in colonists proclaiming themselves to be patriots to their own local Australian territory and nationalists enjoying their place in the widespread British Empire. Henry Parkes used the phrase 'the crimson thread of kinship' to describe the ambivalences embodied in a people who prided themselves on being Australian Britons and perceived no contradictions in such an assertion.

In cultural terms, however, there was a growing movement of artists, writers, and musicians away from a rigid adherence to European forms and appearances, and towards an acceptance that Australia was so different from the parent culture that it demanded a new artistic expression of its own. The Heidelberg group of impressionist artists became the first to give tangible form to native-born sentiment that Australian landscapes were noble and breathtaking, and that they were worthy of depiction in their own right without the filter of European romanticism that had hitherto corrupted the work of most artists in the colonies. Previously, where a romantic gloss had been eschewed, most colonial artists had followed the tradition of the illustrators who accompanied the scientific voyages of Cook and others, and had recorded anglicised depictions of colonial life and landscapes for an English audience. The Heidelberg group was led by Tom Roberts, and included Frederick McCubbin, Arthur Streeton, and Charles Conder. After Roberts returned to Australia in 1885, the members of the group established bush camps in the countryside around Melbourne, one of which was at Heidelberg, where they painted landscapes as they appeared to the artists and according to the light that encompassed them. They abandoned the romantic filter of seeing the bush through European eyes and, instead, portrayed the unique light, colour, and untidiness of the Australian bush and rural life.

Native-born writing also took on a somewhat nationalist hue in the final decades of the nineteenth century when the popular magazine the *Bulletin* was founded in 1880. It produced its own stable of writers who reflected an increasing national awareness and who wrote about Australia for an audience of native-born Australians. Poetry and prose found a place in the new magazine, and it quickly became known as the 'bushman's bible'—as much for the aggressive Australian tone of its writing as for its concentration on rural issues. Writers in the magazine included well-known nationalists such as Henry Lawson, A.B. 'Banjo' Paterson, Joseph Furphy, Victor Daley, Miles Franklin, and Shaw Neilson. The *Bulletin* took a republican political stance and cautioned against too enthusiastic a support for British causes. Australian self-interest was not necessarily identical with British advantage, and the *Bulletin* sounded a warning note of caution to those in the majority such as Henry Parkes who espoused the theme of the 'crimson thread of kinship'.

Such overt settler pride in being part of an empire on which the sun never set did nor imply that colonists applauded everything that Britain did or failed to do. There were times when Britain's failure to act infuriated colonists—especially when dilatory behaviour by the mother country was believed to compromise Australian security. In 1883, the government of Queensland pre-emptively annexed New Guinea on behalf of the British Empire in response to German interest in the area. Unfortunately Sir Thomas McIlwraith, the Queensland premier, had not obtained British permission, and the annexation was repudiated by Britain. When Germany then colonised north-eastern New Guinea in the following year, Australia found itself with a powerful European imperial power as a near neighbour. Colonists began to feel nervous when Britain showed such evident unwillingness to confront Germany on an issue of colonial security, and these feelings became even more pronounced over a similar reluctance to confront France concerning French attempts to colonise the New Hebrides. When the French landed four hundred marines on the New Hebrides, and Britain did not regard the issue as worth fighting a war, colonial governments became aware of their powerlessness and of the degree to which they relied on Britain for their defence and security.

Education, religion, and the Irish

Reliance upon Britain for the defence of the continent did not unduly concern most Australians, but there was a group within colonial society which felt less enamoured of their status as Britons. As usual, that exception was the Irish and, in particular, the Irish Roman Catholics. In matters of religion and education, Roman Catholics of Irish background were highly suspicious of the Anglican and Presbyterian churches. Since the time of Governor Richard Bourke, the education system had persisted as a hybrid whereby colonial governments made grants to all religious denominations in support of their schools. This proved to be both expensive and inefficient, and a time had to come when some form of rationalisation became essential. That time arrived during the 1870s and the 1880s.

In 1879, the move towards a secular system of education had become overwhelming and, in that year, the government of New South Wales cut financial assistance to religious schools altogether. It was a process mirrored in all the Australian colonies, and it roused considerable sectarian bitterness whenever the topics of religion or education came up for discussion. The non-Catholic denominations reluctantly acquiesced in the new scheme, but the Roman Catholics, under the leadership of Archbishop Polding, decided to follow their own path. Polding regarded an entirely secular system of education as a surefire method of eradicating Christianity altogether, and likened it to the administration of poison in small doses over a prolonged period sufficient to prove fatal. He announced that Roman Catholics could not, in good conscience, make use of the education system financed and administered by the state, and called on Roman Catholics to build their own schools, train and equip their own teachers, and prescribe their own textbooks.

The ideal of a free non-denominational education system had been that it would unite the colonists by providing equal access to a basic education for all children irrespective of religion or location. It was part of the 'fair go' ethos that all children should be treated equally, but the effect of the legislation was precisely the opposite. Many Roman Catholics retreated into an educational and religious ghetto that separated them from the general life of the community. Roman Catholic schools were staffed with nuns, brothers, and priests from Ireland who taught huge classes without payment, and who inculcated all the prejudices and divisions of the old world in their pupils in Australia. Irish separatism had existed in the Australian colonies since the time of the first Irish convicts, and was aggravated in 1867 by community outrage when a deranged Irish migrant attempted to assassinate the touring Duke of Edinburgh at Clontarf in Sydney. But the educational division gave Irish separatism a structural importance and a new lease of life which carried it well into the twentieth century.[9]

An urbanised country

Urbanisation dates the very beginnings of European occupation of Australia, which began with the formation of the town of Sydney. It was a process that continued throughout the nineteenth century— such that, by the 1890s, almost two-thirds of the population of Australia already lived in cities and towns, and the proportion of urban dwellers was constantly increasing.[10] The use of towns as administrative centres and ports meant that they inevitably became the centres of commercial life as well. The later development of road, rail, and telegraph links only strengthened this early trend, as did the predilections of countless immigrants who came from urban environments in the old world and sought them out in Australia.

Service industries and manufacturing came behind this population growth and took advantage of it. A multiplier effect operated here, as industries developed to cater to the needs of this large and expanding population, and they, in their turn, attracted more expansion and a further inflow of investment capital.

Protection

Manufacturing industries developed in both New South Wales and Victoria at about an equal rate during the years before 1890—even though New South Wales had nominally embraced free trade whereas Victoria had gone in for tariff protection for its infant industries. New South Wales justified its tariffs by claiming that they were not designed to protect local industries so much as to raise revenue for the government. A revenue tariff was acceptable to the free-trade ideology whereas a protective tariff was not. In fact, no colonial government was about to risk causing widespread unemployment in its cities by allowing local industry to compete openly with mass-produced goods from Britain, and the levels of tariff protection were not very different in the two colonies. Local governments also tried to ensure that at least some contracts were let to Australian manufacturers when railway construction or other large infrastructure projects were undertaken and, on the private market, industrial goods and machinery such as ploughs, harvesters, and threshing machines—which were made to local designs and suited to Australian conditions—were usually preferred by most colonists.

Housing the population

One of the major growth areas after the gold rushes was the housing industry. Melbourne set the pace and became the fastest-growing city in Australia. It earned the sobriquet of 'Marvellous Melbourne' during the 1870s and 1880s when a housing and land boom caused it to become Australia's foremost city.

In both Melbourne and Sydney the population grew in spectacular fashion, as unsuccessful gold diggers flooded back from the goldfields and a rising tide of immigration ensured a continuous supply of people in need of housing. This was in addition to a high rate of natural increase stimulated by a tendency to early marriage common to new settlers and the native-born. But Melbourne proved to be the phenomenon of the age, increasing its population between 1881 and 1891 by almost 100% to 497 000 souls. They had to be housed somewhere, and the building industry boomed. By the end of that decade, nearly half of the city's houses were less than ten years old. Sydney developed in similar fashion and, by 1891, its population stood at 383 333. The additional population also contributed to a housing boom, and new suburbs developed in tandem with the spread of rail and tramway systems.

The cost of this building program was enormous and was funded largely (although indirectly) from overseas borrowings. British investors poured their money into railway construction, banks, and pastoral companies. Some small British investors, attracted by high interest payments, placed their savings with the branches of Victorian Land Banks and Building Societies that had opened in England. In Australia, colonists also ploughed their savings into the Land Banks and Building Societies, but the vast bulk of the money to fuel the boom came from overseas and, in particular, from the continued inflow of capital from Britain. Most of this investment went into suburban development, land speculation, and public works. Comparatively little was invested in productive industries or new production. Land values soared in Melbourne during the 1880s, as they did also, to a lesser extent, in Sydney. In Melbourne some allotments increased in value from five to twenty times over in the space of just a few years. One writer has summed up the situation and the tenuous connection it had with reality in the words: 'the big speculators were selling to the medium speculators, the medium speculators were selling to the small speculators, and madness was in the air'.[11] This dangerous exposure was exacerbated by the extent to which bribery and corruption had become common among the officials and politicians who were supposed to be supervising the situation, but who consistently turned a blind eye to flagrant breaches of the law. For many Melburnians at this time, the old hope of making a quick killing on the gold fields had been replaced by the new hope of making a quick killing on the real estate market.

Silverado

The focus of the speculative hysteria was not restricted to Victoria, and a second mineral provided the impulse for a further period of financial effervescence in New South Wales. A foretaste of what was to come occurred in 1882–83, when rich deposits of silver were discovered at Silverton. Thousands of miners flooded in and smelters were built—before the find petered out in 1885. In that same year, a syndicate of seven men was formed to develop a promising find of silver on George McCullough's station. The shares were worth a nominal amount of £19 each, and when they unearthed rich silver in soft clay, the share value soared to £409 each by February 1888. New smelters were built, miners flocked to the area, and the Broken Hill Proprietary Company hit the big time. By 1891, the town of Broken Hill had become the third-biggest city in the colony, with a population of 20 000 and rising. Speculation in mining shares matched the speculation in Melbourne real estate in its failure to demonstrate any reality checks by its participants, and men seemed prepared to gamble on any piece of share scrip as fly-by-night operators and non-existent companies made the most of the public mania for gambling and the desire to become rich without working. This boom was also founded on false expectations, for the price of lead and silver declined continuously during these years. By 1894 silver brought just a little over half the return it had earned ten years earlier.

Regionalism: a stumbling block for federation

By 1891, the native-born proportion of the total population of Australia had risen to almost three-quarters, and a new generation was coming into its own. This did not mean, however, that a widespread national sentiment also existed. Although locals rejoiced in the defeat of English cricket teams or individual sportsmen by native-born competitors, it did not presage the emergence of any sort of continental patriotism or sense of identity. In fact, in the next decade, colonial particularism was to prove a major stumbling-block to attempts by Australian nationalists to federate the colonies into a single Australian nation. This intense regional rivalry is best illustrated by the stupidity of the adoption of different railway gauges by the various colonies. Instead of all using the same gauge, which would have facilitated trade and communications, Queensland adopted one gauge, Victoria chose another, and South Australia experimented with several gauge sizes—and they all did this so as not to be seen falling into line with the mother colony of New South Wales (which had a gauge size different from all of them!). Nor were the rivalries between the colonies restricted to practical things such as the size of the railway gauges. Melbourne resented Sydney's claim to greater wisdom and experience, and Melburnians smouldered with anger when they were patronised by the press and politicians of Sydney. After all, Melbourne had replaced Sydney as Australia's largest city, and New South Wales' pretensions to superiority were bitterly resented. South Australians regarded all other Australian colonies as possessing undesirable bloodlines because of their association with convictism, while Tasmanians struggled to throw off the shadow of Van Diemen's Land. In Western Australia, the colony stood finally on the threshold of responsible government, having at last been able to pay its way. The years of isolation and stagnation in the west had produced an inward-looking population quite distrustful of the aims and ambitions of the other Australian colonies, and determined to go its own way whatever the other colonies did. In Queensland, the sugar plantations, with their thousands of Kanaka labourers brought the charge of slavery from Britain and from the other colonies—a stigma destined to prove a major bone of contention when federation became a subject for serious debate. One thing that the colonies did share was fear. They feared German and French activities in the region, and their obvious inability to defend themselves or to affect the decisions of the great powers in Europe regarding the regional balance of power. They feared being swamped under an avalanche of Chinese immigrants if restrictive immigration legislation was ever removed. They had become totally reliant on importing capital from Britain to fuel the boom of the second half of the nineteenth century and, as indications began to appear that the source of the capital was about to dry up, they feared the day of retribution when the entire edifice of 'Marvellous Melbourne' and the lesser speculative booms in the other colonies would come to an end, and ruin and bankruptcy would stare them in the face. How would Australian workers, who had become used to a higher standard of living than almost anywhere else in the world, react to the busting of the boom? Was Australia on the eve of one of those great confrontations between capital and labour that periodically convulsed the old world, or would the concept of the 'fair go' be sufficient for colonists to muddle through by relying on sensible men to avoid conflict and work their way through to a compromise? Was a time dawning when the traditional refusal of Australians to take up arms in pursuit of domestic political or economic aims might be subject to revision? Would the apocalyptic vision of Henry Lawson come to pass in the testing time to come, and what would be left of the old ways if 'blood should stain the wattle'?

6

Civilising Capitalism

As Australia entered the 1890s, the economies of the various colonies were characterised by dangerous structural weaknesses, and the roots of the coming collapse can clearly be seen in the years of the long boom that preceded it. Capital had appeared to be in unlimited quantity, and massive indebtedness resulted as colonial governments and private individuals borrowed heavily to finance their investments. Almost by definition, long-term infrastructure projects could not be expected to produce short-term returns. Nevertheless, much of the money that underwrote these projects came from the short-term money market, and from overseas and local investors who wanted quick returns on their capital. The flood of capital into the colonies concealed these structural weaknesses for a time—enabling private and governmental borrowers to meet their interest payments on past loans from current borrowings—but the economies of the two largest colonies of Victoria and New South Wales were in a dangerous state of imbalance. A combination of international and local events between 1890 and 1893 ensured that the inevitable readjustment would be an extremely painful one.

The decline of the economy

During the 1880s, the terms of international trade moved inexorably against the Australian colonies. The decade marked a period of slow but steady decline in the price of wool on overseas markets. Pastoralists, who were heavily in debt themselves and needed to maintain their incomes to meet interest payments, responded to the situation by increasing the size of their flocks and raising the level of production. This flooded an already glutted market with more wool, and accelerated the fall in prices. Australian wool producers had temporarily outstripped world demand for their product, and excess production could no longer be readily absorbed. Silver prices suffered a similar decline throughout the decade, and the price of wheat also tumbled.

In the early years of 1890s, the deterioration in the terms of trade warned British investors that all was not well in Australia, and resulted in a quick contraction of credit and investment finance. A slump in the Argentine and the collapse of Baring's investment house frightened British investors in 1890—preceded as it had been by the closure of the Premier Building Society of Victoria in 1889. The loans that had been floated so frequently by the Australian colonial governments in London failed to attract sufficient subscribers. British investors had grown wary of the continued borrowing of the Australian colonies. As the unease grew, smaller investors began to withdraw their money from the London offices of Australian banks, land banks, and building societies.

By the early 1890s, there was already about £275 million worth of overseas investment in Australia. The interest payments on these loans were met by additional loans because government revenues were insufficient and export prices were declining. When the loans stopped, the public works projects also stopped—producing serious unemployment in the cities and towns. In the rural districts, pastoralists and farmers had already begun a retrenchment policy as their export earnings dried up, and as they battled the continuing influence of El Niño through a period of prolonged drought. As if this was not enough, a plague of rabbits converted many previously viable properties into dustbowls of sand and erosion. The trend towards growing unemployment affected both town and country. It was not long before the shaky foundations of the financial institutions established in the 1880s were exposed for all to see.

Corrupt government officials and financial regulators had turned a blind eye to infractions of the legislation that was designed to protect society from the effects of financial mismanagement. The banks and building societies had effectively escaped regulation in the era of economic free-for-all, and many of the financial institutions were dangerously exposed with a very low level of immediate capital in relation to the total amount of deposits that they had accepted. They freely loaned money for land purchases during the boom years when land values rose continuously. They had never envisaged a situation occurring in which the assets they held in land titles would be valueless due to tumbling prices and a lack of purchasers. They had behaved as though the boom would never end. When it did come to a crisis, they were unable to liquidate enough of their assets to cover the significant proportion of their depositors who queued to remove their money while they still could.

As rising unemployment began to bite, more and more small investors found themselves forced to withdraw their savings to live. Others, fearing that the institutions were unstable, began to withdraw their money, and a run on the banks and societies developed to the point that they began to default—unable to meet their depositors demands and unable to realise the assets in which their capital was tied up. The first collapses triggered a chain reaction and provoked a run on those banks and societies still operating. As they collapsed in their turn, a panic broke out among depositors who saw their lives' savings disappearing without trace. The casualty rate among institutions and depositors proved to be high.

Collapse of the banks

On 3 August 1891, the doors of the Bank of Van Diemen's Land in Hobart remained closed. In Melbourne, during 1891–92, twenty-one building societies, banks, and loan companies failed. In Sydney, a further twenty suffered the same fate. In March 1892, the large Mercantile Bank of Victoria collapsed, to be followed the next year by the Federal Bank. A further eleven banks closed their doors and their depositors lost most if not all of their money. The Bank of South Australia saved itself by merging with the Union Bank, but the Bank of Van Diemen's Land proved to be beyond resuscitation. Many of these institutions ended by paying their depositors only a fraction of their original savings, and thousands of individuals and businesses were bankrupted. In Victoria, where the problem was most acute, the law permitted bankrupts to make secret accommodations with their creditors. There were seventy-eight of these agreements made in 1892 alone—for amounts in excess of £5 million. Nobody could tell which businesses or individuals were sound, and which were on the point of collapse. The upshot of such a lack of transparency was that rumours and gossip weakened confidence still further.

The colonial governments reacted to the crisis in different ways. In New South Wales, budgets had been extensively underwritten by the revenue stream flowing from the sale of Crown lands, but this major source of income temporarily dried up. The Dibbs government rushed emergency legislation through the legislature in the form of the *Bank Issue Act*, which empowered the government to declare bank notes legal tender for one year. This halted the damaging and destabilising run on the banks where customers were demanding that the bank notes be replaced with gold coinage. Some of the banks that had gone to the wall had been banks of issue—that is, they had printed their own bank notes—and the firm action taken by the Dibbs ministry reassured colonists of the soundness of the bank notes and the developing run on the banks soon halted. In Victoria, on the other hand, the Patterson government's policy only exacerbated the crisis. As an emergency measure following the collapse of the Federal and the Commercial banks, the government sought a cooling-off period and proclaimed a five-day bank holiday. Far from dampening down the crisis, this action cast doubt on the viability of the entire banking system in the colony, and precipitated a panic and a further run of collapses.

By 1893 most of the banks were back in business, although substantially restructured. The favoured method of reconstruction involved the compulsory conversion of a proportion of each deposit into shares in the bank, with the balance of the deposit to be available for withdrawal after five years. The moratorium on withdrawals gave the banks time to rationalise and realise their holdings of land and other assets—although it was no help at all to the thousands of small depositors who needed their money for survival. To help such people, both the New South Wales and Queensland governments passed legislation authorising the colonial treasuries to advance up to half the value of their frozen deposits to them.

Trade and industry falter

The whole fabric of society lay in ruins during these years, and the slump in the terms of international trade continued—thus ensuring that primary industry remained at a low ebb and that the building trades (with all their associated industries such as quarries, brickyards, and timberyards) persisted in the doldrums. Factories continued to close, and unemployment to rise. Industrial action by trade unionists to protect their livelihoods only made matters worse. Eventual recovery might well have been certain, but this was no consolation to the thousands of unemployed who suffered severely during the depression. Even skilled tradesmen, especially those in the building industry, experienced high levels of unemployment, and the level for unskilled workers was much higher again. Conditions were desperate because colonial governments, hopelessly short of funds, refused pleas from the unemployed for a public works program to create jobs and begin the recovery. In an era of laissez-faire, the colonial governments refused to accept responsibility for looking after the unemployed and their families. Once the wage-earners' savings had been spent or frozen, the only recourse was to private charity, and to the soup kitchens and refuges run by the religious organisations and the benevolent societies.

Gold in Western Australia

To men in such grim conditions, the discovery of vast alluvial and reef-based gold deposits in Western Australia proved a

godsend. As the depression in the eastern colonies deepened, many men eked out a precarious existence fossicking for gold on the old gold fields of the 1850s, or travelled to the Kimberley gold field— newly proclaimed in 1886 in the far north of Western Australia. But, in 1892, two prospectors, Arthur Bayley from Queensland and William Ford from Victoria, discovered what was to become the Coolgardie gold field. They found alluvial gold and surface reef gold in

Western Australian prospector and his bicycle, 1890s. (Australian History Museum, Macquarie University)

abundance, nuggets were lying about on the surface of the earth waiting to be picked up, and the reefs were so rich that a man could tomahawk hundreds of ounces out in a single afternoon. In the following year, another eastern colonies' prospector named Paddy Hannan and his partner discovered the vast Kalgoorlie field, and further discoveries came thick and fast. Many unemployed men from the other colonies flocked to the diggings in Western Australia and sent substantial sums of money back to their families and dependants. They joined thousands more from all around the globe, drawn like the Australians to the lure of the last big gold rush of the nineteenth century. Gold production went from £226 000 in 1892 to £787 000 in 1894; and by the end of the decade annual gold production in Western Australia had passed the £6 200 000 mark.

Conditions in the difficult waterless region were tough, but most prospectors could make a living and some could strike a fortune. Later on in the decade, when the alluvial gold had been

Miners' camp, Coolgardie, 1890s. (Australian History Museum, Macquarie University)

largely worked out, mining companies set up on the fields, and provided secure and well-paid jobs for men willing to undertake the hazards and discomfort of deep-lode mining or of work in the huge crushing plants. The population of Western Australia doubled and then doubled again during the 1890s, and the desert gold fields boomed. Coolgardie had two stock exchanges, twenty-five registered stock brokers, twenty-six hotels, three breweries, and four clubs (including a Japanese Club). There were three daily newspapers, plus another four weekly papers. Kalgoorlie, Southern Cross, and Boulder competed with Coolgardie for the title of premier gold-field town, and overseas investment flowed in ever-increasing torrents into Western Australia at a time when the other Australian colonies found it impossible to raise money in London. In addition to importing people, Western Australia also increased (by 700%) its imports of food and machinery from the other colonies—thereby helping their industries to trade their way out of the depression. It was a rather grim irony that the newest self-governing colony in Australia should experience an unprecedented and utterly unexpected boom at a time when the older colonies found it difficult merely to survive.

Trade unionism

As if the economic and commercial crisis were not bad enough, conditions in the eastern Australian colonies were rendered immeasurably worse by a major industrial upheaval as the decade began. Trade unions had existed in Australia since 1840, when the Australian Society of Compositors was founded in Sydney, but the early unions tended to be combinations of skilled craftsmen who were as much interested in keeping unskilled labour from poaching their jobs as in improving working conditions and obtaining shorter hours. These small unions were largely friendly societies that concentrated on aiding indigent members and the widows and families of members who had died. There was a number of strikes in favour of higher wages and the eight-hour day, and some headway had been made in achieving these aims during the years of the long boom. By 1860, a Trades Hall Council was formed in Melbourne, and the Sydney Trades and Labour Council was established in 1871. The first intercolonial trade union congress met in Sydney in 1879. The years of prosperity encouraged the extension of the union movement into the ranks of the semi-skilled and unskilled workers in mining and the bush. The bush unions came last and were the hardest to organise, but the job was tackled successfully by William Lane and W.G. Spence during the 1880s.

The prosperity of the long boom had engendered a false sense of security in the trade unions. Many members felt that there was no essential conflict between the aims of capital and the aspirations of labour, and that both could work cooperatively to produce favourable outcomes for workers and capitalists together. Employers, anxious not to jeopardise high profits, would often cave in to union demands for wage increases and improvements in conditions. Prosperity masked the basic differences of position, and produced a veneer of cooperative harmony, but it could not last. Union successes during the boom years led them to believe that organisation and solidarity would always be sufficient to win them the gains they desired. Between 1890 and 1894 a series of major strikes occurred during which the scales fell from their eyes as they all ended in disaster for the unions.

The great strikes

The outbreak began with a seemingly insignificant dispute between shipowners and the Maritime Officers' Association. The employers had refused to negotiate with the small union of marine officers and, in desperation, the union sought affiliation with the Trades Hall Council. Shipowners were horrified that professional men would throw in their lot with the workers. They believed that such a thing would subvert all discipline at sea. The officers walked off their ships in every Australian port and, within a few days, the strike had spread to include wharf labourers, seamen, stewards, and cooks. The miners and shearers quickly came out in sympathy, and the scene was set for a very bruising confrontation.

The economic collapse had already produced a growing pool of unemployed and desperate workers, and conditions were not favourable for the successful outcome of what was close to being a national strike. Pastoralists were able to obtain non-union shearers, and were able to transport their wool to the wharves—where shipowners and their supporters loaded it onto ships under the protection of armed special constables. At Circular Quay in Sydney, the *Riot Act* was read. In Melbourne, troops of the Victorian Mounted Rifles received a warning from their commanding officer, Lieutenant-Colonel Tom Price, that, if necessary, he would order them to fire directly into the crowds of demonstrating strikers, and that, in such an event, he wanted his troops to 'Fire low and lay them out'.[1] Public opinion was clearly divided on the issue. The Victorian chief justice, George Higginbotham, and the Queensland chief justice, Sir Charles Lilley, both agreed that the strikers had a strong case. In New South Wales, the Roman Catholic Cardinal Moran also supported the strikers. In Western Australia, a year or so later, the Roman Catholic Archbishop Clune took the side of the employers whereas his Anglican opposite number supported the workers. By and large, the governments of all the colonies opposed the strikers, and used police and troops against the workers. There was no 'fair go' to be found here, and the episode exploded once and for all the comfortable idea that there was any compatibility between the interests of workers and the interests of employers. It would be an experience that unionists did not forget.

The strike continued from August to October 1890, until the unions collapsed and the marine officers returned to work on the shipowners' terms. In 1891 the Queensland shearers struck again when the graziers repudiated the agreements with the shearers' union and brought in non-union labour to break the strike, while the unionist shearers gathered in large camps of armed men near the larger shearing sheds. Armed conflict appeared ominously close. The conflict was articulated around a division of freedoms. The pastoralists demanded freedom of contract—the right to offer employment to whomsoever they liked on whatever terms they liked. The unions demanded freedom of association—the right of workers to associate together and to bargain collectively. The union was determined to enforce the closed shop (in which only union members could work in the industry), and the employers were just as determined to break the closed shop (by offering employment to non-unionists).

Clashes occurred between strikers and 'scabs' (strikebreakers)—the latter being afforded police protection. Police and troops raided several of the miners' camps. The Queensland government sent in more than 2000 troops armed with artillery and machine guns. It dismissed any railway workers who made donations to the strike funds of the shearers' union, and it secured the appointment of judges and magistrates who would use the anti-union laws of early nineteenth-century Britain against the strikers. Such laws had long since been repealed in Britain, but were still enforceable in Australia—because they had been in force when Australia was settled and had never been specifically repealed. The best-known incident occurred at Barcaldine in Queensland where almost a thousand armed men had established a camp under the Eureka flag. For a moment it appeared that Australians were about to take up arms for a domestic political cause but, when the Queensland police and troops arrived, the movement collapsed like a pricked balloon. Eighty-two men were jailed on trumped-up charges of conspiracy, intimidation, and riot. Here, as at Eureka earlier in the century, radical and revolutionary rhetoric fell far short of action in an Australian political and social confrontation. In 1894, the shearers went out again, and some unionists set fire to a river steamer named the *Rodney* as it carried scabs up the Darling River. The culprits were never arrested, but a further fifty union leaders were imprisoned in the crackdown that followed. Other unionists were jailed at Broken Hill and during further unsuccessful strikes that took place in the coal-mining industry in 1893 and 1896 in New South Wales and Queensland.

By the middle and second half of the 1890s, a combination of factors—unsuccessful strikes, widespread unemployment, the collapse of the financial institutions, the imprisonment of union leaders, and the disappearance of trade unions that could not survive in such difficult circumstances—had left the union movement in total disarray. The failure of the great strikes generally worked to the advantage of those within organised labour who recognised that the opportunity for realising labour's goals lay through politics and not through direct and militant industrial action. It also helped to increase interest among both unionists and liberal politicians in the development of an arbitration system whereby those injurious and bruising confrontations between capital and labour could be managed or avoided altogether. Furthermore, the fact that colonial governments had not hesitated to use military force and the law to repress strikes was not lost on the labour movement. If the state possessed the power to break strikes in such a way, it was obvious that workers would have to find some means of capturing the state and gaining control over the apparatus of power. The ballot box would provide the road forward for a workers' political movement that had met with such calamitous defeat when it tried direct action.

The beginnings of the Labor Party

It is important to realise that the idea of a parliamentary labour party did not follow as an effect from the failures of militant trade unionism—although there is no doubt that the industrial failure gave the movement towards political representation an urgency and a focus that it had not hitherto possessed. But the movement towards organised political representation can be traced back to 1890, when a union leader, Robert Harris, presented the Trades and Labour Council with a proposal that it establish labour electoral leagues in every electorate where practicable, and that a structure be prepared for the organisation and management of these leagues. The council accepted the proposal and, in the following year, the leagues came into existence with an annual membership subscription of two shillings—half of which went to the central body to form an electoral fighting fund.

The development was made all the easier by the passing, by the New South Wales legislature in 1889, of an Act introducing the payment of members of parliament. A salary made it possible for any member of the labour movement to run for office. Hitherto, there had been individuals whose trade unions had paid their salaries while they were members of the Legislative Assembly, but such arrangements were individualistic and *ad hoc*. Certainly, a political party could not be organised on such a basis—particularly one that would be so narrowly sectional as would the new Labor Party.[2] On the other hand, however, there had been payment of MPs in Victoria since the 1870s and a Labor Party had not emerged there. The experiences of the 1890s can be seen as an important stimulus to the formation of a new political movement—but as an accelerator rather than as a generator of its formation.

After 1894, the new Labor Party held the balance of power between free traders and protectionists in New South Wales, and maintained the free traders in office in return for concessions and the partial implementation of Labor policies. Similar developments took place in the other colonies, and Labor appeared in the Victorian legislature from 1892 onwards where it supported the liberal protectionists. In Queensland, the first Labor men appeared in 1891, and the party became the largest opposition grouping with sixteen members in 1893. In 1899, the first Labor government anywhere in the world held office in Queensland under Anderson Dawson for a single week before losing a confidence vote to its combined liberal and conservative opponents. In South Australia, political Labor appeared in 1891 and supported the Liberals, and in Western Australia and Tasmania the first Labor members were not elected until the early years of the twentieth century.

Achievement and reform

Labor's achievements of reform in return for concessions proved impressive. Plural voting was one of the first targets, and this was abolished in New South Wales in 1898, and soon after in all the other colonies. Similarly, property qualifications for members of the Legislative Assemblies were abolished. There were significant advances in social legislation. Between 1894 and 1900 all the mainland colonies legislated for the regulation of factory working conditions, and minimum standards were enacted controlling wages, employment of juveniles, hours of work for women, and the conditions of apprenticeship. Maximum working hours for shop assistants were specified and, in Victoria, the Liberal government—with Labor support—established wages boards empowered to fix minimum wage rates and to ensure that employers passed on to their hands a portion of the financial benefits that they enjoyed under tariff protection. By the end of the decade more than twenty industries came under this legislation. New South Wales went further than this in 1901 when it founded an Arbitration Court—consisting of a judge, an employers' representative, and an employees' representative—which possessed the power to make awards and settle disputes. The resolutions made by this court had the force of law and were binding on an entire industry.

In the fiscal field, most colonies introduced land and income taxes during this decade. In 1900, both New South Wales and Victoria brought in old-age pensions. The concept of land tax

Kanakas in a Queensland cane field, c.1901. (Australian History Museum, Macquarie University)

held a natural appeal to Labor, which found inherently attractive the argument that those who owned the land should pay some contribution to offset that made by the worker with his labour. Naturally, landowners rejected this view and found Henry George's *Progress and Poverty*, and the single tax program that sprang up to implement his ideas, verging on the revolutionary. Finally, all colonies accepted the necessity of excluding the Chinese and developing a full White Australia policy. Queensland shillyshallied because of its reliance on Kanakas in the sugar industry, but the other colonies all passed Acts prohibiting the immigration of all Asians, Africans, and Polynesians. These enactments violated international agreements and treaties between Britain and China, and between Britain and Japan, and insulted the inhabitants of both Asian nations. Consequently, Britain disallowed them. Eventually a compromise was found in the mechanism developed by Natal whereby an immigrant could be compelled to take a dictation test in any European language. Failure in the test resulted in exclusion without any reference to colour or race. It was a mechanism that appealed to the new federal government after 1901.

The Labor parties during these years established a reputation for being pragmatic non-doctrinaire organisations. They were certainly not socialist parties, and seemed more than happy to follow a policy of supporting either free traders or protectionists in return for piecemeal social and industrial reforms. They were not out to overthrow existing society, but to improve it. They did not aim to confiscate and redistribute wealth, but merely to improve the opportunities for their own members to accumulate wealth for themselves. Australian society was to be reformed, not fundamentally restructured.

Towards federation

The late 1890s was more than just an era of small gains and improvements in the aftermath of the depression, and the decision to convert the independent and isolated colonies into a single nation made the decade an indisputable watershed. In retrospect, the case for federation seems to be overwhelming, but contemporaries did not find it so, and it is worth remembering that substantial minorities in all colonies voted against federation in 1898 and 1899, and that if the opposition vote is added to the number of electors who did not bother to cast a vote at all, it could well be argued that federation never enjoyed true majority support.

Basically, there were two cases against federation, the first amounting to an argument for a different type of union, an imperial federation, in which the colonies would become provinces in a Greater Britain, and elect members to the parliament at Westminster; and the second and more popular being in favour of colonial particularism and the status quo. After all, the colonies had been settled at different times and for different reasons, and were in dissimilar stages of economic development. The capital cities were thousands of kilometres apart and, until the recent gold rush Western Australia had been as much *terra incognita*, for most of the inhabitants of the eastern colonies as was China or Tibet. The smaller colonies feared that in any political association they would be swamped by the more populous colonies of New South Wales and Victoria, and the moral pretentiousness of the South Australians led them to look down upon the inhabitants and suspect bloodlines of the former convict colonies. Added to this was the difficulty of conflicting economic systems and values, with Victoria staunchly protectionist in opposition to New South Wales' enthusiastic embrace of free trade. To top it all off, there had been decades of rancour and spleen generated by the rivalry between Victoria and New South Wales, and all the colonies were heavily involved in their own schemes of development and desired to go their own way.

On the other hand, arguments in favour of federation grew stronger as the 1890s progressed. The electric telegraph and the advent of railways had helped to break down the psychological isolation of the various colonies, bringing them to a realisation that they shared the continent with sister colonies that were experiencing similar problems. Trade and labour, especially rural labour, tended to move about freely irrespective of colonial boundaries, and the irritations of colonial customs barriers on the Murray annoyed businessmen and the larger banks who wanted intercolonial commerce to be free of all restrictions. In 1888, the first intercolonial conference of the chambers of commerce issued strong demands for uniform legislation in areas such as insurance, debt recovery, partnerships, patents, and trademarks. The large trade unions were already national in coverage and operated in all the colonies. Intercolonial union congresses and the shared fear of cheap coloured labour made many trade unionists favour federation, but the labour movement was split on the fiscal question, and many labour men were suspicious of a movement that drew such wide support from their political enemies.

Defence

As the decade of the 1890s unfolded, the twin bogeys of defence and coloured immigration ensured that the topic of federation did not slip entirely off the agenda. Defence became a real issue after Japan's success against China in 1895 and the later Anglo–Japanese Treaty and naval agreements. It was one thing to fear being swamped under a tide of coloured labour, but it was quite another to be confronted by an Asian military power where hitherto the only threat had been discerned from Britain's European rivals. Again fear was to prove a major stimulus in forcing the pace of Australian political development.

At an intercolonial conference in 1880 on the vexed question of tariffs, Henry Parkes of New South Wales had proposed the establishment of a federal council to deal with matters of common interest to the colonies. Although such an organisation did eventually come into existence in 1885 by an Act of the Imperial Parliament, it was virtually a powerless debating society which was unelected and restricted to offering advice. In 1889 Parkes tried again and, in a famous speech at Tenterfield in northern New South Wales, he stressed the burning issue of defence and proclaimed his belief that all the colonial military forces should be combined into one great federal army. It was necessary for the colonies to produce an effective system of federal government to achieve this aim:

The great question that they had to consider was whether the time had now come for the creation on this Australian continent of an Australian government—as distinct from the local governments then in existence. (Applause.) In other words, to make himself as plain as possible, Australia had now a population of three and a half millions, and the American people had numbered between only three and four millions when they formed the great commonwealth of the United States. The numbers were about the same, and surely what the Americans had done by war, the Australians could bring about in peace without breaking the ties that held them to the mother country.

(Cheers.) Believing, as he did, that to preserve the security and integrity of these colonies it was essential to amalgamate the whole of their forces into one great federal army, and seeing no other means of attaining the end, it seemed to him that the time was close at hand when they ought set about creating this great national government for all Australia.[3]

As a result of Parkes' passionate advocacy, a conference of colonial premiers met in Melbourne in 1890 to discuss the issue and, although nothing was decided on the federation question, it was agreed to hold a national Australasian convention in Sydney in the following year to take the matter further and to come up with definite proposals.

Producing a constitution

Henry Parkes. (Taken from Jack Cato, *The Story of the Camera in Australia,* Melbourne, 1955)

In due course the convention met, and the Queensland attorney-general and premier, Sir Samuel Griffith, drafted a proposed constitution which was the main work of the convention. Griffith's Bill called for the colonies to cede certain specific powers to a new central government, the chief of these being defence. There should be free trade among the colonies, although the question of a national tariff was not raised— leaving the debate over whether the new nation would embrace free trade or protection still to be fought out. The Bill also attempted to calm the fears of the smaller colonies by calling for a bicameral legislature with a House of Representatives elected on the basis of population and a Senate in which each colony would be equally represented. Although this draft subsequently was altered extensively at the conventions of 1897–98, the fact remains that its basic framework did not change, and Griffith is, in a very real sense, the founding father of Australian federation.

In the meantime, the elderly Parkes lost office and faded from the scene, and the leadership of the pro-federation forces passed to two native-born politicians. In New South Wales Edmund Barton, a protectionist politician

Alfred Deakin. (Australian History Museum, Macquarie University)

and lawyer, became the focal point; and in Victoria, Alfred Deakin, lawyer, former deputy premier, and leader of the protectionist liberals in the Victorian parliament, emerged as the chief protagonist. Both men shared a consuming vision of a single Australian nation, and both worked tirelessly to realise this vision by addressing public meetings and mobilising public opinion. In July 1893, interested groups from both colonies met at a private conference in the border town of Corowa where they passed a resolution that the parliament of each colony should be requested to pass an enabling Act to set up another conference to be composed of elected representatives chosen by the people. This convention would then draw up a constitution which would be put to the people in a referendum. This proposal took the federation issue out of the hands of colonial politicians and involved the people, and the democratic nature of it helped to reconcile labour to the federation movement.

The convention of ten delegates met for the first time in Adelaide in March 1897. The voters had supported the general direction by sending powerful advocates of federation such as Barton, Deakin, and Kingston (the last being the premier of South Australia)—all well-known proponents of the cause. They used Griffith's draft Bill as the starting point for their deliberations, and held additional meetings in Sydney and Melbourne to take further advice from the colonial legislatures. Discussions centred on the role of the Senate and its function of protecting the rights of the smaller states (as the constituent colonies would be known after federation). It was finally agreed that the powers of the Senate would be the same as those of the lower house—except that, although it could reject financial measures outright, it had no powers of amendment over such money Bills. Governments would be made and unmade in the House of Representatives, but the Senate could not be ignored.

The convention's Bill called for complete free trade among the states of the new nation. Because tariffs were the traditional source of government revenue, and the main source of revenue for several colonial governments unable to sell much Crown land, the draft Bill contained the Braddon clause—or the 'Braddon Blot' as it became known subsequently. This clause provided that the new federal government should return three-quarters of its customs revenues each year to the states.

The constitution Bill also vested in the federal government the powers of defence, immigration, external affairs, posts and telegraphs, conciliation and arbitration involving disputes extending beyond a single state, and payment of invalid and old-age pensions. Powers not specified in the constitution were to remain with the states, and it is clear that the federalists had no intention of centralising power and administration, except in certain limited areas. Unification under a single central government was not at all what they had in mind.

The referenda

The Bill was put to referendum in all colonies except Western Australia, which was not interested at this stage. In New South Wales the premier, George Reid, insisted not only that the vote had to win, but also that the majority had to number at least 80 000 votes in total. Reid earned the sobriquet of 'Yes-No Reid' during this referendum by advising the voters that, although he personally intended to support the Bill by voting 'Yes', the people of New South Wales should realise that the Bill as it stood did not entirely safeguard their interests. Many Labor men actively opposed the referendum and complained that it had so many concessions to the smaller states that it was no longer really democratic. They also believed that they had been excluded from having any real input into the process and that the result was a 'toff's constitution'. Other vested interest groups in the colonies opposed federation for their own reasons. Small manufacturers were concerned that they would have to compete with the powerful and well-established industries of Victoria without the protection of a local tariff. They tended to vote 'No' and seem to have persuaded their employees to vote along with them. The situation was similar with Victorian sugar-beet farmers, who knew that they would be unable to compete with Queensland sugar on the open market, and thus voted 'No' in protest.

In the event, colonists obviously recognised that they had more in common with one another than differences from one another. A common language, a common ancestry, and a growing sense of a shared Australian nationality helped to buttress the fears that they also shared. Majorities were recorded in favour of federation in the four participating colonies (Queensland and Western Australia did not participate) but the majority did not reach the necessary figure in New South Wales.

Reid immediately invited the other premiers to a meeting to discuss ways of making the Bill more palatable to New South

Wales electors, and a series of compromises was hammered out to cover his difficulties and to entice Queensland into participation. Perhaps the main amendment of significance was the restriction of the 'Braddon clause' to the first ten years after federation, following which the federal government would decide what was the most appropriate form of revenue-sharing. Another agreement gained by Reid was that the new federal capital would be sited in New South Wales, although it was stipulated that it had to be at least a hundred miles (160 kilometres) from Sydney. Until an acceptable venue was found, the federal parliament would meet in Melbourne.

Reid now declared himself well satisfied and, in a second referendum in 1899, the vote in favour of federation passed in all the eastern colonies. Western Australia proved to be a reluctant bride, but Premier John Forrest found that the other colonies would make no concessions at all to accommodate the colony and that he faced a secession movement on the gold fields of Coolgardie and Kalgoorlie. The miners were determined to be in federation and petitioned the British government to form a new colony to be known as 'Auralia' from the gold fields districts—which would then vote to join the federation. Under heavy pressure from the Colonial Office, John Forrest changed his mind and, at the eleventh hour in 1900, Western Australia voted at a referendum to federate on the same terms as the other colonies.

Federation achieved

The *Commonwealth of Australia Constitution Act* received Queen Victoria's assent after it had passed through the British Parliament in July 1900 and, in September, the queen proclaimed that on the first day of the new century the people of the Australian colonies would be united under the name of the Commonwealth of Australia. It was to be the first continental nation in the world, and realised the federationists' slogan of 'one people for a nation and one nation for a people'.

Accordingly, on New Year's Day, in all the Australian colonies, at the height of an Australian summer, elaborate ceremonies were conducted to celebrate the birth of the new nation. Grand military parades helped to remind the onlookers that the new Commonwealth was at war in South Africa and in China. When the Boer War broke out in 1899, both Victoria and New South Wales had been quick to send volunteers, and the other colonies had ultimately followed suit. Australians fought throughout the South African campaign as colonial volunteers even though they became a federal responsibility as a result of federation. The lure of adventure and a sense of shared British nationalism might help to explain why colonists volunteered to fight a war in which they had no stake. At least in New Zealand, colonists had received a reward for risking their lives in the form of confiscated Maori land, but there was no such reward on offer in South Africa. Nor was anything more tangible offered as an inducement to volunteers to aid Britain by assisting in the international expedition to repress the Boxer Rebellion in China. Both New South Wales and Victoria sent men from their naval brigades, Queensland offered its unseaworthy gunboat, and South Australia's gunboat was actually co-opted into the Royal Navy for the duration of the emergency and steamed north to China. The men in China did not see much action, but the 16 000 Australian soldiers in South Africa confronted a brave and determined enemy defending their homeland against a British invasion. So the new nation began its life with its citizens serving as mercenaries in two foreign locations where they sought to crush resistance to British control from nationalist patriots. It was an irony that did not seem to strike most of the thousands of Australians who crowded the capital cities of the new states to watch the festivities although, in 1899, the radical magazine the *Bulletin* had published a cartoon entitled 'An Ominous Start' commenting on the fact.[4]

The first Commonwealth government

The first business of the new government led by Edmund Barton was the organisation of the first federal elections, to be held at the end of March. There were 75 members to be elected to the House of Representatives in addition to 36 senators, and the elections were conducted under the electoral laws then in force in the different states. This meant that women could vote only in Western Australia and South Australia although, in the interests of uniformity, this was extended to all states in 1902 when all persons over the age of 21 received the vote.

The newly elected members were an experienced and talented group. Of the 75 MHRs there were ten former premiers and twelve others who had ministerial experience. The party system was in its infancy (with the exception of the Labor Party), and there were loose divisions of free traders and protectionists rather than formal political parties. Consequently, it took some time to discern which faction had won the election. Eventually Barton was able to form a broadly protectionist government and George Reid became the leader of the free-trade opposition. Labor, which had won 24 seats, sat on the crossbenches, but continued their tried-and-true policy of support in return for concessions. This meant, in practice, that they usually supported the protectionists, but that they would keep in office any government that was willing to bring forward progressive social legislation. Protectionists and free traders were united into cohesive groups only on the fiscal question, and the members of both groups were reasonably eclectic on other issues. Labor, on the other hand, quickly introduced the discipline of caucus, the 'pledge' (to vote as a bloc in accordance with the majority opinion of the caucus), and the annual conference. On 8 May 1901 the Labor members formed the Federal Parliamentary Labor Party under the leadership of John Christian Watson from New South Wales.

THE FIRST COMMONWEALTH MINISTRY OF AUSTRALIA
(From 1 January 1901 to 24 September 1903)

1. Rt. Hon. Sir Edmund Barton, P.C., G.C.M.G., K.C., Prime Minister
2. Hon. Alfred Deakin, Attorney-General
3. Hon. Sir William John Lyne, K.C.M.G., Minister for Home Affairs
4. Rt. Hon. Sir John Forrest, P.C., K.C.M.G., Post-Master-General
5. Rt. Hon. Sir George Turner, P.C., K.C.M.G., Treasurer
6. Rt. Hon. Charles Cameron Kingston, P.C., K.C., Minister for Customs
7. Hon. Sir James Robert Dickson, K.C.M.G., Minister for Defence
8. Senator Hon. James George Drake, Post Master-General
9. Hon. Sir Phillip Oakley Fysh, K.C.M.G., Honorary Minister
10. Senator Hon. Richard Edward O'Connor, K.C., Vice-President Executive Council
11. Hon. Neil Elliott Lewis, Honorary Minister

First Commonwealth ministry, 1901. (Australian History Museum, Macquarie University)

The new federal politicians represented a combined Australian population of 3 765 894. Because some states did not include Aborigines in their census figures, only about a quarter of the estimated 67 000 Aborigines then resident in Australia were counted in this figure. When the Commonwealth conducted its first population census ten years later, it excluded all full-blood Aborigines as a matter of course. The federal constitution left Aboriginal affairs to the states, and Aborigines were excluded from the federal franchise unless they already possessed the vote for their state legislatures. Very few of them did. Finally, Section 127 of the Commonwealth Constitution held that, in estimating the population of the continent at times of national census, 'Aboriginal natives shall not be counted'. This neatly maintained the exclusion of Australian Blacks from any say in the government of a country in which they had lived for more than 60 000 years.

Early legislation and White Australia

Parliament enacted legislation in two crucial areas that enjoyed a virtual consensus from all members of the new legislature. The first of these was the question of ensuring a White Australia and protecting the population of Australia from contamination by supposedly inferior races and the workers of the country from the threat of cheap labour. It was not that a current threat actually existed from the millions of Asians in Australia's region of the world, but rather to ensure that such a threat never arose. The Chinese population of the country had fallen to fewer than 30 000 by 1901, and there were fewer than 10 000 Kanakas working on the Queensland cane fields. Nevertheless, Australians had become acutely conscious of themselves as a small White enclave that could be swamped by Asians in a very short space of time unless steps were taken to keep them out. The rising military power of Japan also caused concern, and a desire to avoid allowing a large number of Japanese nationals who might become a future security risk helps to explain the uniform support that the *Immigration Restriction Act* received. The Natal system was introduced—which demanded the passing of a literacy test in any European language selected by the civil servant administering the test, before non-European migrants would be permitted to enter the country. The test was not to be applied to Whites, and the officer was expected to select a language with which the coloured migrants were unfamiliar.

In the same year Barton also introduced a *Pacific Islands Labourers' Act* that was designed to end the use of Kanaka labour on the sugar plantations in Queensland. The Act provided for the repatriation of all Kanakas and, although the planters claimed that they would be ruined, the Act became law in December 1901. The sugar planters were compensated in 1903 with a special tariff on imported sugar and by bounties paid on sugar if the cane had been cut by White labour.

Tariffs

The next piece of crucial legislation passed by the Barton government proved far more contentious—because it related to the vexed question of tariffs. All parties recognised the need for a revenue tariff, but even the modest degree of protection for which Barton aimed became the cause of deep divisions and a prolonged debate. Eventually, a tariff ranging from 5–25% *ad valorum* duty was accepted by the Senate where the free traders had a majority and, with the *Customs Tariff Act* of September 1902, a policy of protection became the law of the land.

Supporting the British Navy

At a colonial conference in London during 1902, the subject of defence was discussed and Barton agreed to subscribe £240 000 a year as Australia's contribution to the costs borne by the Royal

Navy in defending Australia. The money was to help maintain a British naval squadron of one armoured cruiser, six light cruisers, four sloops, and a naval reserve of 25 officers and 700 men in Australian waters. The officers and men would be trained by the British and eventually form the nucleus of the Royal Australian Navy—although that development was not one favoured by the British in 1902. The arrangement was cheap, but left Australia with little say in its own defence and was obviously a stopgap measure. Both Barton and Deakin believed that an Australian navy would ultimately have to be formed, for it did not require the gift of prophecy to foresee that Britain's strategic requirements might not always coincide with Australia's needs. But moves in that direction as early as 1902 would have been premature. The scanty colonial naval forces that passed into Commonwealth control in 1901 were anything but a blue-water navy, and consisted of a few colonial gunboats and torpedo boats.

The courts

In September 1903, the High Court of Australia came into existence with Sir Samuel Griffith, the early draftsman of the constitution, appointed as the first chief justice. The prime minister, Edmund Barton, and the leader of the Senate, R.E. O'Connor both resigned from parliament and Cabinet to take up the two positions on the bench of the High Court. All three of the new justices had been actively involved in the federation movement and were expected to apply their extensive knowledge and experience to the judicial interpretation of the new constitution. Deakin succeeded Barton as the leader of the protectionist liberals and as prime minister.

Between 1903 and 1909, substantial strides were made in the area of progressive social legislation. The Labor Party usually supported Alfred Deakin during these years, and even ruled as a minority government in 1904 and 1908. The combination of Deakin and Labor produced legislation that had a profound effect on Australian society. In 1904, a temporary alliance of free traders and some protectionists under George Reid brought forward an Industrial Arbitration Bill that was heavily influenced by proposals introduced by the first Labor government. A federal Arbitration Court was established to exercise the powers granted by the constitution to the Commonwealth in disputes covering more than one state.

New protection

The Court of Arbitration and Conciliation was constituted in 1905 and, under the leadership of Justice Henry Bournes Higgins, it was destined to play a major role during the years 1905–08 in establishing an approach to industrial issues and wages policy that became known as 'new protection'. The new feature of this system of protection was that it became a court-centred attempt to ensure that a manufacturer who benefited from the imposition of protective tariffs against overseas competition should charge a fair and reasonable price for his products, and pay fair and reasonable wages to his employees. Employers were confronted with the demand that protection from competition carried social responsibilities with it, and the new approach argued that protection should be reduced or eliminated altogether from employers who did not pay adequate wages to their workers. In his 'Harvester Judgment' in 1907, Justice Higgins thought in terms of minimum needs of the workforce rather than in solely economic values, and he proclaimed a 'fair' wage to be one that permitted an employee to keep himself and his family in modest comfort. His average worker had a wife and three children to support, and Higgins took into account the amount of money such a family would need for food, clothing, rent, and day-to-day living expenses. Largely by this measure, the Harvester Judgment arrived at a figure of 7 shillings per day as a fair and reasonable wage to pay an unskilled labourer. Skilled workers received additional amounts under a system of margins for skill. The wage was established on the basic requirements of the worker to sustain a decent if modest standard of living, not on the capacity of the employer to pay. The ethos of the 'fair go' underlay the system of arbitration and conciliation, and was about to be enshrined in legislation.

To secure a viable industrial basis for a needs-based wage system, Deakin, with Labor support, extended protection in 1908 via a new tariff that gave a 5% margin of preference to British made imports over those from countries outside the empire. Moreover, although the High Court later struck down most of the new protection legislation, the concept had been established (and accepted throughout the Australian community) that the needs of the worker had to be taken into account when state or federal courts handed down rulings on wages. Furthermore, because the industrial courts would deal only with representatives of organised associations, there was a rapid growth in the number of trade unions, and overall union membership trebled between 1906 and 1914.

New protection undermined the basic creed of the free traders (in the pre-eminence accorded to market forces), and the growing power of the Labor Party had begun to alarm its political opponents on both sides of the fiscal divide. When George Reid resigned as leader of the free traders and was replaced by the more moderate Joseph Cook—a former coal miner and turncoat Labor leader from New South Wales—the ground was prepared for an anti-Labor alliance. In 1909, Labor withdrew its support from Deakin and, to a chorus of Labor denouncements, Deakin responded by negotiating a 'fusion' between the free traders and his own followers—to form the Liberal Party. Labor and its opponents had established the basis for two-party politics in Australia—a pattern that has continued with minor variations ever since. The new party under Deakin's leadership lost the elections of 1910, and the Labor Party found itself voted into power with majorities in both the House of Representatives and the Senate for the first time in its brief history.

An Australian defence force

Defence is another important theme of the first ten years of the Commonwealth. In 1902 Australia had committed itself to a annual payment in support of the British navy's Australian squadron (see page 178), but Deakin soon recognised that the subsidy scheme was not popular and did little to encourage the growth of Australian patriotism. In 1905 he suggested to the Admiralty a scheme for a flotilla of Australian destroyers, only to have it torpedoed by the British who preferred a navy over which they exercised total control. Australian fears of Japan had been enhanced when the Japanese navy crushed the Russian fleet in the Straits of Tsushima that same year, and Japanese naval strength continued to grow.

The Japanese army had also scored landmark victories against China (1895 and 1900) and Russia (1905), and the parlous state of Australia's land defences similarly began to cause alarm. From 1904 onwards, with all-party support, a system of school cadet corps was established in which children learnt the rudiments of drill and rifle shooting; and in 1909 the Deakin fusion ministry brought in a system of compulsory training for junior cadets aged 12 to 14, senior cadets aged 14 to 18, and citizen forces aged 18 to 20.

In 1908, to the great displeasure of the British, Deakin had also secured for Australia a visit from the Great White Fleet of the United States Navy, then on a goodwill tour around the world. The name of the fleet reflected the colour of the ships and not the racial complexion of the American navy, but the general public welcomed the fleet with great exuberance. If a comparatively new nation such as the United States could have such a powerful fleet, why could not Australia have its own blue-water fleet? At the same time, Britain had become engaged in a race to build *Dreadnought* battleships to maintain her advantage over imperial Germany. Dreadnoughts marked such a technological advance that they rendered obsolete most existing warships, and thereby undermined Britain's historical position of naval supremacy. A genuine arms race was now under way and, because Dreadnoughts were extremely expensive to build, Britain began to look more kindly upon Australia's ambitions to possess a fleet of its own. Such a development would certainly relieve Britain of a significant financial strain. In 1909, the Admiralty reversed its previous views and recommended that the dominions be permitted to create fleets of their own and that these should be to a certain extent under local control. At an imperial defence conference on that year, the Admiralty proposed the creation of a Pacific fleet to which Britain, Australia, New Zealand, and Canada could contribute units. The Australian contribution, paid for by the Commonwealth and crewed as far as possible by Australians, was to consist of one armoured cruiser, three light cruisers, six destroyers, and three submarines. The ships were ordered from English shipyards and, in 1911, the king granted the title of 'Royal Australian Navy' to the new fleet. In Australian waters the fleet would be exclusively controlled by the Australian government, but in foreign ports the ships would take orders from the British government and, in time of war, they would automatically become part of the Royal Navy under the control of the Admiralty.

Early in 1910, the army received its equivalent of the visit of the Great White Fleet when Lord Kitchener of Khartoum toured Australia and inspected its military establishment for the Commonwealth government. Kitchener—in an echo of Henry Parkes' Tenterfield speech—recommended the formation of an army of 80 000 men, half to defend the cities and ports, and the rest to constitute a mobile strike force that could be deployed anywhere in Australia. To facilitate the rapid deployment of this force, Kitchener advised the construction of a network of railways and roads linking the entire country together. He also recommended the establishment of an officer training school modelled on America's West Point. In 1911, the Royal Military College of Australia was officially opened at Duntroon.

As the first full term of Labor government began after the 1910 elections, all these earlier strands of development became interwoven. The fears that had underlain the urge to federate the Australian colonies had blossomed into an Australian naval squadron and compulsory military training for all Australian males between the ages of 12 and 20. These institutions came into being as part of an Australian recognition that Japan constituted the main threat in any strategic assessment of this region. But, at the same time, British strategic assessments were identifying Germany as Britain's most formidable opponent. The military forces being brought into existence by Australian fears of the waking Asian giant were ironically destined, again, to be used to support another of Britain's wars in far-off parts of the globe. Nationalistic pride in the British Empire felt by most Australians meant that they failed to perceive the contradictions in this state of affairs. It was purely a matter of good fortune that conflict with Britain over the use of Australian troops was avoided until the 1940s. The seeds of the disagreement were always there—they just took a long time to germinate.

Labor legislation

In 1910, the Fisher Labor government brought in the first fully Labor pieces of legislation, when it introduced a land tax to be levied on unimproved properties of more than £5000 in value. The aim of the enactment was to break up the big estates and to force those who monopolised land to relinquish it and make cheaper land available to the people. Conservatives and some Liberals were horrified at such blatant class legislation, but it produced a useful revenue and subsequent governments found ways of rationalising their refusal to rescind it.

The second distinctive enactment of the Fisher government was the establishment, in 1911, of the Commonwealth Bank. It was to compete with the private banks in both savings and trading areas, and was designed to guarantee that workers would never again lose their savings through banks collapsing as they had during the 1890s depression. The bank was not given central banking functions, although it did become the main bank of issue. The Commonwealth Bank used post offices as its early savings bank branches and became deservedly popular with the lower levels of Australian society—who appreciated a bank guaranteed not to fail in times of depression or recession.

Expansion and growth

The years before the Great War constituted a period of rapid growth in all aspects of Australian development. Natural increase and a rapidly expanding British immigration boosted the population to almost five million by 1914. Cities grew very quickly in these years, as a majority of the immigrants sought work in the rapidly expanding factories growing up under the umbrella of new protection.

In rural districts, the wider use of refrigeration opened up overseas markets for Australian frozen meat and dairy produce and gave a great boost to rural settlement. The area under wheat acreage doubled between 1901 and 1914—largely because of the increasing use of superphosphates to force Australia's fossil soils into artificial fertility. William Farrer contributed by developing disease-resistant strains of wheat better suited to the Australian climate and dry-land farming. In the pastoral sector, the wool clip continued to rise steadily, and the season 1905/06 produced a record clip of more than one million bales, with prices continuing to climb in subsequent years.

By 1914, Australia seemed to be poised on the brink of another one of those waves of pioneering and development that had been characteristic of the nineteenth century. Capital flowed into the country to finance the public works programs required by such developments, and the growing population allowed the burden of annual loan interest payments to be disguised in such a way that it was hardly noticed. The federal system of government was obviously here to stay, and the rate of Commonwealth expansion could be seen in the increasing number of public servants (which had reached 35 000 by 1913), and by the federal government's annual expenditure (which had grown from £3 500 000 in 1901 to £9 million by 1913).

But Australia was no longer quarantined by distance from the rest of the world, and if Australians failed to see any relevance for them in the assassination of the Austrian Archduke Franz Ferdinand at Sarajevo in 1914, they soon discovered that even seemingly minor events far across the world could impinge in a most compelling and brutal fashion on their antipodean idyll.

Australia and World War I

On 5 August 1914, the prime minister, Joseph Cook (Deakin having retired from politics two years earlier, and Labor having lost the 1913 election) called together representatives of the press and informed them that Britain and Germany were at war. Another election campaign was currently under way, and both parties pledged Britain their full support, although the laurels for coining the unforgettable phrase rested with Labor leader Andrew Fisher, who promised that Australia would stand behind the mother country to help defend and protect her 'to our last man and our last shilling'. Australia had no right to declare war or even to choose neutrality. As an automatic result of Britain's declaration of war with Germany and Austria–Hungary, Australia was also at war. The Liberal government offered Britain an expeditionary force of 20 000 men, and placed the ships of the Royal Australian Navy at the disposal of the Admiralty. When Labor won a handsome victory in the elections a month later, Fisher moved quickly to honour the pledges made by the Liberals.

There was great initial enthusiasm for the war among Australians, and something very close to a national consensus existed on the necessity for Australia to be involved. Only the radical fringe of the industrial labour movement stood out against the tide of tribal atavism. The International Workers of the World, a small group of radical trade union syndicalists, called on the workers to resist calls to enlist in the armed services, and urged them not to become murderers of their fellow workers from foreign countries. Between 1914 and 1917, when the leadership was jailed and the organisation proscribed, the 'Wobblies', as they were known, campaigned consistently against the war. Why should workers sacrifice themselves in a conflict from which they stood to gain nothing? In 1915, Tom Barker encapsulated this outlook in a poster which caused him to receive jail terms totalling fifteen months and fines to the sum of £125. Barker's poster contained the words: 'To Arms! Capitalists, parsons, politicians, newspaper editors and other stay-at-home patriots, your country needs you in the trenches! Workers, follow Your Masters!'.[5]

In 1914, however, opposition to the war was minuscule, and men flocked into the recruiting offices of the Australian Imperial Forces (AIF). By year's end, more than 50 000 volunteers had enlisted, and a second contingent was added to the one already promised on the outbreak of war. Few of the men enlisted to protect the world from German militarism or even out of motives of imperial patriotism. That was the language of recruiting agents, clergymen, politicians, and the very group of stay-at-home patriots so clearly identified by Tom Barker—the language of

Tom Barker's subversive poster. (Australian History Museum, Macquarie University)

those who did not expect to have to fight themselves. The vast bulk of the young men appear to have enlisted from a thirst for adventure and the excitement of overseas travel. The pay was good and their mates were joining up. Nobody foresaw the awful carnage of trench warfare, and many felt that the war would be over before the end of the year.

By the quirks of circumstance, Japan had become an ally of Australia's in the war, and Japanese warships helped protect troop convoys conveying Australian soldiers to the fighting on the other side of the world. There were thirty-eight troop transports in the first convoy to leave Australia in November 1914, and they were protected by four cruisers—one British, one Japanese, and two Australian. One of the Australian cruisers, HMAS *Sydney*, temporarily left the convoy to engage the German light cruiser *Emden* on 9 November and drove it ashore on the Cocos Islands, a battered and sinking wreck. It was Australia's second victory of the war and caused enormous celebration and jubilation. Earlier in the war, a hastily raised expeditionary force of three battalions had been sent to capture German New Guinea and it was here that Australia's first casualties occurred in subduing the German garrison at Rabaul.

Gallipoli

Those activities were mere curtain-raisers, however, and the first major campaign for Australians was against the Turks at Gallipoli in the Dardanelles. British strategy was to gain control of the Dardanelles, permitting a British fleet to sail into the Bosphorus and shell Constantinople—thereby driving Turkey out of the war, relieving pressure on Russia, and cutting the enemy's lines of communications. It was an imaginatively conceived plan that foundered on mismanagement and was to involve Australia in one of the worst defeats suffered by British forces during the war. The Australians and New Zealanders (ANZACs) were landed on an

Contemporary cartoon extolling the bravery of the Australian troops at Gallipoli, 1915. (Australian History Museum, Macquarie University)

impossible beach by the British navy, and found themselves confronted by a series of ridges and steep cliffs. Turks were entrenched in the hills overlooking the beach where the landings took place, and casualties were heavy. After eight months of extraordinary heroism and hand-to-hand fighting, the British High Command recognised that the Gallipoli campaign had been a total disaster, and resolved to withdraw. The retreat was carried out with great cunning between 18 and 20 December 1915, and the ANZACs withdrew with only two casualties for the operation. But the toll had been considerably higher in the long months between April and December.

When the British evacuated Gallipoli, the ANZACs left behind almost 10 000 comrades who had been killed during the campaign. Furthermore, another 20 000 of them had been wounded, and the lengthening casualty lists published in Australia caused many to rethink their attitudes towards the war. Domestic political developments assisted this change of view. On the other hand, the bravery, courage, and endurance of the ANZACs had occasioned considerable pride in Australia, and newspapers carried detailed accounts of the exploits of Australian troops. In one month, during the fighting at Lone Pine, seven Victoria Crosses were awarded to Australian soldiers, six in one day, and the people back home gloried in the bravery. In 1916, the day of 25 April was proclaimed as ANZAC Day, and the speeches made at that first celebration demonstrated that Australia was celebrating more than just the soldierly abilities and manly courage of its army. The new prime minister, William Morris Hughes—Fisher having retired to be Australian high commissioner in London—announced that the defeat at Gallipoli was a feat of arms almost unparalleled in the annals of war. When such bravery, nobility, and self-sacrifice could emerge, he asked, how could it be said that the war was wholly an evil? Frequent allusions were also made to the belief that Gallipoli somehow marked a baptism of blood that raised Australia to nationhood. It quickly became accepted as a rite of passage to maturity as a nation, purchased with the blood sacrifice of all those thousands of dead and wounded Australians. The troops had marched off to war in 1914 singing 'Australia will be there', and Gallipoli proved that Australia had been there and had not been found wanting in the hour of trial.

War weariness

Despite the eulogies, however, by 1916 things were not going well for Hughes and his government in Australia. The casualty lists from Gallipoli appalled many people, and caused them to rethink their views of the war. When the ANZACs were transported from the Middle East to Europe where the British High Command seemed to use them as shock troops, the casualty lists grew longer and disenchantment increased. For example, in one nine-day period at Bullecourt, the Australians suffered almost 10 000 casualties. Volunteers no longer appeared in sufficient numbers, and recruitment levels steadily declined. Labour resistance to the war grew as the industrial movement swung more and more towards the views so consistently propounded by Tom Barker and the Wobblies.

The burden of the war fell most unevenly on the Australian populace and, from the end of 1914, living standards fell and wages were frozen while prices soared out of control. Unemployment doubled during the war years, and rents rose alarmingly. The truth of Tom Barker's poster seemed self-evident to many workers who believed that profiteering was rife and that the increasingly conservative government was doing little or nothing to control it. The rising sense of grievance and disaffection erupted in 1916, when the prime minister attempted to introduce conscription for service overseas in the army.

Conscription referenda

In 1916, Prime Minister Hughes returned from a visit to Britain where the High Command had convinced him that conscription was the only way in which the Australian forces could replace the heavy losses that they were suffering in France. Australia had about 100 000 men under arms in France but, if the high casualty rate was maintained, the declining monthly recruitments in Australia would be insufficient to sustain the force. Enlistment figures had dropped during 1916 from just under 19 000 a month to less than 7000 a month by the middle of the year.

Hughes could not just legislate for conscription—although legally he had the power to do so. He knew that he would split the Australian Labor Party (ALP) if he tried and, although he might get a conscription Bill through the House of Representatives with support from the opposition, he also knew it would fail to pass the Senate. The situation came to a head on 24 August when the War Office called Hughes requesting urgent reinforcements for Australia's five divisions in France. They demanded 32 500 men during September and 16 500 in each of the next three months. Volunteer enlistment figures showed such targets to be unattainable under the current system, so Hughes persuaded his government to put the question of conscription to the Australian people in a plebiscite. If he got the overwhelming majority he hoped, it might be possible to bully his opponents within the ALP into line with such a democratic decision.

On 4 September, the New South Wales Labor League expelled

Hughes and the ALP began to fall apart. By October, when the referendum was put to the vote, four of the ministers in Hughes' government had resigned over the issue.

The campaigns in the conscription referenda—a second one was held in 1917—were waged with an enthusiasm, a partisanship, and a virulence that Australia had not hitherto experienced. The community split reflected political divisions that ran along the class, racial, and religious fault lines of the society. Although the main outlines can be delineated fairly quickly, the divisions were often masked and far from clearcut. Archbishop Mannix from Melbourne, for example, became a leading campaigner for a vote against conscription, compounding Irish hatred for English policies towards the country of his birth with the view that Australians ought not be compelled to die in England's war. There is no doubt that Mannix represented the majority of Australian Roman Catholics in putting these views, but the Roman Catholic Archbishops of Sydney, Perth, and Hobart supported the war and advocated a vote in favour of conscription.

The referendum campaigns revealed just how deeply divided was Australia over the issue. Arguments for a vote in favour stressed the ethnic Britishness of Australia and highlighted sentiments of loyalty and the need to defend Australian democracy by fighting German tyranny in Europe. Accusations of treason and disloyalty and of pro-German sympathies were freely flung at opponents of conscription, and old communal divisions of race and religion reappeared. Opponents of conscription concentrated on the argument that Australia had done enough already to help Britain, and that no government had the moral right to compel its citizens to fight in a war outside their own country. The morality of the pro-conscriptionists was attacked and they were described as people prepared to sentence innocent men to death. In 1916 the answer was 'No' by a majority of 72 476. In Victoria (the home state of Archbishop Mannix), Tasmania, and Western Australia the people voted 'Yes', but New South Wales (the home state of the prime minister), Queensland, and South Australia voted 'No'. Farmers might well have decided the outcome of the referendum by voting in the negative for fear of losing their labour force.

The Nationalist Party

On 14 November, Hughes and his supporters in the federal Australian Labor Party walked out of an angry caucus meeting which was about to put a vote of no confidence in the prime minister. Hughes went into coalition with the Liberals, and formed the Nationalist Party, under his leadership, to continue the war. Only twenty-five Labor parliamentarians went with Hughes (of a total of sixty-five). The remainder formally expelled Hughes and his supporters from the ALP, and elected Frank Tudor as their new leader. Similar splits occurred in all states except Queensland, and the split in the party was now nationwide. A deep and abiding bitterness accompanied the split. In the Western Australian branch of the party all files dealing with expelled members and their subsequent political activities were brought together under the simple filing classification 'RATS'. The conscription split was the first of three major disruptions of the Australian Labor Party on a federal level, and the party took many years to rebuild after each one.

In May 1917 a federal election was held, and the Nationalist government under Hughes was returned to office. The electorate clearly distinguished between a referendum and an election, and the majority vote against conscription did not translate into a majority against the war. The Nationalists won 46 seats in the House of Representatives, leaving the ALP with only 19, and the Nationalists won all 18 of the Senate vacancies. Rural districts that had voted against conscription voted to return Nationalist members as the country quickly reverted to its characteristic conservatism once the labour supply had been protected. This swing back to the government did not protect Hughes from another crushing defeat when, in November 1917, he attempted a second referendum to introduce conscription. This time the negative majority reached 165 588, and Victoria also produced a 'No' majority.

War's end

As the casualty lists continued to lengthen, workers' weariness with the war produced the biggest industrial upheaval that Australia had seen to that date. By July 1917 workers had become thoroughly disenchanted with the war and the privations and hardships that they had to endure under wartime restrictions. The strike eventually involved 95 000 workers in the crucial transport, maritime, and mining areas. The Nationalist government in New South Wales, in partnership with the Hughes government, determined to break the strike and called for 'loyalist' workers to keep the industries running. 'Loyalists' was a fancy name for scabs or strikebreakers, and they received preference in employment. The result was a total defeat for the trade unions which were forced to return to work having gained nothing. Friction between unionists and loyalists remained a problem in the workplace for years to come. However, the general strike and the conscription referenda did demonstrate that the earlier consensus on the war had irretrievably broken down on class lines, with the middle class fervently pro-war and the working class vehemently opposed. Declining enlistments—despite the best efforts of official tub-thumping, flag-waving recruitment campaigns—lend support to this view.

As the war ground finally to its conclusion and towards German surrender, the cost to Australia justified the feelings of weariness. Australia's combined casualties in the war had been higher on a per capita basis than any other country's, with 65% of its total expeditionary force having become casualties during the war—compared with 51% for Britain, 50% for Canada, and 59% for

New Zealand. With a population of less than 5 million, Australia lost almost 60 000 dead and returned over 152 000 wounded. In money terms the war had cost Australia almost £377 million and had saddled the country with a level of indebtedness that dwarfed pre-war figures. In 1918 alone, the war cost Australia nearly £81 million, and this was £3 250 000 more than Britain spent in the same period. The money to meet these expenses had been borrowed largely from Britain, which effectively charged Australia for the sacrifices made on behalf of the mother country.

Aside from the dubious honour of participating in the final victory, these sacrifices gained Hughes separate representation at the Peace Conference, which met in Paris on 18 January 1919. The United States of America had become involved in the war in its final months, and President Woodrow Wilson's fourteen-point proposal formed the basis for discussions. Some of Wilson's points struck directly at Australia's interests, for they were theoretical maxims of behaviour based on humanitarian idealism. Three in particular, relating to 'freedom of the seas', 'no indemnities', and 'no annexations' were lost by the president, and he clashed many times with Hughes' unashamed assertion of Australia's aspirations to annex New Guinea. The prime minister's reminders that Australia's casualty rate gave him a privileged position over the commander-in-chief of the late-arriving Americans wounded Wilson's sense of *amour propre*, and Hughes himself was singularly unimpressed by Wilson:[6]

> He was an idealist, but his ideals had feet of clay! His notes about peace based upon justice and right were beautiful to read, but justice and right counted for nothing with him, when force, strongly arrayed, threatened them. He was bold, but not too bold; his word was his bond, but when his personal interests were involved he abandoned those who, relying upon his support, had committed themselves to a policy which he himself had suggested.

Perhaps Wilson did not understand that he was facing, in

Hughes, a man determined to show that the losses Australia had sustained had not been entirely in vain. Moreover, in addition to his determination to secure New Guinea for Australia and to make certain that no Japanese-sponsored statements of racial equality impinged on Australia's sovereign right to implement an immigration policy of its choosing, Hughes viewed Australia's participation in the Peace Conference as a symbolic and formal recognition by Britain and other foreign powers that Australia had become a fully autonomous nation entitled to enjoy equality of status with all other countries in the world.[7]

Hughes secured a 'C' class mandate over New Guinea for Australia in the teeth of President Wilson's opposition, and Hughes needled and provoked Wilson unmercifully to the great amusement of the other delegates. The prime minister enjoyed less success with his argument that the entire costs of the war should be levied against Germany, and Australia's war debts could not therefore be written off against German reparations. The debt owed to English bondholders as a result of Hughes' failure on this point would come back to haunt Australian governments during the next depression. And this amounted to the sum total of benefits Australia received from four years of war and a 65% casualty rate. No wonder Hughes commented to the House of Representatives that the true gains were national safety and liberty—they at least could not be quantified. But the spectacle of the prime minister taking refuge in such vague generalities to justify four years of sacrifice was not an edifying one.

And what of the returned soldiers? What sort of a country did they find when they returned home? Many of them seemed to be confused by the divisions in society brought about by the war. Where they had left mateship, they returned to strife between unionists and loyalists in the labour force. Continuous industrial conflict in 1919 made it the costliest period—in terms of days lost—since statistics had been kept. Returned soldiers found themselves in opposition to 'Bolsheviks' and 'shirkers' who allegedly had stirred up trouble at home while they were away fighting. In Queensland, where a number of radical Russians had lived since the failure of the 1905 anti-Tsarist revolution in Russia, a confrontation occurred between returned soldiers and men bearing red flags of revolution. A march was organised on the Russian Workers' Association and shots were fired from the Russian building. Police dispersed the crowd. The returned soldiers and their supporters marched on the Russian building again a few nights later, only to be halted by a row of police with fixed bayonets. Shots were fired on both sides and nineteen men were injured. Similar demonstrations of disaffection marked the behaviour of returned soldiers in other states, and pitched battles were fought between returned soldiers in alliance with waterfront strikers against the loyalist National Workers Union in Western Australia.

Strikes and civil disorder flared spasmodically as Australia made the rapid adjustment to peace. Prices had continued to rise, and wages lagged far behind, so there were genuine reasons for agitation and discontent. Employers and the middle classes tended to label this legitimate activism as evidence of Bolshevik sympathies and a willingness to engage in bloody revolution. Friction between returned soldiers and the police sometimes boiled over in riots and violence, to the horror of many well-to-do Australians who could not understand how yesterday's heroes could sink to such depths. The men were already tasting the 'ashes in the mouth' that their victory had secured, and more and more would question as the next two decades unfolded, whether all their sacrifices and endurance had been for nothing. The appeal of fascism and communism to such men as these in Europe was not to be without its parallels in Australia.

7

A Land Fit for Heroes

The aftermath of war in Australia was accompanied by widespread social and economic dislocation. During the 1920s, the Commonwealth government made repeated attempts to honour its promises to the returning soldiers while, at the same time, it confronted a rising tide of industrial militancy from the trade union movement which had come to distrust the federal government and regard it as a creature of the employers. One of the most intractable difficulties for both state and federal governments was how to reintegrate the thousands of returned servicemen into society and the workforce.

Repatriation

Prime Minister Hughes had ensured that, by the end of 1919, the vast bulk of the soldiers had returned to Australia, but post-war reconstruction and resettlement proved difficult. How could employment be provided for more than 100 000 extra men in twelve months? How could soldiers be reabsorbed into the community without disruption? And what of the soldiers themselves? They had been through up to four years of hell on earth—many of the younger ones having gone straight from school into the army and having known nothing but childhood and war. How could a grateful government train such men for useful lives in the community? The problem was worse for men who had been clerks, because women now occupied their jobs. Women were cheaper to employ, and many soldiers found it very difficult to obtain work in their former professions. The economy had adjusted to new conditions and a different labour force during the years of war.

A Repatriation Department had been established to coordinate this effort to ease the men back into civilian life. It paid them a weekly allowance that was less than the basic wage, but at least it was something. The department also undertook to set up returned men in their own businesses if that was what they desired, or to train them for a profession or a trade and provide the necessary tools and equipment. Passages for wives or sweethearts from overseas were paid, together with a grant towards the cost of building a house and buying furniture. Disabled and incapacitated soldiers and their dependants were to be supported with pensions and allowances—which, by 1931, had risen to just under £8 million. One major way of helping soldiers back into employment was to grant preference to returned men when job vacancies occurred. The Commonwealth and all the state governments (except Queensland) inserted such a preference clause into their industrial legislation. Queensland's Labor government maintained its stance of preference for trade unionists but, since thousands of the ex-soldiers were also union members, the conflict was more apparent than real. As the 1920s progressed, however, the preference for returned servicemen became a real bone of contention on the waterfront, where employers attempted to use it to dispose of men they regarded as union troublemakers.

Soldier settlers

Probably the most popular choice of the returned men was for a piece of land of their own on which they could set themselves up as small-scale farmers. The longevity of the myth of Australian land ownership is again apparent. Most of the soldiers who settled on the land were not farmers or the sons of farmers, yet the myth of the superiority of rural occupations in bringing happiness and security to a man and his family refused to die out in Australia. The Commonwealth and the various state governments cooperated with one another in this endeavour, with the states providing the Crown land and the federal authorities subsidising the soldiers with loans, fertiliser, roads, and water bores. Almost 40 000 men elected to become 'soldier settlers' in this way—but, by and large, they met with the same lack of success achieved by all previous attempts to place a yeomanry on the land. There seemed to be a refusal to learn the lessons of experience in the persistence with which urban Australians hungered for their own piece of rural Australia, and the pertinacity with which they clung to the rural myth of self-supporting independence demonstrates the difficulty of shifting such deep-seated cultural notions—even after almost a century of demonstrated failure.

In Western Australia, the soldiers worked in groups clearing the land before each man received his allotment for his own farm. This 'Group Settlement Scheme' was designed to produce a viable dairy industry in the southern areas of the state. The enthusiastic support of the premier was such as to earn him the nickname of 'Moo-Cow Mitchell'. The men worked extraordinarily hard, and the dairy produce from the area did improve supplies in the state, but at a very great cost. Consumers paid more, and the farms were marginal. In New South Wales the situation was so bad that it was estimated in 1929 that the Commonwealth had lost £24 million. Thousands of the soldier settlers had already walked off their farms and the condition for those who remained were very hard. Some areas, such as the Griffith district in the irrigation area, proved to be successful, and 700 soldier settlers made a go of their properties there. However, overall, despite enormous efforts by the soldiers, the schemes amounted to very little. Later in the decade, the Australian government signed agreements with the British

These men are convicted of having served their Country.

Contemporary cartoon depicting the vicissitudes of soldier settlers, c. 1920s. (Australian History Museum, Macquarie University)

government to encourage British ex-soldiers with a similar settlement scheme as part of a campaign to populate the interior of Australia, but these attempts proved to be just as expensive and unsuccessful. Except in limited fertile regions, the Australian climatic cycles and fossil soils do not really suit the European-style small-scale peasant farming model, but lack of success has never stopped such attempts being made, and the prospect of owning a small property in the country continued to attract urban Australians for the rest of the twentieth century. In the 1920s the schemes for soldier settlement were predicated on the underlying assumption that Australia possessed an almost unlimited capacity to absorb farmers. Moreover, they relied upon the application of vast quantities of borrowed capital to unproductive land, and involved an enormous outlay in public works such as railways, water supplies, roads, and so on to bring the produce of the new districts into the market structure of the states. By the end of the decade, government persistence had resulted in a high level of rural indebtedness—as surviving farmers struggled along on credit, relying on the maintenance of stable, high prices on overseas markets for their produce. Many farmers were dangerously overextended and they and their creditors came to grief when falling export prices for primary produce heralded the start of the Great Depression.

The losses sustained on the soldier resettlement schemes alone were estimated in January 1929 by Mr Justice Pike (who conducted an official inquiry into soldier settlement) to be in the vicinity of £23 500 000. The Pike report produced a devastating analysis of the scheme in which he highlighted shortage of capital, declining prices, and the unsuitability of the would-be farmers as the main reasons behind the failure.[1]

These rural activities were not the only large expenditure undertaken by governments to resettle the ex-soldiers. All demobbed soldiers received a gratuity from the state in the form of bonds when they arrived back in Australia, and many soldiers used this to help establish themselves in small businesses. The state also took on the support of all ex-soldiers' dependants in the event that a digger died from causes related to war.

New political parties

Two new political parties appeared during these years at opposite ends of the political spectrum. In September 1920 small groups of socialists, former Wobblies, and admirers of the revolution in Russia, came together to form the Communist Party of Australia. Branches were established in Sydney, Melbourne, and Perth, and the program of action outlined in the party manifesto was put into action, especially the educative work of raising the social consciousness of Australian workers. The organisation was beset with factionalism, and did not become a significant political force in the land until the rapid gains it made during the 1940s in the trade union movement.

The second party, which enjoyed considerably more success, was the Country Party—under the leadership of Dr Earle Page. The party came into formal existence in 1919 from a loose collection of conservative farmers' associations, all of which felt that the Nationalists led by Hughes no longer adequately represented rural interests. The Country Party initially favoured removing tariff protection for manufactured goods on the grounds that tariffs increased costs to the farmers, and tariffs on agricultural equipment and fertiliser also antagonised them. To add fuel to the fire, Earle Page had a particular and personal dislike of the prime minister. The Nationalists were returned to office at the elections of 1919, but the farmers' groups managed to win eleven seats in the House of Representatives. These elections were the first in which preferential voting was used—rather than the 'first-past-the-post' system. The preferential method permitted an exchange of preferences between conservative groups such as the Country Party and the Nationalists. This exchange of preferences did not split the anti-Labor vote (as a second conservative candidate would have done under the old system) and it allowed the conservative parties to combine and maximise the anti-Labor vote. The Country Party might well be described as the child of the preferential voting system.

The Hughes' Nationalist government retained office in 1919, but with a greatly reduced majority. The government was supported by the Country Party despite its hostility towards Hughes whom it regarded as unreliable, autocratic, and dangerously sympathetic to state-run enterprises such as the national shipping line and the Commonwealth Bank—which Page regarded as tantamount to socialism. In 1922, Hughes accepted a gift from anonymous sources of £25 000—an enormous sum in those days—for services rendered to the Commonwealth of Australia. This caused deep shock and outrage to many politicians on both sides of the house. The ALP claimed that Hughes was being paid off for bringing down the ALP government and splitting the party. Conservatives were unhappy that the gift gave the impression that the prime minister could be bought.

In the elections of December 1922, Hughes led the Nationalists to victory, but with a further reduction in seats. The need arose for a coalition with the Country Party which had increased its representation to fourteen seats. In these circumstances, the Country Party tail actually wagged the Nationalist Party dog, and Page announced that his party was quite willing to enter into a coalition, but they would have no truck with any government led by Hughes or in which Hughes held a ministry. Page maintained this veto for several weeks of wheeling and dealing and, eventually, Hughes resigned as prime minister and leader of the Nationalists and retired to the backbenches. Stanley Melbourne Bruce, a Victorian businessman and Hughes' treasurer, became the leader of the National Party and prime minister of the Bruce–Page government which lasted until 1929.

Rising militancy

The years of the Bruce–Page government were a time when it appeared to many middle-class Australians that the trade unions were intent on pulling the country down around their ears. Although this was a period of great industrial tension and militancy, the formation of the Communist Party had very little to do with fomenting the problem, despite the conservative government discovering in 1925 that there were electoral benefits in promoting the 'red' scare.

There was a significant difference between political Labor and industrial labour as the decade progressed, marked by the apparent willingness of industrial labour to attempt to change society from below by union muscle rather than through the medium of electoral politics. The reasons for this disillusionment with political Labor were a legacy of the war years, when the ALP, and then the Nationalists led by the renegade ALP leader Hughes, systematically alienated the trade union movement by the conscription campaigns and the employment of scabs during the general strike of 1917. Moreover, wages had been frozen by former Labor politicians such as Hughes and the New South Wales premier William Holman while prices and rents had been permitted to sky-rocket. By the end of the war, real wages had fallen by almost £1 per week, and unionists felt betrayed. Preference to returned soldiers also cut at the very basis of trade unionism and, in New South Wales and Victoria in particular, such preference turned unionists into enemies of the ex-diggers. Hughes' acceptance of his reward money caused enormous disgust and did nothing to enhance the reputation of politicians. Finally, the Bruce–Page government seemed obviously to be a government of the ruling classes. Bruce was an English-educated gentleman who drove a Rolls-Royce, wore spats in the cold weather, and spoke with a carefully modulated English accent. The gulf between industrial labour and the federal government had never seemed so wide.

Industrial unrest became endemic during these years, in the Seamen's Union, on the waterfront, and in the coal-mining industry. The Bruce–Page government swung like a weather cock in the strengthening industrial breeze, and attempted to deal with the problem initially by strengthening the system of Commonwealth arbitration and passing legislation allowing it to deport foreign-born industrial agitators. When this attempt demonstrably failed, the government then attempted to pass back to the states nearly all the Commonwealth powers in the area of industrial arbitration. Eventually this inconsistency over the arbitration issue brought the government to electoral defeat at the hands of an exasperated populace on the eve of the Great Depression.

Financial rationalisation

The story of the Bruce–Page years is not entirely a negative one, however, and it is worth noting the extent to which this conservative administration had reconstructed the country's finances and cleared the way for the Commonwealth government to take a position of financial leadership that had never been envisaged by the founding fathers of the constitution in 1901. During the war, the Commonwealth had introduced an income tax and, after 1920, had continued to pay the states a per capita grant of 25 shillings. The states also continued to tax incomes under the powers retained in the constitution, and the federal government tried without success to get the states to agree to give up the per capita payments. The public at large regarded the double taxation system as an unnecessary burden and demanded change. The Bruce–Page government in 1926 proposed to abolish the per capita payments and, as a *douceur* to the states, it offered to withdraw from the field of income taxation altogether. The states rejected this offer. In the following year the federal government imposed another solution on the states which involved a fundamental restructuring of Commonwealth–State relationships.

Since federation, the Commonwealth and the states had competed with one another to raise loans overseas. The effect of this competition had been to raise interest rates and increase the cost of development in Australia. In 1924 Bruce had managed to persuade the state premiers to establish a Loan Council to coordinate approaches to overseas money markets and to agree on such issues as the total amount to be raised each year and what proportion of this amount each government should receive. In 1927 he threatened to abolish the per capita payments and forced the states to formalise the Loan Council and the financial restructuring by passing identical legislation in every state. The Financial Agreement of 1927 gave the Loan Council legal status and power as a permanent entity to control the methods of government borrowing. In return, the Commonwealth assumed responsibility for both the past and future debts of the states, and the states and the Commonwealth undertook to make regular payments to a sinking fund designed to cover the costs of all debt incurred as a result of governmental borrowing at both state and federal levels. As a result of the Loan Council, Commonwealth power dramatically increased at the expense of the states—for the prime minister needed to obtain the support of only two of the premiers to impose his policies upon all the states. In addition, although the council had been established for the specific and narrow purpose of coordinating government borrowing, it soon came to exercise authority over the whole range of the states' financial affairs. The pendulum of power had swung strongly in favour of the central government.

Unyoking the Commonwealth Bank

In 1924, Bruce's government also passed important legislation to render the Commonwealth Bank independent of political control. Previously, the single governor of the Commonwealth Bank had been directly responsible to the treasurer of the day but, under the new legislation, the governor became answerable to a board of directors of whom the secretary to the Treasury was only one. The other six directors were to comprise men connected with manufacturing, agriculture, or commerce, and two with banking. The bank also became the sole bank of issue for banknotes. This change removed, at a stroke, the ability of the government to control the policy of the central bank, and the ALP was horrified that any government would voluntarily relinquish control over such a major component of the economy. However, Earle Page of the Country Party, who also held the Treasury portfolio, pointed out that it was an express purpose of the Act to render the operations of the Commonwealth Bank independent of government interference. It was an enactment that was to haunt the incoming Scullin government and hamstring its attempts to deal with the depression.

The price of protection

At federation, Australia had embraced a policy of protection of industry, and the system had become an entrenched part of Australian life. But this did not come cheaply, and the extension of protection to primary products—which was a significant focus of the Country Party and led to the gibe that its policy was to privatise gains and socialise losses—helped make Australia more vulnerable when the severities of the Great Depression began to impact during the early 1930s. Although manufacturing was essentially restricted to the domestic market, the tariff wall behind which it sheltered continued to affect the domestic economy. The costs of protection added to the price of imported goods, allowing a margin for the costs of domestic goods to be increased. The result was that the general public paid higher prices for both. Because Arbitration courts took prices into account when they set wage levels for the community, the cost of protection was a higher cost of living. For as long as Australia's exports of primary produce and minerals continued to earn well overseas, the community could afford the social costs of protection and absorb them. During the 1920s, however, the power of the Country Party, and the anxiety of the government to provide markets for the produce of the soldier-settler farmers, led the government to extend protection by way of subsidies to many primary industries. Since 1905 sugar had been a special case in which the government, for historical reasons, paid subsidies to keep the industry afloat and permit it to sell its produce internationally. It was joined in the 1920s by other products, such as butter, which gained a similar advantage to keep the local dairy industry going and ensure that it did not have to compete on even terms with New Zealand dairy produce (which could be shipped to Australia and still sold cheaper than the local product). The same situation arose in relation to dried fruits, timber, and other rural industries. In 1928, it was calculated that protection to industry cost £26 million per year, and protection to primary producers £22 million per year. But, without protection, the standard of living would undoubtedly fall.[2]

Militancy and the ALP

The ALP was in opposition in federal parliament during these years, and it mirrored its links with the trade union movement by going through a short-lived period of radicalism—which, typically, was modified in the interests of political survival. The years after World War I were a time of industrial militancy and disenchantment with the political process. This militancy took tangible form in 1921 when the ALP adopted what became known as the 'socialist objective'. At the annual conference of the party in Brisbane that year, a motion was carried to the effect: 'That the socialisation of industry, production, distribution, and exchange be the objective of the Australian Labor Party'. This objective was carefully modified by the rider: 'That the party does not seek to abolish private ownership even of any of the instruments of production where such instrument is utilised by its owner in a socially useful manner and without exploitation'—but this precaution did not stop Labor's opponents from seizing upon the objective as proof that the party was dangerously revolutionary. The new objective bedevilled the ALP for the next fifty years by saddling it with a form of words that antagonised electors and gave a weapon to its opponents. Moreover, although it was an objective that encapsulated the ideal of the 'fair go', the party never seriously attempted either to implement it or to explain it.

Other signs of militancy during the decade were: the success of Queensland's ALP government in abolishing the state's upper house, the Legislative Council; the Lang government's introduction of child endowment in New South Wales; the formation of a national organisation of trade unions—the Australian Council of Trade Unions (ACTU)—which was to act as a federal executive of the industrial labour movement and present a united front to employers; and the already mentioned formation of the Communist Party. The Australian Workers' Union (AWU), which covered most of the workers in primary industry, refused to join the Australian Council of Trade Unions (ACTU) on the grounds that the new organisation would bring the trade union movement under the domination of communists and wreckers. It reflected within the ranks of labour those distinctions between town and country that had produced the Country Party at the political level. Rural Australia was seen as increasingly conservative, and the cities as hotbeds of progressive thinking.

An era of domestic change

The older generation clucked with disapproval as the age of jazz and flappers, the Charleston, and short dresses became established, and as drinking, smoking, and having a good time became the prevailing sentiments of the generation which had gone through World War I and survived. The foundations of life seemed to be under attack, with conventional morality overthrown, religion mocked, and women elected to parliament—such as Western Australian Edith Cowan's winning a place in the state's Legislative Assembly in 1921. When federal parliament moved to its new home in Canberra in 1927, one of the many worries concerned the effect of unsupervised hostel living on the single young women who followed their jobs to the new capital—although the vision of Canberra as an antipodean Sodom and Gomorrah did not eventuate.

The subversion of moral conventions was not the only change. The aeroplane played its part in making the 1920s a decade of accelerated change. Australians had been flying in the Middle East and Europe during the war, and the application of the plane to breaking down the isolation of distance in Australia moved apace. In 1919, the first transcontinental flight from Point Cook to Darwin took place, and Bass Strait was crossed the same year. Ross and Keith Smith made the first flight from England to Australia. In 1920, the first regular passenger service was inaugurated between Charleville and Cloncurry by the Queensland and Northern Territory Aerial Service (QANTAS). In Western Australia in the following year, Charles Kingsford-Smith and Norman Brearley began regular flights between Geraldton and ports on the north-west coast as far as Broome. By 1928, Kingsford-Smith had crossed the Pacific from the United States to Australia in the famous *Southern Cross* aeroplane, and the historical isolation of Australia from the rest of the European world, which had begun to break down with the electric telegraph in the 1870s, was finally over. The sense of being isolated was a distinctly Australian psychological phenomenon, and it remained ingrained as part of the national ethos until World War II when Japan demonstrated very clearly that the continent was much closer to Asia than was comfortable—whatever Australians might think about their distance from Europe or America.

International relations

The 1920s also marked a rapid change in Australia's formal relationships with the wider world. In 1922, when Britain and Turkey wrangled on the brink of war over the Charnak Incident, the Hughes government offered to send a 20 000 man expeditionary force to Britain's aid if it were needed. Australia knew nothing about the incident and the unreserved support for the United Kingdom was very much a personal response from the prime minister. Stanley Melbourne Bruce had been most unimpressed with Hughes' automatic response and, when he became prime minister, he determined to ensure that Australia would be better informed about events in Britain and would never again find itself on the brink of war without adequate warning. To this end, he secured the appointment of Richard Casey as a liaison officer in London who would be attached to the British Foreign Office and keep the Australian government apprised of changes in British policy and the state of affairs in Europe. Casey was appointed to a position in the office of the secretary to Cabinet and, from then on, Bruce had an inside account of the international situation and of the state of British politics.

In many ways, the appointment of Casey marks the beginning of the Australian diplomatic service. In 1926, the Balfour Declaration heralded a major alteration in the relationship between England and her dominions which were henceforth to be regarded as fully independent sovereign nations. This was formalised in 1931 when the British parliament passed the Statute of Westminster and gave legislative force to Balfour's declaration of intent. The Statute of Westminster, however, was not ratified by the Australian government until 1942, when the ALP under John Curtin formally accepted for Australia a place among the independent nation states of the world. During the 1930s, Australian governments of whatever political persuasion were in no hurry to cut the painter that bound Australia and Britain together.

The spectre of depression

Fripperies such as the embryo diplomatic service, or Australia's legal status as a dominion in a British empire composed of autonomous states, were far from the Scullin government's mind when it assumed office after the 1929 elections. To be sure, Scullin insisted successfully on the government's right to recommend the appointment of the first Australian-born governor-general in 1930, even in the teeth of the king's obvious disapproval of the chief justice of the High Court, Sir Isaac Isaacs. But the state of the economy preoccupied the government, as the country plunged deeper into depression with every passing day.

It was the old story all over again. Australia had borrowed

The unemployed queue for the dole in Sydney, 1930s.

approximately £225 million between 1919 and 1929, and nearly three-quarters of it had been used on long-term development projects. Originally Australia's overseas debts in London stood at £400 million. The money required an annual interest payment of £27 million, and there were no returns from such development investment in the short term to help pay this. Moreover, interest still had to be paid on the large loans raised during the war. While the prices of Australia's primary produces remained buoyant in world markets, the unbalanced Australian economy could survive and even continue to deliver a higher standard of living to its people than most other countries in the world. The structural weaknesses within the economy were exposed for all to see when prices earned by Australia's exports fell dramatically between 1928 and 1931, and the country slumped rapidly into depression.

Wool and wheat accounted for three-quarters of Australia's exports, and prices tumbled to only a quarter of the pre-depression price by 1931. Overseas loan funds were unavailable, and this increased the impact of the depression and made the recovery a slow, painful, and drawn-out affair. Australia was hit harder than most countries by the Great Depression and the gap between conditions of life before and during the depression was more marked than for most other peoples.

Australia fared only marginally better than Germany in terms of unemployment—and, in Germany, the hardship produced Adolf Hitler and Nazism. Unemployment in Australia rose from about 8% to 30% during the winter of 1932, and the annual average during the depression period was 23.4%.

Despite the misery and the hardship, interest on overseas loans still had to be paid. The Loans Council and the establishment of the federal government's' statutory control over the borrowings of the states had come too late to help in averting the depression. How to pay the overseas interest bills from a declining revenue base became one of the major problems confronting the Scullin administration when it came to office, but there were others that rendered the job even more difficult, if not well-nigh impossible.

The effect on government

The ALP, under James Scullin, had come back to office after more than ten years in the wilderness following the split over conscription. Two of the legacies left to the new administration by Bruce caused immeasurable concern and helped, only two years later, to destroy the government. The first of these poisoned wells was a hostile Senate controlled by a large Nationalist majority. The ALP had again found itself in office but not in power. Bruce himself recognised the strong position in which he had left the Nationalists in the Senate, and he advised them not to waste it. It had become obvious to him that no government could avert the depression, and that conditions of life would deteriorate so badly that the voters would turn on whatever government happened to be in office during these years. The astute Bruce correctly foretold the fate of every government, state and federal, in Australia during these years, irrespective of its political coloration. They all fell from office at the next elections. The Senate could block Labor's more radical attempts to come to grips with the depression and the ALP, thus inhibited, would collapse and allow the Nationalists to sweep back into power. 'If they are given a reasonable time they will destroy themselves by their own actions and their own failures.'[3]

The Senate was crucial because Labor could not amend the Commonwealth Bank Act without a majority in both houses. Bruce had altered the Commonwealth Bank to a position where it was no longer answerable to government—but only to its own conservative board of directors. The ALP recognised that regaining control of the Commonwealth Bank was essential if the government ever hoped to gain any significant leverage over the Australian economy, but the newly elected members displayed a great resistance to risking their hold on the spoils of office, and shied away from the prospect of forcing another double-dissolution election while the party still retained the goodwill of the electorate. To the despair of more radical members such as Frank Anstey, the Cabinet decided not to call the Senate's bluff, although the writing was on the wall, and Robert Gibson, the governor of the Commonwealth Bank was already proving difficult by Christmas 1929. Anstey foresaw that Bruce's legacies would bring down the ALP government in ruins—but, to his great distress, he was unable to carry Cabinet with him.

Doing it tough

Ruin was a spectre that stalked the land during these years of the Great Depression and, although the lower levels of society bore the brunt, it was felt severely by those higher up the social scale as well. Many small businesses went bankrupt during this time and those more genteel members of society who relied upon interest payments and investments for their income found themselves badly hit. Similar hardships were experienced by landlords, who were by no means always the black-hearted villains of society that they appeared to be to the members of the Unemployed Workers Union and to all workers and their families who lived in daily dread of the descent of the bailiffs and eviction.

There is no doubt, however, that the social hardships of the depression fell most unevenly upon Australian society and, as always, those at the bottom of the heap fared worse. The general necessities of life, such as food and lodgings, could no longer be guaranteed, and the stress on families was particularly savage. Social relief, sustenance payments, and charitable handouts might have been sufficient to ensure that nobody actually starved to death in Australia during the Great Depression, but this does not mean that people did not go hungry, or that women and children did not suffer from malnutrition and the want of clothing and shelter. Evicted men and their families lived wherever they could, and shanty towns of hessian-sack humpies grew up in Sydney's southern suburbs on vacant Crown land: the largest being at Brighton-le-Sands, Rockdale, Long Bay, and La Perouse. In such camps, unemployed huddled for warmth in humpies while, closer to the city, others squatted in caves in the Domain around the local beauty spot known as Mrs Macquarie's Chair. Police were instructed to move the cave-dwellers on so that they did not affront the eyes of the more respectable members of society. The *Labor Daily* newspaper attacked the Nationalist New South Wales government for ordering such a policy, and interviewed several of the men who claimed that they had nowhere else to sleep.[4]

Many families found themselves evicted from their lodgings and living in huts and old cars while the breadwinners searched for work. The use of newspapers as bedding and blankets became distressingly common. No one could afford medicine or special dietary supplements for sick children or adults, and many men were forced into pilfering and burglary to feed and clothe their dependants. Camps like these existed on the outskirts of all the capital cities and some of the larger rural towns. In Western Australia, the camp at Blackboy Hill at the foot of the Darling Range behind Perth housed well over a thousand men by the end of 1930.

Anxiety over jobs increased the stresses in society, as those still lucky enough to have employment worried about its continuity and those out of work applied more and more desperately for the few positions that were advertised. Families often separated as the men rolled a swag and went 'on the wallaby'—looking for casual work in the rural districts, or seasonal jobs during the fruit-picking, wheat-harvesting, and shearing seasons. It was policy to keep such men moving, and local police stations would refuse to issue ration certificates once men had been in the district for a couple of weeks, thus forcing them to move on to some other town. Many men went fossicking for gold on the old alluvial diggings. It kept them busy and some made pocket money, but it was no substitute for regular work.

The bitterness among the sufferers was increased by reminders of the propaganda that had lured them off to war in 1914–18. The labour newspapers took the opportunity of pointing out that, during the war, the soldiers had been told that they were fighting to make the world safe for democracy and a place well worth living:[5]

> Patriots, who howled for conscription and the fight to a finish with the last man and the last shilling, are silent nowadays at this dreadful aftermath of the war. The Bugle no longer sounds, and the swashbuckler has no use for the slaves of jingoism. The filibuster no longer walks the avenues of life with his goosestep and rattle of spurs. The profiteer has filled his coffers, and is now hatching fresh schemes of exploitation by which he can accumulate more wealth at the expense of Mugwumps.

Fear of violence

Resentments often boiled over into riots during this period, particularly over the matter of evictions, and members of the radical Unemployed Workers Union occasionally fought pitched battles against police and bailiffs to keep workers and their families from being evicted. Shelter, even in a house devoid of furniture, was infinitely preferable to being dumped onto the streets with nowhere to go. Riots also occurred, sometimes under communist leadership, as men protested against a range of measures—including the dole system (known as 'susso'); the restriction of foods under the food-voucher system; the mindless silliness of some of the work required of them to qualify for sustenance payments (those on 'susso' not being permitted to do work that might be done by someone already in employment); and the incompetence or lack of action of the various state governments in ameliorating the effects of the depression.

Apprehensions about violence were shared by many, and rioting in the streets aroused a fear of revolution. With hindsight, it is clear that Australia was never in any danger of revolution and anarchy, but contemporaries lacked the comfort of hindsight. They felt threatened. One reaction by some middle-class returned servicemen began in the 1920s, and continued into the middle of the following decade, with the formation of quasi-fascist secret armies. This bore certain superficial similarities to the reactions of other conservatively minded ex-servicemen in Germany. Perhaps the best known of these were the New Guard in New South Wales and the White Army in Victoria, but there were others,

Contemporary cartoon depicting New Guard thugs attacking a suspected communist, c.1932. (Australian History Museum, Macquarie University)

including a small branch of the Nazi Party in the Barossa Valley of South Australia. The members of these clandestine organisations dedicated themselves to upholding the established political system and to resisting any radical or communist government that might threaten their own enjoyment of the comfortable status quo. The ethic of the 'fair go' did not extend to governments, even elected governments, which might engage in a redistribution of wealth from the people at the top of the social pyramid to those needy souls at the bottom. The rise of the New Guard and its eventual decline paralleled almost exactly the rise and fall of the second ALP government in New South Wales under Premier Jack Lang.

The Lang phenomenon

Jack Lang dominated the years of the Great Depression in New South Wales. He roused passionate hatred in his opponents and equally passionate support in his followers—who were to campaign in 1932 under the slogan 'Lang is greater than Lenin'. In October 1929 the ALP was returned to office in New South Wales and the Nationalists under Bavin were thrown out as part of a general reversal of political fortunes across Australia at the time. Lang had promised brighter times, and swept into office determined to put his own plan for recovery into operation. Basically this involved refusing to pay the interest due on overseas loans until times had improved, and using the money thus saved to encourage the employment of Australians. As far as Lang was concerned, it was preferable to cause hardship to British bondholders rather than have Australians experience adversity by sending the payments out of the country. Lang's hectoring and belligerent manner frightened his opponents, and his plan alarmed the orthodox financial leaders of the day who regarded repudiation of the interest payments as revolutionary.

In April 1931 the Lang government defaulted on the interest due on the overseas loans, and this brought New South Wales into head-on confrontation with the Commonwealth government. To fulfil its obligations under the terms of the 1927 Financial Agreement, the Commonwealth government had to pay the overseas bondholders itself. In an effort to recover the money, the Commonwealth then sued New South Wales. A run on the New South Wales Savings Bank forced it to close its doors and to freeze more than £55 million of deposits. The Commonwealth Bank took over the New South Wales Savings Bank and honoured all deposits, thus restoring confidence in the country's banking system.

Jack Lang, in combative mode, 1930s. (Taken from Ross McMullin, *The Light on the Hill: The Australian Labor Party 1891–1991*, Melbourne, 1991)

In February 1932, New South Wales defaulted a second time, and again the Commonwealth had to step in and make the payment. The Commonwealth again took legal action to recover the costs of the payment, and resolved to seize money collected by the state as income tax. Lang appealed to the High Court for a ruling that the federal government was not entitled to garnishee the state's revenues and, in an effort to provide sufficient money for his administration, he directed that all state revenues should be deposited with the state Treasury and not with the banks where the Commonwealth could seize it. Lang then proceeded to fortify the Treasury building with barricades. In April, the High Court ruled in favour of the Commonwealth and held that, in the circumstances, it was legally entitled to confiscate state revenues. The federal government then issued an order that income tax payments were to be made directly to the Commonwealth Bank instead of to the official receivers appointed by the state. In May,

Lang defaulted on a further interest payment on overseas loans, and the Commonwealth government insisted that the state hand over most of its revenues via the Commonwealth Bank to cover the costs incurred. Lang responded with a defiant circular instructing state civil servants to continue depositing the revenues with the Treasury. He had finally gone too far. His circular was illegal because it instructed civil servants to break the law, and the NSW governor, Sir Philip Game, dismissed Lang from office and called an election. Lang was soundly beaten by the Nationalists. In his wild and reckless career Lang had not only brought about his own defeat, but had also participated in destroying the Scullin ALP government in Canberra and in splitting the Labor Party into three irreconcilable factions. Lang must also bear part of the responsibility for the eruption of the New Guard's right-wing thugs onto the streets of New South Wales. It is difficult to think of any other individual in those depression years who did more harm to the Labor movement than Jack Lang, and it was to be another decade before Labor returned to office in Canberra.

Federal measures and the Great Depression

The government did what it could to deal with the depression and to cut its expenditure. The immigration agreement with Britain was suspended, compulsory military training for all adult males was abolished, and heavy cuts were made in defence spending. In an effort to discourage imports, Scullin raised tariffs, but this had the unlooked-for side-effect of reducing federal revenues at the same time. Income tax was steeply increased, and a sales tax introduced which horrified business. All private gold exports were suspended, the currency was devalued (from parity with sterling to £125 Australian to £100 British, Australia came off the gold standard, and bullion was shipped overseas to help pay off the country's debts. This, and rising gold prices, gave a new lease of life to the gold industry, especially the Western Australian gold

Contemporary cartoon depicting the Bank of England strangling Australia, 1930s.
(Taken from Ross McMullin, *The Light on the Hill: The Australian Labor Party 1891–1991*, Melbourne, 1991)

fields such as Kalgoorlie and Coolgardie, and many men found work there as a result of the expansion.

In 1930 Sir Otto Niemeyer was sent out from the Bank of England to confer with the prime minister and the state premiers—although it must be said that Scullin had invited the Bank of England to send out an expert adviser. Niemeyer did not sympathise with concepts like the 'fair go' or a wages system based upon the needs of the workers, and took the view that budgets must be balanced, and that Australians had been living above their means for some time and must accept reduced standards of living. It was harsh medicine, but the premiers agreed unanimously to make strenuous attempts to balance their budgets for the financial year 1930/31, and to maintain balanced budgets thereafter. They also agreed that the Loan Council raise no overseas loans until the existing debts had been paid off, and that any internal loans were to be spent on projects that would realise quick financial returns. This exercise in belt-tightening became known as the 'Premiers' Plan', and its stress on deliberately lowering living standards caused enormous resentment among those already on the razor's edge of survival. Undisguised disillusionment characterised the reaction of most working people to the Premiers' Plan and helps explain the support for the more radical solutions offered by Jack Lang. The political Labor movement was seen to have betrayed its supporters:[6]

> We have recently had the ignominious spectacle of the Premiers of the great Australian nation sitting like a class of schoolboys to be lectured to by an emissary of British moneylenders, and told how they should govern their own land. It made one hang ones head in shame . . . while our governments seem to govern, in fact they are meekly taking instructions from a long distance outsider who hadn't seen Australia a few hours ago . . . We owe a lot of money to England's money lords, and they are going to screw it out of us remorselessly . . . rapacious hands are reaching across the seas and stripping us bare.

There was another plan put forward in opposition to Niemeyer's orthodox restraint and Lang's repudiation. This bore the name of its proposer, the federal treasurer Edward ('Red Ted') Theodore. Briefly, Theodore's more imaginative proposition involved stimulating the economy with careful injections of capital to revive it and get it moving again. It was radical thinking for the times — although, in later decades, much of what Theodore suggested became accepted financial orthodoxy. Theodore proposed that the Commonwealth Bank expand credit and that the volume of money circulating in the community should be increased by additional printing of currency which was to be backed by the Commonwealth Bank to preserve public confidence. The idea was to reinflate the economy and get people back to work. Two factors militated against the adoption of Theodore's plan—the Senate and the board of the Commonwealth Bank. Theodore pushed legislation through the House of Representatives, only to have it defeated in the Senate;

and Robert Gibson and the board regarded suggestions of expanding credit in a time of depression as quite irresponsible. To add to Theodore's troubles, a royal commission into his behaviour while premier of Queensland found that he had a case in law to answer on charges of fraud. Theodore stood down from federal parliament to clear his name. He was found not guilty and returned to office, but lost his seat in the big swing away from Labor in 1931.

The Australian Labor Party limped into 1931 on the verge of another split. This time it was a three-way division. The majority continued to support Scullin and Theodore, but a substantial minority threw in its lot with the demagogue from New South Wales—becoming the 'Lang Labor' faction. A third group, including some ministers who regarded Theodore as dangerously left wing, coalesced around the disloyal and ambitious Joseph Aloysius Lyons—the postmaster-general in Scullin's Cabinet, and a former premier of Tasmania. The stresses and tensions of the Great Depression were beginning to shake the Scullin government to pieces.

The implementation of the Premiers' Plan began in June 1931. The practical impact of the plan included: a 10-per cent cut to all wages fixed by awards, and to the state and federal public servants; a reduction of 20% in all government expenditure; a reduction in interest paid on government bonds to Australian investors by 22.5%; increased taxation; a moratorium on private mortgages where repayments caused hardship; and devaluation of the currency. In New South Wales, Lang ignored the Premiers' Plan, although he had agreed to it, but the other states went ahead. New South Wales fell into line following Lang's dismissal in 1932. The Premiers' Plan became the accepted nostrum for dealing with the depression in Australia, and was justified to sceptics on the grounds that it ensured equality of sacrifice because all sectors of society would be affected by its provisions.

The United Australia Party

The Australian Labor Party (ALP) had already begun to split. In January 1931 the federal parliamentary caucus had recalled Theodore to the ministry—although he had not yet been cleared of the fraud charges. This caused the resignation from the party of Joe Lyons and James Fenton, two of Scullin's ministers. With three other ALP members they formed an alliance with the nationalist Party and, ultimately a new party, the United Australia Party (UAP). Lyons, following in the footsteps of Hughes, became leader of the new party, and Latham, the former leader of the opposition, became deputy leader. Meanwhile, Lang's followers in the federal party also began to move openly to undermine the position of the Scullin government over its adherence to the Premiers' Plan. As the serious confrontation between the federal and state governments developed during 1931, it was widely held that Lang had gone too far. A special federal conference of the ALP met in March 1931 and expelled the New South Wales State Executive from the party. Lang's power base within the party had been outlawed, but his influence over the federal Labor members from New South Wales remained significant, and seven of Lang's followers in the ALP federal caucus formed a breakaway

Joseph Aloysius Lyons, ALP turncoat and Nationalist prime minister, c.1935. (Australian History Museum, Macquarie University)

group under the leadership of J.A. Beasley—although they initially continued to support the Scullin administration.

Continuous obstruction from Robert Gibson characterised 1931 for the Scullin government. In April, Gibson announced that he would cut credit to any state or federal government that did not reduce its deficit, and he campaigned publicly against the Theodore plan to expand the money supply and to ship gold out of the country to meet the next tranche of interest payments then coming due. In June, Gibson refused to provide £5 million credit to the Commonwealth for relief works for the unemployed, although he did relent a little later on.

By November, the Lang group in federal parliament moved to deliver the coup-de-grâce to the Scullin government by calling for a royal commission to investigate allegations of corruption in the disbursement of unemployed relief funds in Theodore's electorate of Dalley in New South Wales. Lyons and the UAP supported this move and the government was defeated by a combination of its opponents led by former members of the ALP. In the ensuing election, the ALP won only thirteen seats, the Country Party held sixteen, Lang Labor five, and the UAP found itself in the happy position of being able to govern in its own right. Lyons' new party had swept to a remarkable success.

The UAP owed much of its achievement to the national inclination of voters to turn all governments out of office during the depression years, but there was no doubting the appeal of Joseph Lyons himself. Unlike the former Nationalist leader, Bruce, Lyons came across as a man of warmth and humanity with a large family and humble origins. He was a man of the people and he did not wear spats. Bruce returned briefly to parliament at this election, and summed up the conservatives' attitude of admiration and lofty disdain for Lyons:[7]

> He was a delightful person. He couldn't run a government but he could win elections. His resemblance to a cheerful koala, his eleven children, his family-man appeal and his essential humanity were

irresistible to the voters. He did, however, need someone to hold his hand in the early days and I did it, although I had to be careful to be discreet about it.

Relief in sight

Lyons came to office when the slow haul out of depression had already begun. Although unemployment figures continued to show almost half a million men out of work, and although an armed insurrection by the New Guard to topple the Lang government in New South Wales had remained a distinct possibility until Sir Philip Game dismissed the unruly premier later in the year, there were distinct signs of improvement. Prices for wool and wheat at last began to rise on the international market, and the rapid increase in the price of gold added to the value of the increased output from Western Australia. As a result of the Ottawa Economic Conference and the general acceptance of imperial preference in tariffs, a wide range of Australian primary produce—especially meat, wine, dairy products, and canned fruit—began to find overseas markets. The high tariffs established by the ALP were lowered, stimulating efficiency in secondary industry. This pleased the Country Party which believed in the protection of primary industry through subsidies, but found secondary protection via tariffs unacceptable. Furthermore, as a result of an initiative from the United States president, the former Western Australian gold-mining engineer Herbert Hoover, an international moratorium was declared on interest payments on war loans until the depression was over. This helped Australia stabilise the economy, and freed up, for domestic use, funds that had hitherto been earmarked for overseas interest payments.

Such improvements were quickly reflected in the budget figures. Within its first year of office the Lyons government managed to complete the 1931/32 financial year with a surplus in excess of £1 million, and Australia's overseas trade position had gone from a deficit of £33 million in the preceding year to a surplus of £31 million. The combined deficit of all the Australian governments had reached only £18 million instead of the estimated £40 million. Despite the lowering of tariffs, receipts from customs duties remained a growth area in the budgets for the years 1933 and 1934 and indicated that a sustained pick up in economic activity had begun. Slowly reductions in the high depression levels of taxation occurred, and income tax, land tax, and company tax were progressively reduced. Pensions and public service salaries were slowly increased and, in 1934, the federal Arbitration Court rescinded the 10-per cent emergency reduction in the basic wage, and restored the margins above the wage for possession of a trade qualification or a skill.

Meanwhile, the former prime minister, S.M. Bruce, had been sent to London as resident minister, and then high commissioner for Australia, to negotiate a conversion of the interest rate on Australia's overseas debts. Throughout 1933 and 1934, Bruce badgered and harassed the London money market and the governor of the Bank of England, and succeeded in converting most of the high interest loans to rates between 3.5% and 4%. It was a significant accomplishment and a great saving to Australia.

Secessionist sentiment

While the slow haul out of the depression proceeded, conditions of life in Australia remained extremely difficult, and hardship aroused passions about issues that, in the normal course of events, would not have caused such a furor. Western Australia had been a reluctant and last-minute participant in the original federation and, as early as 1906, the WA Legislative Assembly had passed a vote in favour of the state's withdrawing from the Commonwealth. Nothing had eventuated, but the difficulties of life in the depression years led to a revival of secessionist sentiment and a widespread feeling that the state suffered because of federal mismanagement and favouritism towards the other states. A referendum was held in 1933 in Western Australia on the question of secession, and a large majority was secured in its favour. Because the federation legislation was an enactment of the British parliament, a request was then forwarded from Western Australia to Westminster praying that the enactment be amended to permit the state to withdraw and become an independent country.

After delays and discussion in Britain it was decided that such an amendment could not go forward without the agreement of the other states. By this time it was 1935 and the country and the state were well on the road to economic recovery. The issue was dropped and not raised again until the 1970s. In Tasmania and New South Wales the depression produced movements for secession and new states—but they also ran out of steam once the economy began to pick up.

Prime Minister Lyons had been premier of Tasmania earlier in his political career, and this background undoubtedly made him more sympathetic towards the problems experienced by the states with smaller populations. The recognition that population provided an unsatisfactory base upon which to allocate federal monies emerged quite early in Lyons' first term of office. Since 1925, the Bruce–Page government and its successors had made additional grants to the states with large territories and low populations (such as South Australia and Western Australia), to encourage development. A system of grants based solely on population amounted to a permanent and self-perpetuating advantage for New South Wales and Victoria at the expense of the rest of the country. Consequently, in 1933, Lyons established a Grants Commission that was to comprise three commissioners who would be empowered to advise the Commonwealth government on the merits of special cases for additional grants to the small states. The objective was to move from allocating money on a population basis alone to distributing development funds on the basis of needs. The establishment of the Grants Commission owed something to the popularity of the Western Australian secession movement, but it seems that Lyons' own background also came into play.

Lyons under challenge

In the elections of 1934, the UAP was returned to office—although, this time, Lyons needed Country Party support and went into coalition with Dr Earle Page. The coalition won all the Senate seats and entered the new triennium in a strong position. The ALP held eighteen seats in the House of Representatives, and Lang Labor nine. Latham retired at this election as attorney-general and, in the following year, was appointed a justice of the High Court. Latham's replacement as attorney-general was a rising young Victorian politician named Robert Gordon Menzies. Menzies had been state attorney-general and deputy premier in a UAP–Country Party coalition that had taken office in Victoria in 1932, but had resigned to contest Latham's seat of Kooyong in the federal elections of 1934. Menzies came from a poor background, but had made his way in the world by winning scholarships for school and university. He had developed into a brilliant trial barrister and a highly respected constitutional lawyer before he embarked on a career in politics in 1928. The party elders, and Menzies himself, expected that he would go far.

The world intrudes

During the Great Depression Australia had become an introverted country. The rigours of economic collapse and recovery had concentrated people's attention on their own domestic affairs, whereas Japan's aggrandisement in China and the rise to power of Mussolini and Hitler in Europe had failed to capture public attention. As the pace of recovery quickened, the focus of Australians broadened to include affairs in the wider world.

In 1935 the Department of External Affairs was formed as a separate department with its own minister in Cabinet. Hitherto External Affairs had been a section of the Prime Minister's Department but, after Bruce's appointment of Richard Casey, the trend had been inexorably in the direction of expansion of function and the appointment of Australia's own diplomatic representation in foreign countries. Bruce, as high commissioner in London kept Australia well informed of events and developments there, but the time was obviously coming when Australia would no longer be able to avoid looking after her own interests in a world that was not always friendly. Moreover, Bruce's negotiations on loan conversions during the 1930s had shown that Australia's best interests were not necessarily served by subservience to the mother country, and the establishment of the new department was yet another sign of increasing maturity. That said, there is absolutely no doubt that Australia cravenly followed British policy through every shift and turn of the discreditable appeasement period, and happily echoed Britain's views as its own. Sanctions against Italy over its invasion of Abyssinia in October 1935, and in support of the League of Nations, were implemented to remain in step with Britain, but even the Labor newspapers recognised that the League of Nations represented the best chance of avoiding the old system of military alliances that had resulted in the carnage of 1914–18.[8]

The rising power of Japan had always concerned Australia, and Japanese atrocities in China, together with the activities of Hitler and Mussolini, led Australia into a new policy of rearmament and a reconsideration of defence needs. As part of this reassessment of potential threats to northern Australia, the government began negotiating with prominent Jewish spokesmen for the establishment of a Jewish home state in the Kimberley region of Western Australia. Both federal and state governments pursued these negotiations, and considerable progress was made before the outbreak of World War II intervened and the discussions became academic. A Jewish state in northern Australia was to have provided population, to have produced a buffer between Japan and the remainder of the continent, and to have become a useful strategic shock-absorber in the event of an invasion.[9]

In 1937 the defence vote, which had been drastically cut during the Great Depression, underwent a dramatic expansion when a decision was taken to begin development and construction of Australia's own military aircraft, to be built entirely in Australia. The new defence program also involved an upgrading of the navy. This increased expenditure was a step in the right direction, but nowhere near enough to satisfy the new federal leader of the ALP, John Curtin, who had campaigned during the 1937 federal election for a rapid build-up of the airforce to at least parity with the number of aeroplanes capable of being carried as part of any Japanese carrier-borne strike force. The new plane, the Wirraway, was to prove tragically inferior to the Japanese Zero in combat during the early 1940s.

European refugees

Refugees from Europe began arriving in Australia throughout 1938 and 1939 to a sympathetic welcome. The disruption caused by the Spanish Civil War and the increasingly expansionist activities of Hitler and Mussolini, paled to insignificance alongside the brutal treatment meted out to the Jews across much of German-influenced central Europe. The refugees came without government assistance and either paid for their own passages or were assisted by family, national groups, and religious organisations already in Australia. In 1938 the Australian government decided to take 15 000 refugees over a three-year period—a policy that won bilateral support from the ALP. The coming of the refugees served to heighten feelings of apprehension within the community about the turn of events in Europe and the possibility of war. Meanwhile, Japanese methods of subduing China caused alarm and, in 1939, wharf labourers at Port Kembla in New South Wales went on strike and refused to load pig-iron for shipment to Japan. They argued that the pig-iron would be used to make armaments for use against the hapless Chinese and, perhaps, at no distant date, against Australians as well. Robert Gordon Menzies, as attorney-general in the Lyons government, attempted to force the wharf labourers to load the pig-iron by threatening them with punitive legal action if they continued to refuse. From this action, and a well-publicised visit to Port Kembla where he received a boisterous jostling from angry wharfies, Menzies gained two things—first, a reputation for being pro-fascist and, secondly, a life-long nickname that he abhorred: 'Pig-iron Bob'. In the end a compromise was reached, by which wharf labourers loaded only 23 000 tons of pig-iron rather than the 300 000 tons for which the Japanese had contracted.

Prime Minister Menzies

In April 1939 Prime Minister Joe Lyons died in office, leaving the UAP without an heir presumptive. Menzies had been the obvious candidate, but his impatience to replace Lyons had led him into an indiscreet (although veiled) attack on the prime minister's leadership abilities. He had subsequently resigned from Cabinet and amid charges of disloyalty, and had departed to the backbench. The Country Party leader, Dr Earle Page, attempted to form a replacement government, but everybody could see that the UAP, as the larger party in the coalition, should provide the prime minister. Page's attempts were thus ultimately unsuccessful. Approaches were then made to Bruce in London to give up the position of high commissioner and take up the prime ministership again, but Bruce could not be persuaded. Finally, Menzies was elected and took office as prime minister on 26 April 1939.

Page detested Menzies almost as much as he had hated Hughes, and he attempted, by refusing to serve in any ministry headed by Menzies, to repeat the veto that he had successfully exercised against Hughes. In the House of Representatives, Page launched a vitriolic personal attack on Menzies in which he accused him of treachery to Lyons and of cowardice in resigning from the army reserve during World War I to avoid having to fight overseas. This was especially hurtful, as Menzies had been a prominent advocate in favour of conscription. On this occasion, Page was unsuccessful, and the UAP stood by Menzies and refused to buckle under to the Country Party—as the Nationalists had so cravenly done in 1922. Eventually Menzies became leader of a minority UAP government and, shortly thereafter, in an act of almost poetic symmetry, Page was voted out of the leadership of the Country Party which he had created and led for twenty years.

Soon after becoming prime minister, Menzies spelt out the essence of the relationship between Britain and Australia as he understood it. He made no reference to Australia as a mature, independent, and autonomous nation, but wrote in terms of an Australian obligation to defend Britain's interests and Britain's peace—which he regarded as identical to Australia's. 'If she is at war we are at war—defending our own shores.' Despite this, however, he went on to point out that what was the 'Far East' to Britain was the 'near north' to Australia, and he foreshadowed the urgent necessity for Australia to establish and maintain her own lines of communication and intelligence in the region, and to inaugurate her own diplomatic contacts with foreign powers.[10] In the Menzean vision, such developments were to take place within a framework that did not compromise Australia's position as a minor province in a global British empire. Given the overall primacy of Britain in the Menzies view of the world, it came as no surprise to most Australians that, on 3 September 1939, when Britain and France declared war on Germany, the prime minister sonorously announced:[11]

> It is my melancholy duty to inform you officially that, in consequence of a persistence by Germany in her invasion of Poland, Great Britain has declared war upon her and that, as a result, Australia is also at war.

8

World War and Cold War

There were doubts in the minds of many Australians over the suitability of Robert Menzies as a wartime leader. In 1938 and 1939 he had been unashamedly in favour of appeasement, and had managed to discern 'a really spiritual quality in the willingness of young Germans to devote themselves to the service and well-being of the State'.[1] His sympathy for Germany extended to a belief that Australia ought not support Czechoslovakia against Hitler's territorial demands, and to statements that young Australians had much to learn from the fascist countries in the area of enthusiasm for service to the state and that fascist engagement of the young could well form a role model for Australia.[2] These sentiments, together with his obvious desire to appease Japan, and the ill-feeling within the ranks of his own party caused by his earlier attacks on Joseph Lyons, combined to cause serious uncertainty and weakened his ability to unify the country for an all-out war effort.

Australia in another world war

Public enthusiasm for the war did not reach the celebratory level achieved in 1914. Perhaps there were too many who remembered the horrors of the war of 1914–18. Many workers were still unemployed, and some of these responded to the communist arguments that they owed nothing to a country that had treated them so badly, and that the war was a capitalist struggle without real relevance to the workers. Lack of worker enthusiasm for the war was a problem destined to bedevil the Curtin administration even when a Japanese invasion appeared imminent.

On the other hand, the army offered the unemployed the first regular employment since the Great Depression had begun, and there was no shortage of volunteers to join the 2nd AIF which began recruitment following the declaration of war. The original plan had been to send the expeditionary force for advanced training to the Middle East and then to use them on the battlefields of Europe. The speed of the German blitzkrieg, and the rapid fall of Europe under German sway, made it plain that land battles in Europe were years away. The declaration of war by Italy, and the advance of Italian armies in the Middle East and Greece, ensured that the Australian troops had plenty to do before they contemplated fighting Germans in Europe. Australian forces were sent to the Middle East to fight Italians. They won great success but, when Erwin Rommel and the German Afrika Korps became involved, the early successes were reversed and were followed by several years of heavy fighting. In the event, Australian troops were not destined to participate in the great land battles of World War II in Europe.

Conscription

The Australian government faced massive problems in preparing for war in 1939. The tide of volunteers was obviously sufficient to recruit successive divisions of the AIF, but this did not address the problem of home defence. The AIF was expected to fight overseas, and volunteers naturally flowed into that organisation. Accordingly, in October 1939, the government reintroduced military conscription for the local militia which was designed for domestic defence. All single men who were due to reach 21 years of age before 1 July 1940 were called up for three months of military training. The objective was to bring the militia up to a strength of 75 000 men who would be available for duty in the event of an invasion of Australia.

Prime Minister Menzies was at pains to reassure the electorate that training for the militia imposed absolutely no obligation for service abroad, and that the scheme was for Australian defence only. Despite such reassurances, many trade unionists were thoroughly sceptical and regarded the plan—correctly as it turned out—as the 'thin edge of the wedge' for the introduction of conscription for overseas military service.[3]

Menzies proposes a coalition

Robert Menzies. (Taken from Jack Cato, *The Story of the Camera in Australia*, Melbourne, 1955)

In Britain, the emergency of the war had resulted in the formation of a national government composed of Tories and Labour—who agreed to work as a team until the war was over. Winston Churchill became the prime minister of this composite government, and the leader of the opposition became deputy prime minister. Menzies regarded such an arrangement as the only sensible one for a country at war, and repeatedly requested the ALP under John Curtin to join him in a similar venture— even offering to relinquish the leadership in favour of Curtin for the duration of the war.

The ALP believed that Australia would be better served, both in war and in the subsequent peace, by a fully committed Labor government—although Curtin and a number of his frontbenchers did agree to serve on an Advisory War Council with the government, at which they were fully briefed concerning the state of the war and to which they contributed support and advice. The government was under no obligation to accept the views of this Advisory War Council, but it at least provided a mechanism whereby the opposition could be kept up to date on the war and able to submit advice to the government on how it should be conducted. In August 1941 Menzies again offered Curtin an all-party government in which the ALP could provide the leader and hold half the portfolios. Curtin rejected the offer brusquely, suggesting that it demonstrated Menzies' inability to offer stable government, whereas the ALP could. The reference to the lack of stability by Curtin drew attention to the embattled position of Menzies within the UAP and his tenuous hold on the leadership. Curtin demanded that Menzies resign and that he advise the governor-general to call on Labor to form a new government.

It was not open party warfare, however, and the extent to which there was bilateral support for the war effort during those first months of the war can be seen in the ALP's support in June 1940 for amendments to the *National Security Act*, which gave the government of the day complete control over the country's resources, production, manpower, and people for the duration of the war—provided only that it did not have the power to conscript Australians, either military or civilian, for service beyond Australian territory. The amendments conferred full executive authority to do whatever was necessary to prosecute the war. The revised *Act* authorised civilian conscription of services, and many skilled tradesmen found themselves directed to far-distant regions of Australia where their skills were needed to buttress the war effort and to perform necessary defence works. After December 1941, for example, when Japan entered the war, many tradesmen found themselves drafted for war work in the far-north of Australia where extensive military construction had been urgently undertaken.

In September 1940, elections produced a hung parliament—with the ALP and the UAP–Country Party coalition holding 36 seats apiece, and the balance of power resting with two independents. This further loss of seats eroded Menzies' hold on the leadership and, in August 1941, he resigned as prime minister. W.M. Hughes replaced him as the leader of the UAP but, because of Hughes' advanced age. the Country Party leader Arthur Fadden became prime minister. Menzies stayed on in the Fadden Cabinet as minister for Defence Co-ordination. The Fadden government lasted only a short time. Fadden claimed that he had reigned for forty days and forty nights, but his time in office was not without incident. Fadden lacked the exaggerated respect for all things British that was already a hallmark of the Menzies style and, at the suggestion of General Thomas Blamey, he demanded that the 9th Division of the AIF, which had been under siege in Tobruk for almost a year, should be relieved. The Rats of Tobruk had become a legend in Australia for their heroic resistance to German attack and their resolute refusal to surrender. Churchill reluctantly agreed to relieve the Australian garrison and, when Tobruk fell to the Germans later in the war, the 9th Division did not go into captivity as did the 15 000 men of the ill-fated 8th Division following the fall of Singapore to the Japanese. The 9th Division was to play an important role in the famous battle for El Alamein, where Rommel's army was soundly defeated, and they then returned to help defend Australia against the Japanese thrust southwards. Fadden's demand had at least ensured that the 9th Division was still extant when the recall to Australia came.

The Fadden government lost the support of the two independents early in October 1941, and the governor-general commissioned John Curtin to form a government. It was the first federal Labor government since 1931, and the former prime minister, James Scullin, proved of inestimable assistance to Curtin whose Cabinet contained only two men—Frank Forde and Ben Chifley—with previous ministerial experience. The incoming government held office on the support of the independents until the elections of 1943 gave Curtin a comfortable majority in both houses. Reliance on independents did not inhibit Curtin from giving strong leadership, and he announced from the beginning that he expected the same constructive support in the Advisory War Council from Menzies and Fadden as he had extended to them. He was not destined to receive it for long. Early in 1944 Menzies led his followers out of the Council, although Fadden refused to follow this example and pledged that the Country Party would support the government in the full prosecution of the war.

Australians in battle

John Curtin. (Australian History Museum, Macquarie University)

When Curtin came to office in 1941, the Australian forces were extended. The 6th, 7th, and 9th Divisions of the AIF were serving in the Middle East, and the bulk of naval and airforce personnel were also deployed on the other side of the world. On 7 December 1941, when the Japanese launched their surprise attack on the American naval base at Pearl Harbor, Australia had the war in its own backyard rather than comfortably in the northern hemisphere.

Three days after the disaster at Pearl Harbor, the Japanese sank the two battleships HMS *Prince of Wales* and HMS *Repulse* and reduced the Allied naval forces in Asian waters to impotence. Within two months the Japanese army had flung back the British, Dutch, Indian, and Australian troops opposing them, and had occupied Guam, Wake Island, Hong Kong, British North Borneo, Rabaul (New Britain), the Netherlands East Indies, Burma, and the entire Malay Peninsula. The so-called impregnable fortress of Singapore surrendered on 15 February 1942 and, within a week, Japanese planes had bombed Darwin. Before the month was out, HMAS *Perth* had gone to the bottom in the Battle of the Java Sea. The Japanese onslaught seemed irresistible, and the new Australian government faced the situation of a national nightmare come true—the 'yellow peril' seemed likely to submerge the country just as the propagandists from the 1850s onwards had always foretold.

Labor reacted to the news of Pearl Harbor by declaring war on Japan for itself—without waiting for a British declaration. It was clear that Australia could not expect significant help from the British who were fully engaged in defending themselves against Germany. Indeed, Churchill regarded the war in the Pacific as a side-issue, and took the view that the most important task was to defeat Hitler. After that had been achieved, the Japanese could then be dealt with. If this strategy resulted in the loss of Australia to a Japanese invasion, this was regrettable, but Australia could always be recaptured. Naturally this sanguine view dumbfounded the Australian government and, in December 1941, the prime minister responded with an historic declaration in which he refused to accept that the struggle in the Pacific was of secondary importance, or that Australia was dispensable:[4]

> Without any inhibitions of any kind, I make it quite clear that Australia looks to America, free of any pangs as to our traditional links or kinship with the United Kingdom . . . We are, therefore, determined that Australia shall not go, and we shall exert all our energies towards the shaping of a plan, with the United States as its keystone, which will give to our country some confidence of being able to hold out until the tide of battle swings against the enemy.

The call to America aroused resentment in Churchill and in Curtin's political opponents in Australia, who were offended by the throwing over of more than 150 years of deference. Ironically, unbeknown to Curtin, President Roosevelt of the United States had already agreed to Churchill's 'beat Hitler first' strategy, but Australia did have attractions as a base from which the reconquest of the Pacific could be launched. For this reason, the US general, Douglas MacArthur, was ordered to leave the besieged American forces on Corregidor and proceed to Australia where he would take command of the new army that was being gathered to hurl back the Japanese and punish them for their aggression. MacArthur arrived in Australia in March 1942 and established his headquarters in Melbourne. He was accepted by all the Allied governments as supreme commander in the South-West Pacific Area but, because the only soldiers available at that time were Australian troops, the Australian general, Thomas Blamey, was to command all land forces. In the same month as MacArthur's arrival, Japanese forces landed in New Guinea and began their advance on Port Moresby. They were not destined, however, to get much farther.

Growth of an independent spirit

When Singapore fell, the greatest strength of Australia's armed forces was still in the Middle East. To meet the oncoming Japanese, Australia possessed the militia of about 200 000 men and 50 000 AIF volunteers who were better trained but without battle experience. The Australian General Staff recommended that the three battle-hardened veteran divisions be brought home from the Middle East to help defend Australia. Curtin's Cabinet agreed unanimously and cabled Churchill. Churchill proved to be exceedingly difficult. He suggested sending the 7th Division to Burma, and had even ordered the fleet bringing the men home to head for that country when, to his astonishment, Curtin insisted on their return to Australia. This was not the sort of deferential behaviour to which British statesmen had become accustomed from Menzies, and Churchill had Roosevelt bring pressure to bear on Curtin—but to no avail. In Australia, the opposition—led by Menzies, Fadden, Hughes, Spender, and McEwen—supported Churchill against Curtin in this confrontation, but Curtin would not be moved. With very bad grace, the order was sent to the fleet to change course again for Australia and, to the great delight of both government and people, the transports arrived without mishap. These AIF veterans made a major difference to the action in New Guinea and played an important role in defeating and throwing back the Japanese threat to Port Moresby. Indeed, they were responsible for inflicting the first major defeat of the war on Japanese land forces. Had Churchill and Menzies had their way, a further two divisions of the AIF would have joined the 8th Division as guests of the Japanese when Burma fell soon afterwards, and the consequences for Australia could well have been disastrous.

By the end of 1942 Curtin was still pressing for the return of the 9th Division. It had fought with distinction at Alamein and the prime minister wanted it back in Australia to support the other two divisions. When Curtin insisted that the 9th Division return to Australia, Churchill grudgingly acquiesced with the message that he would not oppose Australia's wishes; to which Curtin tartly replied that he had expected support and not mere absence of opposition. When the 9th Division did return to Australia in February 1943, Churchill churlishly refused to allow its equipment to go with it as it would place too serious a strain on shipping. Australia had to re-equip the entire division when it arrived.

In the light of Curtin's difficulties with Churchill during 1942, and the more Australian-centred outlook that the ALP possessed, the government quietly ratified the Statute of Westminster, thereby making Australia a fully autonomous and independent nation. The days of cringing deference to Britain at government level were over, at least for a time, and the government concentrated its attention on mobilising Australian society against the Japanese.

Civilian involvement

In January 1942, new regulations were issued under the *National Security Act* which declared certain industries to be 'essential industries', and certain occupations to be 'reserved' occupations. Men working in these areas were not permitted to enlist in the AIF because their labour was deemed essential to the war effort. Iron-founding and heavy industry were two such areas, and others were added to the list as required. Every employable man and woman came under the new manpower plan, and had to work wherever they were directed. Some were maintained in munitions industries, some were released for military training, and some were directed to essential civilian occupations. Munitions production was streamlined and placed under the direction of Essington Lewis, the former managing director of BHP, whose job was to oversee production and distribution of munitions in the most efficient way possible. Despite a great deal of trade union suspicion about a man from Lewis' background, all the evidence suggests that his appointment was a signal success.

As men were progressively called up for military training, more and more women flooded into the workforce. They took jobs in all sectors that had hitherto been the province of men and performed extremely well. For example, the Women's Land Army kept agricultural production levels up despite the shortage of males, and thereby freed men for service in the armed forces. As the war continued, Australians found themselves unable to escape its effects. Income taxes rose alarmingly, and so-called luxury items —such as petrol, tobacco, and imported wine and spirits—felt the weight of restrictions. Day-to-day items —such as butter, eggs, clothing and, eventually, even meat—were rationed. Of course enormous quantities of these goods were produced in Australia, but the war effort had first call on all items. The need to use wool cloth for uniforms and foodstuffs for feeding two armies (American and Australian), together with the need to send food and wool to

Britain, left precious little to distribute among the civilian population. Manpower restrictions meant that practically no new housing was built for the private market, and rents were frozen for the duration of the war. Young couples had no option but to live with parents or friends until conditions improved. Paradoxically, wages also rose during the war years—in contrast to the collapse of real wages during World War I—not as a result of salary rises, but as a result of the amount of overtime worked in all the essential industries. Because war-workers laboured around the clock in some industries (such as munitions), public transport operated 24 hours a day to take them to and from their jobs. In 1942, the Commonwealth government took over sole income-taxing rights from the states and raised the levels across the board to help finance the war effort. Nevertheless, one of the effects of war on the civilian population was an increase in prosperity. There was full employment and overtime for nearly all workers. In the rural sector, farmers were similarly well off. They had a guaranteed market for everything that they could produce as the government bought up all the wool, wheat, meat, and dairy produce at agreed prices. People certainly complained about the high taxation levels, but the complaints were muffled when returning AIF soldiers waiting for transport to take them to New Guinea pointed out that they were being paid at the same rate as the 1st AIF soldiers in World War I, and that they received no overtime.[5]

Some of the extra money undoubtedly went on the black market. As rationing restrictions affected most aspects of everyday life, a thriving black market built up to supply the demand. Cigarettes and alcohol were the main items available, but clothing and food could also be obtained. Even a little petrol was occasionally available for those who knew where to look for it. Many Australians attempted to beat the cutback in beer production by making their own home brew, and illicit stills proliferated in a way that had not been seen since the very early days of the convict colony. The American servicemen received a substantially higher rate of pay than did the Australians, and they could obtain American cigarettes very cheaply at their military PX stores. The Americans also possessed sufficient money to purchase expensive and illicitly distilled spirits, and the nightclubs and dives of all the capital cities overflowed with soldiers, sailors, and airmen from America celebrating and on leave. Australian servicemen resented the differential in pay, and the success that Americans seemed to enjoy with Australian girls. Occasionally such frictions led to fighting and riots, the best known of these being the Battle of Brisbane which involved hundreds of soldiers from both armies. During this fracas one Australian private was killed and another seven were wounded as a result of American military police using shotguns, and about forty soldiers from both armies required medical attention for their injuries. Fighting between the armies was not the norm, however, and hundreds of marriages occurred between American servicemen and Australian girls during the years of World War II.

The tide turns

Hostilities against the Japanese during 1942 presaged the turning of the tide of battle for which Curtin had hoped when he had called on America for assistance. Australian troops flung back the advancing Japanese in New Guinea while, at sea, American and Australian ships inflicted two heavy defeats on the Japanese in the Battles of the Coral Sea and Midway. In fact, Allied losses had been heavier than Japanese in the Battle of the Coral Sea, but they could be made good, whereas the Japanese fleet was being slowly ground down by attrition. In the Battle of Midway, the Japanese lost four aircraft carriers that were irreplaceable, and their ability to supply their far-flung armies and to protect convoys of supplies was seriously weakened. Similarly, the Japanese ability to mount further offensive operations and to threaten Australia with invasion was also destroyed. From 1943 onwards, the Japanese were on the defensive as the Allied forces remorselessly began to drive them out of their conquered territories.

American conscripts were involved in this war of attrition, and pressure to make Australian militiamen share the risks proved well-nigh impossible for Curtin to resist. The Australian militia had been used in New Guinea without breaking the guarantee not to use conscripts overseas—on the technicality that New Guinea was actually Australian territory since the mandate won by W.M. Hughes in 1919. The militia had fought with distinction alongside the AIF in New Guinea and, in 1943, Curtin introduced legislation that authorised the use of conscripts against the Japanese as far north as the equator. Curtin found it impossible to support the contention that it was all right for American conscripts to die fighting the Japanese north of New Guinea but it was not acceptable for Australian conscripts. The irony was that Curtin had been one of the foremost agitators against conscription for overseas service during World War I. Now, the fortunes of World War II had placed him in a position where he had to introduce the policy that he had previously opposed. The threat from Japan was so immediate, however, that conscription did not prove divisive among the civilian population. The UAP, the communists, and the Roman Catholic hierarchy all endorsed conscription, and were united behind the war effort—so there was little of the communal strife that had characterised the issue in 1916 and 1917.

The Liberal Party

In 1944, the government, as part of its planning for the post-war period, sponsored a referendum in which it sought to gain for the Commonwealth the exclusive right to legislate for a period of five years in four areas that had hitherto been controlled by the states—employment, housing, primary production, and social security. The opposition campaign was led by Menzies and proved to be most effective, playing on the people's weariness with the controls and regulations of government. The success of this negative campaign emboldened Menzies to attempt the formation of a new political party to replace the array of disparate anti-Labor groups with a single nationally organised entity under his leadership. At a conference of anti-Labor forces in Canberra, he proposed the formation of a completely new party that would mirror the successful organisational structure of the ALP, with party branches and a mass membership of rank and file who would all have an input into policy formulation.

Menzies also recognised that to attract members to his new party, it would have to offer more than just opposition to the ALP, and he carefully spelt out the ideology of the Liberal Party. The new movement aimed to secure for Australia an environment in which all who had risked their lives in its service could enjoy honour and security; in which constant employment at good wages was available to all who were willing and able to work; in which the unavoidable minimum of unemployment arising from sickness or change of occupation was provided against by adequate unemployment benefits; in which citizens enjoyed the rights of freedom of speech, religion, and association, together with the right to choose their own way of living and of life; and which looked primarily to the encouragement of individual initiative and enterprise as the dynamic force of reconstruction and progress.[6]

The stress on individual initiative, rather than the state, as the motive force for reconstruction and change, clearly distinguished the Liberal Party from the ALP in ideological terms—although the record was to show that, in practical affairs, the Liberal Party could be quite as committed to state welfarism as was the ALP. The new party also comprised a strange mix of arch conservatives and genuine liberals who were united solely by their shared hostility to Labor. In this sense, the Liberal Party can be seen as a direct lineal descendent of Deakin's Liberal Party following the fusion of 1909.

Curtin replaced by Chifley

As the war ground on to its inevitable conclusion, John Curtin's health finally gave way under the strain and he died of a heart attack in July 1945. Curtin had been an unashamed nationalist who had put the

welfare of his own country above all other considerations. In the process he had incurred the hostility of Churchill and Roosevelt and had established the basis of an undying legend within the Australian Labor Party. At the same time, his sincerity and wholehearted devotion to Australia had won him the respect of his political opponents despite their ideological differences, and his loss was deeply felt by his country. The measure of Curtin's commitment to Australia, rather than to the ideological position of his own party, can be seen in his courageous introduction of conscription for overseas service in

Joseph 'Ben' Chifley. (Australian History Museum, Macquarie University)

1943. Moreover, his towering stature in the ALP can be gauged by the fact that when he offered his resignation to the federal caucus over the issue, he won a unanimous vote of support—even from known opponents within the party. Curtin was that rare politician who was prepared to put the welfare of his country above a strict adherence to the platform of his party, but it is ironic that in going beyond the ALP platform on conscription he cemented the basis of his legend within the Labor movement.

After an interim six days as prime minister, Curtin's deputy, Frank Forde, was replaced at the next meeting of the caucus of the Federal Parliamentary Labor Party by Joseph Benedict (Ben)

Chifley, former treasurer in the Curtin government. Chifley automatically became prime minister, since Labor enjoyed a comfortable majority in both houses of parliament. It fell to Chifley to see out the final months of the war and to handle the vast task of post-war reconstruction for which Labor had been planning since 1942. When the war in Europe ended in May 1945, and in the Pacific three months later, Australia had lost almost 34 000 dead. This was only half the total of military dead from World War I, and the population had risen to just on seven million so, in terms of service deaths, World War II had less impact on the Australian community than had World War I. Nevertheless, it would also be fair to say that the Australian population had been conscripted, rationed, and controlled during World War II in a way that had never before been experienced. By the end of the war more than half a million Australians were in uniform and large numbers of civilians had been conscripted under manpower regulations. These had all to be reabsorbed into the general community. The Chifley government faced a most daunting task.

Ben Chifley was the product of two depressions. He had experienced the depression of the 1890s as a small boy living on his grandfather's farm, and he had been a member of the Scullin government during the Great Depression of the 1930s. In both cases, he had witnessed ordinary people suffering as a result of banks' collapsing and of bank policies. He had seen the Scullin government hamstrung by the opposition of the Commonwealth Bank in its attempts to mitigate the worst effects of the 1930s depression, and he had come to regard the private banks and their relentless pursuit of ever-higher profits as parasitical growths on the economy. Control over the economy was a necessary part of Chifley's plans for reconstruction after the war because of the ALP's commitment to maintaining full employment while reabsorbing demobilised servicemen. Since 1942, extensive government works had been planned by the government to handle this transition if the private market proved unable to manage the task. Chifley was also very aware that, during the Great Depression, the Commonwealth Bank board had vetoed similar plans and refused to provide the necessary funds. Controlling the banks became a core component of government policy for the post-war era.

Financial nationalism

Even before the war ended, Chifley had introduced two banking Bills into federal parliament which were designed to lay the financial groundwork for reconstruction. The Commonwealth Bank board was abolished and the bank was placed under a single governor who was directly responsible to the treasurer of the day. In addition, the Commonwealth Bank was to function as a Reserve Bank and superintend and control the activities of all private banks; and all state and local government instrumentalities were to bank with the Commonwealth or with one of the government-run state banks. This final provision was ultimately ruled unconstitutional by the High Court in 1947, but the basic provisions establishing firm governmental control over the banks and the monetary system remained unaltered. Despite subsequent tinkering with the system by Liberal–Country Party governments, the basis established by Chifley's legislation remained unaltered until 1986.

The private banks were appalled at what they described as Chifley's policy of 'creeping socialism' and, for the rest of its period in office, the government faced the combined and powerful opposition of vested financial interests anxious to bring it down and to secure the reversal of the banking legislation. It was an issue destined to play a major role in the eventual downfall of the Chifley administration. Despite Menzies' best efforts on behalf of the Liberal Party, the Chifley government won the general election of 1946, and was returned to office with a handsome majority in both houses. Clearly the electorate found it hard to equate the transparent honesty and integrity of Ben Chifley with the socialist ogre portrayed by Menzies and the banks, and the dry humour and folksy style of the prime minister stood in marked contrast to the flashing wit and urbanity of the leader of the opposition.

Demobbing the troops

In contrast to the dislocation and unemployment returning servicemen experienced after World War I, the period immediately following the cessation of hostilities in World War II coincided with an economic boom that provided more than enough job opportunities for everyone. Moreover, the government offered a wide range of services to the ex-servicemen whereby they could equip themselves for a return to civilian life. Free tertiary training was available to all with entry qualifications to universities and colleges, and living allowances were paid as a low-interest loan to those who undertook further full-time training. Free training was also on offer for those who opted for skilled trades and semi-skilled occupations. Although the attractions of the land were not as great as they had been after World War I, thousands of ex-servicemen opted to take up the rural life, and they were assisted with loans, land grants, and free training and assistance until they managed to establish themselves. The El Niño phenomenon was still unknown, but the land had been chosen with greater care, and the size of the allotments was adjusted to take into account local conditions, the nature of the soil, and the rainfall patterns. In the long run, however, most of these ventures failed and, after years of hardship, the survivors often walked off their properties with nothing but the clothes in which they stood.

The economy booms

In 1946 the country experienced booming economic conditions in both primary and secondary industries. The war had led to a massive increase in Australia's industrial capacity and these plants changed-over rapidly to peacetime production. The building industry took off with an insatiable demand for private housing and for the household goods that had been unavailable during the war. Items such as radios and motor cars, hitherto regarded as unessential, were snapped-up as soon as they came onto the market. Full employment and a booming economy meant that there were very few problems absorbing the demobilised servicemen into civilian life, and the public works programs that the ALP had planned for post-war reconstruction were largely unused.

There were, however, social problems aplenty. Five years in the armed forces changed many men, and they found it difficult to readjust to civilian life. Moreover, they encountered a weariness with the war and a reluctance to talk much about it. Because soldiers, sailors, and airmen had known nothing but war, this often made conversation and the resumption of former friendships difficult. Fathers found themselves confronted by children they had never seen, and by wives and sweethearts who had become independent of spirit and used to looking after themselves during the long years of war. Women found it difficult to revert to the pre-war roles traditionally assigned to women and to give up their jobs and economic independence.

In primary industry, the profitable times continued after the war. Much of Europe was in a devastated condition and many countries were unable to feed or clothe themselves. Australia's exports of wool and wheat remained buoyant and much additional land was brought into production to cater for the increased demand. British consumption of meat and dairy produce remained high, and exports of canned fruits and dry fruit also increased.

Assisted immigration

By 1947, the economy was performing so well that the government decided to embark upon a major program of assisted immigration. The conflict with Japan and the rising power of the communists in China raised old fears in many Australians of being swamped by Asian hordes. Both sides of politics agreed that Australia's population needed to be increased substantially—as much for defence purposes as anything else. The minister for Immigration, Arthur Calwell, attacked the problem with great energy. The first choice of migrants was obviously British, and Calwell made strenuous efforts to attract as many Britishers as he could. The government offered a passage scheme that essentially amounted to free travel to Australia for any British migrants willing to make the journey. In addition to the British Isles, Calwell pointed out that the refugee camps of Europe contained almost one million people made homeless by the war, including people of Baltic, German, Polish, Italian, and Yugoslav origin who included professions and skilled trades among their accomplishments. Such people were needed in Australia and could make a real contribution to the country in return for their passages. This was the beginning of a program that came to play a major part in the development of Australia. In return for a free voyage to Australia, the immigrants from the displaced persons' camps agreed to work for two years, at regulation wages, wherever the Commonwealth government directed them. In this way a labour force became available for major construction works such as the Snowy River Development Scheme, which was to divert the waters of the Snowy River into a series of dams and tunnels to provide hydro-electric power to both New South Wales and Victoria, and irrigation waters to farmers on the other side of the Snowy Mountains. It was a mammoth development and could not have been undertaken or completed without the thousands of European immigrants. Similar (although less ambitious) projects were undertaken in other parts of the country, and the program served the dual purposes of populating Australia and providing a workforce for large projects of national importance. Preference was still given to Whites, however, and Blacks and Asians were rigorously excluded.

The Department of Immigration grew astronomically between 1946 and 1949, from a staff of twenty-four to about five thousand, as approximately seven hundred thousand immigrants landed in Australia. Subsequent Liberal–Country Party governments continued the program. By 1959 the national population had reached ten million, and by 1970 more than two-and-a-half million immigrants had arrived in Australia with a minimum of fuss and dislocation. Many of these post-war migrants experienced some level of hostility and prejudice from the Australian populace, but words of abuse such as 'Dago', 'Reffo', and 'Balt' were quickly replaced by the more acceptable term 'New Australian'. The offensive terms have now largely passed out of use. The feeling that migrants who had been through what most of these had suffered were entitled to receive a 'fair go' in Australia eventually prevailed, and assimilation of the children via the school system worked quite effectively. Periodic cricket contests ensured that 'Pom' remained popular as a derogatory word for people from England but, over time, it came to be used with a sense of affection rather than venom.

Creeping socialism: medicine and banking

Two areas where Chifley's nationalism and sense of fair play brought him into head on confrontation with powerful vested interests were his attempts to nationalise medicine and banking. During the war years, the medical profession had resolutely opposed attempts to establish a system of free medical attention and free pharmaceutical benefits paid from the tax revenues. They regarded such developments as dangerously socialistic and used the teething problems of the new British public health system to claim that it would produce a bureaucratic nightmare if anything similar were to be attempted in Australia. The British Medical Association (Australian Branch), soon to become the Australian Medical Association, set a standard for selfish and irresponsible behaviour when its members made plain their resolution to defend their privileges and incomes, whatever the cost to their patients.

Nationalised medicine would permit governments to limit and control doctors' incomes, and such socialistic interference would not be tolerated.

However, Chifley's plans to nationalise banking produced the most vitriolic and ferocious opposition. Chifley regarded the banks, on the basis of his experience of their behaviour through two depressions, as speculative parasitical growths on the economy. Although his 1945 legislation had escaped almost unscathed from the High Court appeal against it, and although his attorney-general, Dr Herbert Vere Evatt, strongly advised that there was no need to proceed further (because the banks were already subject to the overall control of the government), Chifley was determined to press ahead and crush the banks altogether. A conservative government could always reverse the controls and again make the Commonwealth Bank independent and capable of sabotaging an elected government—as had happened to Scullin during the early 1930s. It was better to scotch the financial snake while it was still possible. Chifley proceeded to attempt full nationalisation. It was to be a fatal mistake.

The banks and financial interests responded with one of the most bitter and sustained attacks on a government ever seen in Australia—far surpassing the abuse heaped on Jack Lang during the 1930s depression. Their customers were deluged with propaganda claiming that the government had designs on their savings, and their employees were told that their jobs would be endangered in the event that nationalisation went ahead. The newspapers joined in and Chifley was portrayed as a crazed socialist. To ram home the point, cartoons were published of a pipe-smoking Ben Chifley alongside a pipe-smoking Joseph Stalin. As the 1949 elections approached, the banks gave extended paid leave to many of their managers and executives so that they could work for the election of the Menzies Liberal party. It was a thoroughly professional and overwhelming campaign, and it did much to unseat the government.

Australia in the Cold War

The campaign against socialism, and the attempt to connect socialism and communism in the public mind, did not take place in a neutral environment, but in a world already fearful that it trembled on the brink of another war. The cooperation among the victorious Allies that had carried them through to victory against the Axis powers and Japan did not survive the peace. Increasing hostility between Soviet Russia and the West from 1947 onwards heralded the beginnings of the Cold War. In the Far East, the communists under Mao Tse-Tung continued to win impressive victories over the corrupt Kuomintang regime. It seemed only a matter of time before all China fell to the communists. In Europe, the Russian sponsored communist regimes in Hungary, Poland, Estonia, Latvia, and East Germany quickly showed themselves to be as repressive and as brutal as any collaborating Nazi sympathisers. In particular, the attacks on the sick and frail Hungarian prelate, Cardinal Mindszenty, aroused the horror of Roman Catholics throughout the world, and non-Catholics who valued the right of free speech and free association spoke out vehemently in his defence. At the United Nations, the recently elected president of the General Assembly, Dr Evatt, earned the enmity of the Soviet delegation by his protests on behalf of Mindszenty. But, back home in Australia, Evatt was a man pilloried by conservatives for being much too favourably inclined towards communism.

As the world increasingly came to resemble two armed camps, the smaller nations began to align themselves with one or other of the superpowers. American policy was dominated by the need to contain communism. Australia, as a loyal ally, soon fell into line with this world view. Indeed, it was a view that proved to be wholly congenial to Menzies and the more conservative politicians in the Liberal Party and the Country Party, but it posed real problems for the ALP which paid lip-service (at least) to the socialist objective. As the international situation deteriorated, anything which smacked of socialism or communism became progressively easier to depict as treasonable. The Communist Party of Australia had ended the war with more than 20 000 members, and party members were in control of many of the country's largest and most important trade unions. Membership of the party fell rapidly as international tensions escalated, but communists proved harder to dislodge from the trade unions. First, many communist union officials were highly regarded by the rank and file for their militancy and their efficiency in obtaining concessions from the employers; workers remembered with gratitude the prominent role taken by communists in the Unemployed Workers Movement during the Great Depression, when Labor governments appeared to have abandoned them. Second, many communists were entrenched in power within the union bureaucracies and used all the facilities of head office to maintain their positions. Third, some communists did not hesitate to defend their positions with stand-over tactics, violence, and general bullying of their opponents. Fourth, opposition to communism within the industrial labour movement was not as well organised as were the communists—at least, not until the later 1940s.

The extent of communist influence within Australia's trade union movement has always been difficult to quantify. One of their leading opponents at this time has stated that, by 1945, communists controlled four out of the five state Trades and Labour Councils, and exercised an all-but-controlling influence on the councils and conference of the federal organisation the Australian Council of Trade Unions (ACTU).[7] In the years after the war, many trades unions in the public sector struck in favour of shorter hours and greater pay. Strikes in the areas of public transport, coal mining, and power supply greatly inconvenienced Australians who found it easy to blame the communist scapegoats who were deemed to be responsible by the newspapers and conservative politicians. A tide of public opinion soon began to run against the trade unions, and especially those under communist leadership. At least some of these strikes involved genuine industrial grievances but, after five years of war, the public was in no mood for strikes in public utilities.

Public discourse was further poisoned by startling revelations from former Soviet agents in Canada, the United States of America, and even Victoria—revelations indicating that a far-flung and sinister network of communist infiltration, masterminded by the Soviet Union, existed throughout the 'free world'. These agents were working from within to undermine the capacity of the West to defend itself via a network of secret cells in government departments and key industrial trade unions. Committed socialists were described as 'fellow travellers' with the communists, and their beliefs were felt by many Australians to be dangerous to national security. Thus, when trades unions in the public utilities went out on strike after 1945 they met with little sympathy and increasing hostility as the decade progressed. The conservatives hammered the theme that the ALP was a socialist party and therefore must be unreliable on communism. In the growing Cold War climate, to be soft on communism was to become an electoral kiss of death.

This was the context in which Chifley's attempts to nationalise the banks and the doctors were fought out after 1947, and the longer the issues dragged on the less sympathy the government enjoyed. Events culminated in the industrial arena with the great coal strike of 1949, when miners under communist leadership in New South Wales went on strike and coal miners in all states quickly joined in. The miners claimed a 35-hour week and certain other privileges which the Chifley government adamantly refused. This last great strike of the 1940s brought almost the entire industrial life of the country to a stop, for other industries were unable to function without coal. Eventually, the Chifley government froze the bank accounts of the striking unions so that strike pay could no longer be supplied to their members, and it sent in the army to work the coal mines and get industry started. It was firm and resolute action and the strike was broken, but Menzies and the rabid anti-communists were the long-term winners.

On the eve of the election in October 1949 the final touch of anti-communist publicity was generated by Lawrence Sharkey, chairman of the Communist Party of Australia, who was found guilty of uttering seditious words with a seditious intention earlier in the year when he had informed a startled public that, if Soviet forces in pursuit of aggressors entered Australia, Australian workers would welcome them. It was a stupid, thoughtless, and inflammatory thing to say, and he received a sentence of three years in jail. Sharkey had been prosecuted by Dr Evatt, Chifley's attorney-general, but even this did not help the ALP shake off the taint of being pro-communist—a taint so assiduously being fastened upon it by the doctors, the banks, and the opposition.

There were other lesser irritants that helped to swell the feeling that the government was well past its prime. Chifley believed that it was necessary to continue wartime rationing and restrictions to assist in the process of reconstruction, but these were only marginally useful and not worth the ill-will they caused in a community that had grown heartily sick of government intervention in their lives. Menzies promised to remove the restrictions and restore value to the currency that had eroded due to inflation during the post-war economic boom. At the end of the election, the Liberal–Country party coalition had secured 74 seats in the House of Representatives to Labor's 47, although the ALP still retained control of the Senate. Robert Gordon Menzies became prime minister of Australia for the second time, and the Australian Labor Party began twenty-three years in the political wilderness.

The Age of Menzies

For the next sixteen years Robert Gordon Menzies presided over the fortunes of Australia. By the time he retired in 1966 there were young adults who could not remember a time when Australia had had any other prime minister. The period became known as the 'Menzies era', and had some notable distinguishing characteristics. It was a time dominated both domestically and internationally by fear of communism. Menzies proved to be the supreme political opportunist in appealing to the Australian electorate time after time on a rabidly anti-communist platform. Election campaigns throughout these years became exercises in 'red-baiting' or 'kicking the communist can' as they were colloquially described. Anti-communism had been a political weapon in Australia since the time of Billy Hughes. Combined with traditional fears of Asia—especially after China became communist in 1949—anti-communism became an extremely potent electoral asset for Menzies and the conservatives. The ALP was routinely and regularly attacked for its trade union links with communist agitators, and for the allegedly pro-communist foreign policies which such links produced in the ALP platform.

To this must be added a recognition of the utter inadequacy of ALP leaders, after Chifley, to match Menzies in any field of political endeavour. Chifley died of a heart attack in 1951, and neither of his successors, first Dr Evatt and then Arthur Calwell, was up to the job of confronting the prime minister in parliament or on the hustings.

The ALP split yet again in 1955. The split was on sectarian religious lines, and a small but fanatical group of mainly Roman Catholic zealots formed their own political party with the single express purpose of denying office to the ALP by the distribution of their electoral preferences. In this they proved eminently successful. Moreover, their virulent attacks on the ALP for its softness on communism played right into the hands of the prime minister, and there is evidence to suggest that the Liberal-Country Party coalition assisted such a useful electoral asset with financial donations during election campaigns.[8]

Prosperity and stability

Part of the secret of Menzies' continued success lay in the fact that he delivered prosperity and stability, or that he was fortunate enough to be in office at a time when such conditions became the accepted norm for much of Australia. There were periodic fluctuations of employment but, overall, the Menzies era was characterised by full employment and rising prosperity domestically, amid turmoil and misery abroad. The large migrant population from war-ravaged Europe wanted stability and freedom from terror and persecution. Such people tended to become avid supporters of the prime minister, and his anti-communist rhetoric appealed to their well-founded prejudices. But to Australians in general, the Menzies appeal—even the virulent anti-communism— was entirely pragmatic. Export prices for primary produce and industrialisation of the domestic economy delivered a way of life and a standard of living that were equal or superior to those of almost any other country in the world. There was a great (if *ad hoc*) expansion in social services—with contributory medical insurance, subsidised pharmaceutical benefits, increased child endowment, and other welfare measures—and a vast increase in federal government spending on education from primary to tertiary level. Menzies broke the mould of entrenched anti-Catholicism on the conservative side of politics, and his administration began the shifting of substantial resources to support the Catholic school system. His government seemed to accept that it was the proper role of government in Australia to ensure a 'fair go' for all members of society, or at least those parts of society that were electorally significant. Poverty and prejudice continued to affect the lives of some Australians, particularly the Aborigines. However, because most Aborigines were not citizens and could not vote, they continued to suffer the trauma of forced assimilation policies and the state-sponsored kidnapping of their children.

Whatever might be said about the Menzies era, it must be kept in mind that the prime minister remained in office because he gave a majority of the Australian people what they wanted.

Coalition foreign policy

As the Liberal–Country party coalition took over the running of the country in 1950, one of the hallmarks of the new administration was its handling of foreign policy. During 1949 Mao Tse-Tung had taken the communists to power in China, and the Chifley government had prepared the grounds for extending diplomatic recognition to the new government of China and had intended to do so after the election at the end of the year. Menzies, however, would not recognise the new Chinese government as legitimate and refused to proceed with the plan. Instead the new government of Australia accepted the American approach of attempting to contain and isolate communism like some sort of infectious disease. The initial step in this policy was withholding recognition from communist China, and the second was the arrangement of a series of treaties and diplomatic agreements that was designed to strengthen and support anti-communist regimes in countries to Australia's north. Where the ALP had sought alliances that brought a buffer zone between Australia and Japan, the Menzies government followed a similar policy directed against China.

The first brick in this defensive structure was laid as early as January 1950 when the new minister for External Affairs, Percy Spender, proposed to a joint meeting of foreign ministers from the British Commonwealth—with a view to organising concerted action to raise the living standards of people in South and South-East Asia. The idea was to improve conditions of life for the people of the region and thereby make them less susceptible to the allurements of communism. In essence it was an attempt to do internationally what Menzies was to do domestically, and to give the residents of the region a vested interest in maintaining and protecting the status quo. The scheme became known as the

'Colombo Plan', and the originating members agreed to offer finance for capital equipment and technical assistance to the governments of undeveloped nations. The plan was not restricted to Commonwealth countries but included a large number of non-Commonwealth undeveloped countries. Australia contributed more than £31 million in the first six years and sent expert advisers to the countries concerned. Australia also expended £3.5 million on scholarships to bring students from these countries to Australia for tertiary training before returning them to their own countries to assist in development.

In the following year, in return for Australia's acceptance of a peace with Japan that was significantly less punitive than Australia had wanted, the cornerstone of post-war Australian security was laid with the signing of the ANZUS Treaty among Australia, New Zealand, and the United States of America. Although the wording of the treaty is deliberately vague, Australia has always interpreted it to be a guarantee of American assistance in the event of any attack being launched upon Australia. The days of any independence in foreign policy, such as that enjoyed by Dr Evatt in the years immediately after the war, had now passed, and the ANZUS Treaty marked Australia's recognition of its strategically precarious position in a world divided into armed camps and ideological conflict. Added point had been given to the search for security in June 1950 when communist North Korea invaded South Korea and the United States assumed leadership of the United Nations forces opposing the invasion. The Australian government pledged 'the closest possible collaboration' with the United States, and Australian military forces later joined in the war to resist the tidal wave of 'volunteers' from communist China who came south to assist the North Koreans. General Douglas MacArthur was appointed commander of United Nations forces in Korea and planned to carry the war to China by using atomic weapons. President Truman overruled him and ordered him back home where he was relieved of his command, but the episode does provide a measure of the degree to which the world had polarised into hostile camps that were fully intent on destroying one another. By the time that an armistice in the Korean War was signed in 1953, Australia had lost 42 pilots and 1538 soldiers killed, wounded, or missing in action.

Australia's preoccupation with erecting a defensive buffer zone of allies and friends between China and itself received further impetus in September 1954 with the signing of the South-East Asia Collective Defence Treaty (known as the South-East Asia Treaty Organisation, SEATO). The signatories were Australia, France, New Zealand, Pakistan, the Philippines, Thailand, Britain, and the United States, and the treaty bound them together in a defensive alliance against communist governments in the region. The treaty nations undertook to defend not only themselves but also any other country in the region that might be threatened by communist aggression. From Australia's perspective, the treaty complemented ANZUS because it committed America to defend not only Australia but also Australia's neighbours in the *cordon sanitaire* that the government was constructing to Australia's north. Countries that were not signatories to the treaty could be 'designated' as being within the ambit of the treaty if all the treaty nations unanimously agreed, and a special protocol at the end of the treaty 'designated' Cambodia, Laos, and French-occupied South Vietnam as being areas covered by its provisions. It was under SEATO that Australia's involvement in the imbroglio of Vietnam took place after 1962.

Under an agreement among Australia, Britain, and New Zealand, Australian troops were also committed to fighting communist insurgents in the Commonwealth country of Malaya during the early 1950s and, later on, in defending the borders of the new Commonwealth state of Malaysia against Indonesian attacks during the period of 'Confrontation'. China's invasion of Tibet and India, and the stunning defeat suffered by the French in Vietnam at Dien Bien Phu, helped to produce a siege mentality in many Australians who feared the loss of a comfortable and affluent way of life to outside invasion from Asia, aided and assisted by a shadowy fifth column of communist agents and sympathisers within Australia itself. This combination of greed and fear lay at the heart of Menzies' success in convincing enough Australians to keep voting for him to maintain him in office.

Kicking the communist can

One of the first measures brought forward by the Menzies government in 1950 was a Bill to outlaw the Communist Party. This had already been done by regulation under the *National Security Act* in the early days of World War II when communists opposed and sabotaged the war effort, but the ban had been lifted in 1942 in recognition of the new status of Soviet Russia as an ally against Germany. At that time, Australian communists had switched from opposing the war to giving it their fullest support. Inconsistency never worried Australian communists at this time, and they seemed prepared to mouth whatever platitudes their master in the Kremlin directed them to utter. But the years after 1945 had brought most Australians to the point where communists were seen as an identifiable threat to the country. Consequently, when Prime Minister Menzies introduced his Bill to dissolve the Communist Party, it received the reluctant support of the ALP and passed both houses of parliament. The Labor Party was averse to the declaratory provisions of the new Act—that anybody could be declared a communist and thereby deprived of employment on the uncorroborated assertion of the Australian Security Intelligence Organisation (ASIO) (which had been established by the Chifley Labor government in 1949). It was then up to that person to prove that he or she was not a communist. This reversed the normal onus of proof in favour of the accuser, and caused considerable concern to the former attorney-general, Dr Evatt. So-called 'declared persons' were to be prohibited from holding any government position or any office in any major trade union. The ALP was not united, however, and a significant minority of Roman Catholic members strongly favoured the legislation. They had been working within the trade union movement since 1937 in a campaign to defeat entrenched communist leaders, and communist persecution of Roman Catholics throughout the Soviet Union fired their zeal.

A secret organisation had grown up, led by a Roman Catholic lawyer and journalist, B.A. Santamaria, and financed at least in part by the Roman Catholic Church. Known as the 'Catholic Social Studies Movement' or more simply as 'the Movement', this small band of men had used the communist tactics of secrecy and infiltration to form a nucleus of cells dedicated to ending once

B.A. Santamaria. (Australian History Museum, Macquarie University)

and for all communist leadership in the trade union movement. They were strongest in New South Wales and Victoria, and did not limit their attentions to the trade unions, but extended their organisation into the branches and various executives of the ALP. As a consequence, they were able to control ALP preselections and ensure that their own members won preselection as parliamentary seats became vacant. They also sought to eliminate the socialist objective from the ALP platform and to replace ALP policies with

new ones modelled upon the various social encyclicals of the Popes. The Movement succeeded in obtaining official ALP endorsement for its anti-communist crusade in the trade unions by sponsoring official ALP bodies known as 'industrial groups'. These groups (or 'groupers' as they were known), within which the Movement provided the nucleus, permitted anti-communist trade unionists to run for office as endorsed ALP candidates against communist officials in trade union elections, but the groups soon extended their campaigns and opposed any officials who dared to disagree with them. They were fanatics and had been described by Ben Chifley as 'all those mad buggers';[9] but given their prominence in the party and in the House of Representatives, Chifley and Evatt decided to accept the communist dissolution Bill rather than risk splitting the party.

The law was immediately challenged in the High Court by the Communist Party and a number of trade unions. One of these unions, the Waterside Workers Federation, briefed Dr Evatt to appear as counsel on its behalf. Evatt had a long history of concerned interest in civil rights issues and had been a renowned barrister. However, he was a former ALP attorney-general and Chifley's heir presumptive to the leadership of the federal party. His acceptance of this brief constituted the first of the monumental blunders that were to bedevil the remainder of his parliamentary career. Certainly it made it very easy for Menzies and other coalition ministers to label Evatt and, through him, the ALP, as being pro-communist. How could the deputy leader of the ALP appear before the High Court without the appearance of involving his party? As far as the Movement was concerned, Evatt's role in securing a six-to-one rejection of the Act by the High Court meant open war.

Within ten days of this verdict, Menzies had secured a double dissolution from the governor-general on the basis that the ALP-controlled Senate had refused to pass his banking legislation. That the issue was merely a ruse was shown by the fact that banking played practically no part in the subsequent election campaign—which was fought predominantly over the communist issue. Prime Minister Menzies promised that if his government were returned he would ask the people of Australia in a referendum to give him the power to outlaw the Communist Party. Earlier in the month the prime minister had solemnly announced his belief that another world war would occur within the next three years.[10] These tactics proved eminently successful, and the Liberal–Country Party government was returned to office with a majority in both houses. In June 1951 Ben Chifley died of a heart attack and the unstable and erratic Evatt succeeded to the national leadership of the ALP.

The referendum on communism was fixed for 22 September 1951, and Evatt flung himself into the 'No' campaign with all the vigour at his command. He stumped the country from end to end and, in the face of adverse opinion polls and press hostility, held fast to the belief that Australians could be persuaded to vote against outlawing a party for its beliefs. Evatt argued that the attempt against the communists violated the ethic of the 'fair go' because it was an attack on free speech. People ought not be punished for holding unconventional or unpopular beliefs. Menzies and supporters of the referendum denied that they were attacking the freedom of speech of ordinary Australians—after all, communists would be the only people affected. The 'No' case won a small majority of the votes cast but, in political terms, Menzies won a handsome victory. The leader of the opposition had totally identified himself in the public eye with a defence of the civil rights of communists, and being sympathetic towards communism was an accusation that haunted Evatt and his party for decades to come. Menzies had been handed a weapon against the ALP that he and his successors would use thereafter with telling effect.

The great split

The ALP became increasingly inconsequential after 1951 and turned inwards in a factional confrontation between the Movement and those who opposed it. Evatt attempted to play both sides against the middle. At first he favoured the Movement and flattered Santamaria. Then he swung in the opposite direction and attacked the groupers—describing Santamaria, his main episcopal supporter

(Archbishop Daniel Mannix), and their followers, as 'clerical fascists'. Evatt's behaviour became increasingly unpredictable.

Another of his errors of judgment occurred in 1954 during what became known as the Petrov Affair. In April 1954, Prime Minister Menzies announced to a stunned House of Representatives that Vladimir Mikhailovich Petrov, third secretary of the Soviet embassy in Australia, had defected and had sought political asylum in Australia. Petrov brought with him certain documents that demonstrated that Soviet espionage was occurring in Australia. Menzies then announced that a royal commission into Soviet espionage would immediately be established. The following week, Petrov's wife was rescued in Darwin from the clutches of two armed escorts who were taking her back to the Soviet Union. The publicity was too good to waste, and Menzies called an election for the following month—which he won with a reduced but comfortable majority. Then it emerged that certain of the documents that Petrov had brought with him contained references to members of Evatt's personal staff. An incensed Evatt demanded the right to represent his staff before the royal commission, where he hectored the commissioners to the effect that the royal commission was nothing more than a political stunt dreamed up by Prime Minister Menzies to destroy his reputation. The commissioners were not amused at accusations of being accessories in a political stunt, and responded by pointing out that Evatt seemed to have confused his political role as leader of the opposition with his legal role as counsel for his own staff members. After further clashes they refused to allow him to appear again before them.

To pre-empt the groupers from attempting to remove him from the leadership of the ALP, Evatt went public with an attack in October 1954, in which he denounced right-wing members of the ALP for disloyalty and for taking their orders from an organisation that was outside the Labor Party. In these basic charges, Evatt was undoubtedly correct. Groupers had been disloyal, and they were involved in subversion of both political and industrial wings of the labour movement.[11]

In 1955, the crisis split the ALP again, and resulted in the formation of a new political party, the Democratic Labor Party (DLP), consisting largely of Roman Catholics. The split caused ALP governments to fall in Victoria in 1955, Queensland in 1957, and Western Australia in 1959, and the DLP was able to keep the ALP out of federal office until 1972 by the distribution of its preferences. In the Senate, the proportional voting system permitted the DLP to elect senators quite effectively and, on occasion, the party held the balance of power by virtue of the small group of DLP senators it managed to get elected.

The ALP replaced the unstable Evatt with his deputy, Arthur Calwell, in 1960. Although Calwell, as a Roman Catholic, proved more difficult to smear as a crypto-communist, he was quite unable to match Menzies in the cut and thrust of parliamentary debate or in electioneering.

Menzies' last years

In 1962 Prime Minister Menzies authorised the dispatch of a small number of military advisers to South Vietnam and, three years later, sent an entire infantry battalion. The decision to commit Australia's armed forces to fight alongside American troops in Vietnam followed logically from the treaty relationships with America and the underlying purpose of those treaties to obtain a United States' commitment to the defence of Australia. It seemed only reasonable that this would demand a reciprocal response from Australia when American soldiers were fighting in Asia, and the government accepted the proposition that American protection had to be purchased by Australian participation in the quagmire of Vietnam. The issue which, in 1966, became further complicated by the question of conscription for service in Vietnam, split the Australian community throughout the 1960s and made foreign policy critically important in elections. The Americans were delighted to receive support in such an unpopular war, and a Melbourne newspaper soberly summed up the situation from the perspective of protecting Australia's best interests: 'An act of support for our American allies, limited though it is by our resources, is the far-sighted course to take at this critical stage. It may have grave consequences, but it deepens the friendship we need.' [12]

The final step in Australia's increasing involvement in the tragedy of Vietnam occurred in November 1964, when the government announced a massive build-up of the defence establishment and the introduction of conscription. However, it was a partial conscription as not all those born in a particular year would be called up, but only those unfortunate enough to have their birth dates drawn in a ballot. The so-called 'lottery of death' was to divide the Australian community almost as deeply as did the earlier conscription conflicts of World War I, but the issue in the 1960s did take time to build up. In the Senate elections held soon after the prime minister's announcement, the issue seemed to be electorally unimportant. As the decade progressed, however, public agitation and demonstrations against the war became more numerous and attracted an increasing following. By then, of course, the man responsible for reintroducing conscription onto the political bill-of-fare had retired, leaving his hapless successors to reap the whirlwind he had sown.

The end of an era

On 10 January 1966, Prime Minister Robert Menzies retired. He was 71 years of age and had held office continuously since 1949, establishing an all-time record for any Australian leader or for any prime minister within the British Commonwealth. His opportunism had brought many Roman Catholic voters across to the coalition from the ALP, but his pursuit of short-term political gains was to leave his successors with a series of intractable headaches. Menzies had built on the foundations laid during World War II and had presided over an economic boom almost as long as that in the second half of the nineteenth century. When necessary, for electoral popularity, he had been able to be a non-doctrinaire socialist—as, for example, in extending state aid to the Roman Catholic school system. For the same electoral reasons, he had been capable of being quite reactionary on other issues. Aside from keeping himself in power he did not seem to have believed in anything very much. Even his anti-communism did not hinder good business when it came to selling Australian wheat to communist China after 1961. Ben Chifley had perceived the Labor platform as being a 'light on the hill' for all mankind, but Menzies was never a man who could be said to have had a great vision in his heart concerning the future of his country. Australians tended to admire him and respect him, but not to like him very much. During the war years, there had often been spontaneous applause when the figure of John Curtin appeared on the newsreels. Nothing similar can be said about Menzies, whose aloof and slightly patronising air discouraged easy familiarity, and whose oft-repeated pride in his Britishness had, by the time of his departure from public life, made him something of an anachronism to young Australians.

9

The Turbulent Years

The Liberal PartyA Land Fit for HeroesA Land Fit for Heroes at the time of Menzies' retirement amounted to a coalition of conservatives and liberals that was held together by opposition to the ALP rather than by any overarching sense of ideology--aside from anti-communism tempered by economic pragmatism. Menzies had provided a federal structure that ensured the party's survival in an administrative sense, but the party had not been really committed to a belief that the state should play a lesser role in the daily life of the community, and Menzies himself had been like an old Deakinite liberal who was more than happy to use state power to advance liberal social policies and for his own electoral advantage. The innate tensions between liberals and conservatives within the party had been held in check by the towering figure of Menzies, and the years following his departure proved to be a testing time for the party he had created.

The Liberal Party chose Menzies' loyal deputy, Harold Holt, as the prime minister's replacement. Holt had been Menzies' heir-apparent for a considerable time. He had been in parliament for thirty-one years, had spent eighteen years as a minister, and had been deputy leader of the party for the previous ten years. His loyalty to his chief had been unquestioning and there had never been any suggestion that he was impatient or prepared to challenge Menzies for the leadership. He was friendly and personable, and was an avid sportsman who still engaged in swimming and spearfishing whenever he could find the time. It pleased him enormously that he had come to the leadership of his party and his country without having to walk over the bodies of any political rivals. Holt's basic decency and amiability of character made him popular with his colleagues in the government and, later in the year, these characteristics also proved to be strong electoral assets with the general public. There were, however, some doubts as to whether he would be ruthless enough to survive at the top in Australian politics. Would he be able to withstand pressure from the leader of the junior partner in the coalition, the formidable John 'Black Jack' McEwen, or was he likely to be another Joseph Lyons—popular with the public but in need of careful minding or hand-holding (as Bruce had put it) by his less favoured colleagues?

Prime Minister Holt

Harold Holt's views on leadership had been honed and refined during the long years he had served as Menzies' deputy, and he had clearly defined views concerning the sort of leadership that he would offer. To begin with, he resolutely rejected any suggestion of introducing an elected ministry like the ALP's. The prime minister must have the right to choose his ministers, said Holt, so that he could ensure a balance of talents and introduce selected younger members of parliament who could be groomed for leadership. Holt had chosen a style of leadership that suited him perfectly: 'There is the leadership which can lead but, at the same time, be close enough to the team to be a part of it and be on the basis of friendly cooperation. I will make that my technique of leadership'.[1]

Although it could be argued that Holt's brief term of office really marked the final years of the Menzies era, the new prime minister did make alterations in style. Menzies had despised the press and avoided it wherever he could, but Holt introduced weekly press conferences at which reporters were able to question him freely. These quickly highlighted certain of Holt's deficiencies, in that he was an unimpressive speaker and inclined to be vague and imprecise. While his opposition was only the ageing Arthur Calwell this did not much matter, but it became a serious problem in 1967 when the articulate and gifted Edward Gough Whitlam took over the leadership of the Federal Parliamentary Labor Party.

Another change in style became apparent in the new prime minister's attitude to Asia and South-East Asia. Menzies had always avoided Australia's northern neighbours, merely flying over them on his way to Europe or North America, but Holt actually seemed to like Asians and visited all of Australia's South-East Asian neighbours in his first year of office. His personal friendship with the leaders of these countries stood in marked contrast to the reserve with which they had been treated by Menzies. Holt made personal contact in this way with the heads of government in South Vietnam, Malaysia, Singapore, and Thailand.

During 1967, the last vestiges of the White Australia Policy were quietly disposed of, and the final barriers to skilled Asian immigration were removed. Racial prejudice had no place in Harold Holt's makeup, and this approach also affected his outlook on policies towards Aborigines. In May 1967, the Holt government, with bipartisan support from the ALP, took a referendum to the Australian people that proposed to give the Commonwealth government power to legislate for Aborigines. The intention was to put a stop to discrimination against Aborigines and to ensure that they would be included in any future census as Australians. Since federation, Aboriginal welfare had been a state concern and, by and large, the states had done very little for the indigenous people. After all, they did not vote, so why waste money on them? Aboriginal health, housing and education were scandals, and segregation was openly practised in rural areas. Following the American lead in Negro civil rights during the 1960s, these customs were challenged by freedom riders from Sydney led by an Aboriginal activist named Charles Perkins.

Enormous publicity resulted, and urban Australians were horrified to find that in country towns the Blacks were not permitted to share hotel bars or cinemas with Whites, and that Aboriginal children were not permitted to swim in the local council swimming pool with the White children. Moreover, as workers on the northern pastoral stations, Aborigines received rates of pay that were much lower than the wages paid to White pastoral workers, and their working conditions were vastly inferior. This was clearly discrimination on the basis of colour and, in September 1966, Aborigines at Wave Hill station in the Northern Territory had appealed to the United Nations for protection. As a consequence of all this exposure, the Holt-sponsored referendum obtained overwhelming support from a conscience-stricken populace and passed with a large majority in all states.

The Vietnam imbroglio

One of the legacies that Menzies had left to his successors was Australia's involvement in the war in Vietnam, and his decision to commit conscripts to that war brought into focus a sharp divergence of opinion—not only on the question of using conscripts but also, by implication, on Australia's increasing reliance on the United States of America for a guarantee of military protection. In March 1966, Harold Holt announced that Australia would treble its commitment in South Vietnam to 4500 men, who would constitute a self-contained task force under Australian command and who would include conscripts unfortunate enough to be drawn in the 'lottery of death'. The prime minister commented that the task force had been increased to match a rapid and much larger increase in the numbers of American soldiers serving in Vietnam. After all, he said, 'while the Chinese communist philosophy of world domination persists, the whole free world is threatened'.[2]

The opposition took the view that the government was

cynically manipulating events for its own political advantage. If communist China was really such a rogue state and a threat to world peace, then what was the Holt government doing in trading raw materials with China that were essential components of an atomic bomb delivery system? By accusing China of hostile intentions, the Holt government was enabled to build up a war atmosphere for its own electoral advantage while, at the same time, its trade with China won it votes in rural areas.[3] Holt's administration definitely seemed to have the best of both worlds.

The American alliance

The American alliance became inextricably intertwined with the Vietnam debate, and the government usually labelled any opposition to the war as anti-Americanism, thus leading to the ironic situation that the ALP, which had initiated the turn to America against conservative opposition during World War II, became suspected of being opposed to the United States of America and its policies. Since the signing of the ANZUS pact, Liberal–Country Party governments had made the treaty with America the cornerstone of Australia's defence planning. They would do whatever it took to secure an American commitment to the defence of Australia, and if that meant sending conscripts to fight and die in Vietnam, then so be it. The ALP vainly protested that it was opposed to American policy not to America, but it proved to be too subtle a distinction for most people, and the Holt government was able to play with considerable success upon traditional Australian fears concerning the danger from Asia and the absolute need for American protection. The downside of such a policy stance, however, was that the conservative government found itself trapped into an unthinking and automatic support of American policy on the war and Asia in general which, on occasion, descended into sycophantic posturing.

In June 1966, Prime Minister Holt visited the United States

of America and, in a speech before the American president, Lyndon Baines Johnson, announced that Australia would go 'all the way with LBJ'. He meant to refer to the war in Vietnam, but the claim was so all-embracing and uncritical that it implied support for Johnson personally and for the American Democratic Party. Many Australians were disappointed to find that the obsequious kowtowing of Menzies before Britain's Queen Elizabeth II had been transferred, by his successor, to the president of the United States. Many, however, also shared Holt's affection for the president, and they gave him a tumultuous welcome when he accepted Holt's invitation to tour Australia later that year. Holt took care to accompany Johnson whenever he could, and basked in the reflected glory of his friendship with the world's most powerful man. Johnson's visit also brought demonstrators onto the streets of Australian cities, and anti-war activists jostled and scuffled with pro-Johnson supporters as the president's cavalcade drove past. At one stage, Johnson was driving in a car with the Liberal premier of New South Wales, Robin Askin, when demonstrators laid down in front of the vehicle. Askin urged his chauffeur to 'drive over the bastards'. That such a comment could be made by the leader of a popularly elected government indicates the extent to which the Vietnam War had already polarised political opinion in the country. It marked the beginning of another deeply divisive community debate on conscription for overseas service. This time, as in World War II, the Roman Catholic Church supported conscription to fight Asians.

Conscription revisited

Harold Holt called an election just one month after President Johnson's visit, and focused the campaign squarely on the issues of the war, conscription, and the American alliance. He also continued the Menzies push to attract the Roman Catholic vote by promising massive increases in state aid to private schools. The

ALP under Calwell agreed that the war was the important issue of the election, and promised that conscription would be abolished immediately and Australian troops withdrawn from Vietnam if they were voted into office. The government won overwhelmingly, with 82 seats to the ALP's 41 in the House of Representatives. Holt had read the mood of the electorate very shrewdly and recognised that it would support the war against Asian communism in Vietnam, and would support conscription to fight that war. His judgment was also vindicated in that Menzies' understanding, that no party could win government in Australia if it was suspected of being anti-American, had been spectacularly reaffirmed. In any situation where war was being waged to the north, to be anti-American in Australia was tantamount to treason.

Calwell had been shot at during the campaign, and broken glass had cut his face. He campaigned on bravely, but even the sympathy vote was unable to moderate the electoral verdict. In 1967 he reluctantly resigned in favour of his ambitious deputy Edward Gough Whitlam. The rout had been so comprehensive that, in many ways, Whitlam's job was rendered easier, for the party could only improve on its 1966 showing.

After the election, the prime minister of South Vietnam, Air Vice-Marshall Ky, visited Australia at Holt's invitation. Ky did not possess the crowd-pulling power of President Johnson, but he was a personable and dashing figure given to sporting a fighter pilot's scarf. He also proved to be a fluent speaker, both modest and articulate. He did not come to seek further military aid, he said, but to thank Australians for the aid already sent. Calwell described the South Vietnamese prime minister as 'a pocket Hitler' and 'a moral and social leper', but Australians did not see him that way, and were quietly inclined to agree with the South Vietnamese ambassador that Calwell's denunciation emanated from a desperate old politician at the tail-end of an unsuccessful career.[4]

Australia's links with America and with regional allies such as

South Vietnam and Malaysia became even more important during 1967 when Britain finally announced its intention to withdraw altogether from South-East Asia. It planned to vacate its bases voluntarily in Singapore and Malaysia by the middle of 1970. The decision was not unexpected, but it further highlighted Britain's decline as a world power and Australia's reliance on the United States to fill the power vacuum left behind. In the event, Australia was to take over some of the bases in Malaysia and maintain stability in the region by guaranteeing that country's independence.

Economic autonomy

In November 1967, Britain devalued the pound by 14.3% and, for the first time, the Australian government did not devalue to maintain the traditional connection between the currencies. Britain's move had been anticipated, and Australia had taken steps to limit the amount of overseas reserves held in sterling. The Country Party demanded that Australia devalue to protect rural markets and rural interests. The Country Party leader, John McEwen, nearly touched off a crisis by criticising in public the government's decision not to devalue the dollar, and enabled Harold Holt to demonstrate that there was plenty of steel under that affable exterior. The prime minister rebuked McEwen publicly for breaking Cabinet solidarity, and pointedly noted that the Country Party was the *junior* partner in the coalition. The Liberals had come within an ace of being able to govern in their own right, and Holt believed that if McEwen attempted to take the Country Party out of the coalition—as Page had threatened to do to Hughes and Menzies—enough Country Party members would stay behind to give his government a stable majority.[5]

McEwen's arguments were based on the need to protect rural incomes, which had been badly hit by the effects of a prolonged El Niño drought cycle between 1964 and 1966. The drought impacted with particular severity in New South Wales and Queensland and had already led to unemployment and relief works in the affected areas. The dairying industry accumulated losses of $400 million and, in Queensland, farmers had lost more than four million sheep and half-a-million head of cattle. These were not minor considerations, but Holt took the view that the government had to do more than protect the incomes of a supporting group when it came to defining economic policy, and he convinced Cabinet that it would be to Australia's absolute economic disadvantage to cave in to Country Party pressure in favour of devaluation. Overall, the economy would benefit more from not devaluing, even if this inconvenienced some major stakeholders.

Indeed, the general strength of the Australian economy was demonstrated during 1967 when the Conciliation and Arbitration Commission altered the entire basis of wage-fixing decisions and replaced the concept of basic wage plus margins, established by the Harvester decision in the early years of the century, with a 'total wage'. The judgment handed down by the commission referred to the blurring of the rationale behind the basic wage that had eventually reached the stage where it meant many different things to different people. For some it stood for the minimum wage paid in any particular industry; for others it meant the lowest wage paid for unskilled work, and some continued to regard it as an assessment of a living wage for a family. The new approach absorbed the margins into a wage package for each industry, and future national wage increases would apply to this total wage.

The commission believed that the new system gave flexibility and permitted both the protection of the lowest-paid members of the workforce and the passing on of economic gains to the workers each year. It also made it easier to set a statutory minimum wage. The new practice was justified on the implicit assumption that there would be economic gains to pass on to workers each year, and the expectation of sustained economic growth was built into the system. Similar optimistic expectations underlay the drive to bring married women into the workforce. Women had been liberated from their traditional roles of childbearing and housework by the arrival of cheap reliable contraception in the 1960s, and Australian women proved to be among the most enthusiastic in the world in their readiness to embrace the new opportunities that scientific advances had made available. Spokeswomen began to argue that females were also entitled to expect a 'fair go' in the workforce, and that there was nothing gender-specific in the concept.

The Liberal Party—leadership changes

Since its overwhelming success in the 1966 elections, the government's position had been slipping. It had lost several by-elections and a Senate position in the Senate elections of 1967. Holt himself was clearly having difficulties in matching Gough Whitlam in the cut and thrust of parliamentary debate, and the prime minister was a man with much on his mind on 17 December 1967 when he went swimming at Cheviot Beach, Portsea, near his home in Melbourne. He disappeared into the surf and was never seen again. Despite a two-day search, no trace could be found, although a helicopter crew reported sighting a huge shark in the area where the prime minister had been swimming. A memorial service was attended by President Johnson and the Prince of Wales, the current and former prime ministers of the United Kingdom, and heads of state from South Vietnam, the Philippines, South Korea, New Zealand, Singapore, Malaysia, and Thailand. The attendance attests to the popularity of Harold Holt and to the attempts he made to establish personal relationships with other world leaders. Never had so many Asian heads of state been in Australia at the same time. It was an obvious reflection of the changes in the country over which Holt had presided during his brief tenure in office.

The former Liberal Cabinet minister, Richard Casey, had been appointed governor-general before Menzies retired, and he faced a difficult situation. The deputy leader of the Liberal Party was the treasurer, William 'Billy' McMahon and, by rights, Casey should have sent for McMahon and asked him to form a government. Casey knew, however, that McMahon was unacceptable as prime minister to McEwen and the Country Party. The two men represented opposite sides in the debate over economic policy, and McMahon was opposed to Country Party pretensions of ensuring that the interests of primary producers always took precedence over those of secondary industry. McMahon had strongly supported Holt in his confrontation over devaluation with McEwen, and the Country Party would not serve in a McMahon administration. McMahon stood aside in deference to McEwen's threat and the Liberal Party cravenly permitted the Country Party to dictate to it over the matter of its own leadership. McEwen became temporary prime minister until the Liberals worked out the succession. In the event, four candidates stood for the position and the eventual winner of the balloting was the surprise candidate, Senator John Gorton, the minister for Education and Science.

John Gorton. (Australian History Museum, Macquarie University)

Gorton was the first prime minister to come from the Senate. He resigned his position in the upper house and won the by-election for Holt's seat in the House of Representatives. John Gorton marked a departure from the usual pattern of conservative political leaders in Australia. He was an unashamed Australian nationalist and possessed a streak of larrikinism that was to make him popular with the public, but also an electoral risk. As government leader in the Senate he had acquitted himself well, whereas

Holt had received a thorough mauling from Whitlam in the lower house. Gorton had supporters in the Liberal Party who believed that he was one of the few Liberal members of parliament who might be able to match the formidable Whitlam. Gorton was a returned fighter pilot from World War II, and Liberals hoped that his combative nature and aggression might curb the leader of the ALP who was establishing an ascendancy in the House of Representatives that bade ill for the government.

Prime Minister John Gorton

The new prime minister made few changes to Holt's Cabinet initially, but must have been relieved in February 1969 when Paul Hasluck—his main rival for the leadership—resigned to accept the position of governor-general to which Gorton had nominated him. The prime minister appeared intent on withdrawing Australia from the increasingly unpopular war in Vietnam but, after a few days in office, was making typically bellicose speeches like any other Liberal leader. The communal divisions caused by the war were beginning to tear the country apart. Thousands of young men refused outright to register for the conscription ballot and were sentenced to jail. Others claimed conscientious objection or medical incapacity. Of those who were called up, many refused to be inducted into the army and were sentenced to jail. Some fled the country or went into hiding. Public demonstrations against the war grew more violent as police and anti-war protesters confronted one another in the streets of Australia's capital cities.

Opposition to the war and to conscription flowed into other areas of life, and the universities became hotbeds of radicalism and anti-government activism. Much of this took the form of general anti-authoritarianism, and bewildered university administrators and some academics found their offices occupied by students who berated them for using examinations as grading devices, indulging in coercive essay marking, and imposing outmoded and authoritarian beliefs in things such as academic standards and basic literacy. The government was in danger of losing touch with the rising generation and the intelligentsia.

Gorton floundered in office. He visited the United States where he met the newly elected president, Richard Nixon. At a dinner for the president, Gorton concluded his speech with another of those obsequious statements that seemed the hallmark of Menzies' successors when he informed a somewhat bemused president that Australia 'will go a-waltzing Matilda with you'. Such reiterated statements of uncritical support did not receive an enthusiastic reception at home, where the war in Vietnam had become increasingly unpopular.

The mining boom

The Gorton years marked the beginning of a huge burst of speculation on Australian sharemarkets connected with the mining sector. Share prices soared for companies that had anything to do with mining and exploration. In a repeat of earlier patterns, entrepreneurs from overseas rushed to invest in a secure and stable environment such as Australia, which possessed apparently unlimited mineral resources. Huge contracts were signed with Japan for the provision of enormous volumes of coal and iron ore for Japanese industry. In 1967–68 the share-price index on the Sydney Stock Exchange jumped 66% while, in Brisbane, oil shares jumped by 189%. Private investors rushed the market, all anxious to make a killing without having to work for it, and people borrowed heavily against their assets to obtain money to speculate in shares. The Poseidon company illustrated the rapidity with which a struggling company could become an overnight success. In 1966 Poseidon shares could be purchased on the open market for four cents each. The company began drilling for nickel in September 1969 and made a good strike. By December 1969 the shares had reached $100 each on the Perth sharemarket. Similar stories could be told about many of the hundreds of tiny mining companies that mushroomed during these years, and many small investors were badly hurt financially when the correction came, the companies went under, and the bubble finally burst. The contracts with Japan were impressive, but too much of the boom was based on hope and a desire to make money easily, and many investors were sadder but wiser after the event.

The government falters

Opposition to Gorton from within the ranks of his own party was exacerbated by his boorish and unacceptable behaviour in private, and by his tendency to be autocratic and masterful in Cabinet. Holt's leadership had relied upon persuasion and teamwork, whereas Gorton expected that the views of the prime minister must always prevail in Cabinet discussions. This tendency ruffled the feathers of his ministers, as did his relationship with his private secretary, Ainslie Gotto. Some ministers felt that Gotto was far too protective of the prime minister, that she manipulated his timetable so that they could never get to see him, and that she reflected Gorton's dislike for some of them by insulting them with impunity. Ainslie Gotto's attractions as a woman became the main issue in the media's treatment of this, and the real question of whether a prime minister had an obligation to make himself available to his ministers—whatever his private feelings about them—disappeared from the discussion.

Gorton's reputation as a hard drinker also received attention, as did his alleged partiality for attractive women. Harold Holt had similar proclivities, but possessed a sense of decorum, whereas Gorton's appreciation of the charms of a visiting American singer, Lisa Minelli, and a local female journalist, Geraldine Willesee, achieved instant notoriety. In the latter case he was charged by a member of his own party, the backbench lawyer Edward St John, with behaviour that made him unfit to remain as prime minister.

St John was forced out of the Liberal Party, but some of the mud stuck.

The communist bogey

These were mere straws in the wind when, in 1969, a major storm broke following a suggestion by Gorton's minister for External Affairs, Gordon Freeth, that Australia and the Soviet Union might usefully cooperate within the region to the detriment of communist China. A desire to stop 'the downward thrust of China' had drawn Australia into the Vietnam War and, because China was the bogey most often called upon by Liberal politicians during elections, this suggestion had a superficial attraction. But Freeth ignored the more simple-minded of his fellow Liberals, and he antagonised most Roman Catholics who had been taught to see the Soviet Union as the main threat to their co-religionists throughout the world. Nevertheless, the government happily sold wool, wheat, and minerals to both Russia and China while, at the same time, proclaiming the communist monolith as the main threat to the country's continued survival. The DLP threatened Gorton with the loss of its preferences at the next election if he did not immediately disown his minister, and Gorton obliged with a statement that Freeth was expressing private views and not government policy, which remained one of rigorous anti-communism. But it was too late. Allen Fairhall, aggrieved by the fact that Gorton had allowed Freeth to make the speech in the first place without consulting Fairhall (who was defence minister), announced his intention to retire from politics at the forthcoming election.

When the embattled Gorton government went to the polls in October 1969, it faced a revitalised opposition led by Whitlam. Gorton, with a nod in the direction of the DLP, campaigned on defence with special stress being placed on the threat posed by the Soviet Union. Whitlam announced that an ALP government would withdraw all Australian soldiers from Vietnam by the following June. The extent to which public opinion had shifted on Vietnam can be gauged from the very strong swing to Labor, and Holt's record majority was reduced from thirty-eight to seven.

The recriminations fell thick and fast upon Gorton. One minister stated that he would refuse to serve in any government led by John Gorton, and Billy McMahon launched a challenge for the leadership. The party meeting re-elected Gorton by a narrow majority, and then elected McMahon as his deputy. Gorton was clearly on probation as far as his party was concerned. On the other hand, Gough Whitlam rode the crest of the wave in the ALP. He had brought them to within striking distance of government, and the party backed him when he launched a strike against the corrupt Victorian state branch of the party and reformed the power structures of the state branch. The contrast with the increasingly unconvincing performance of Gorton was obvious, and Whitlam looked very much like a prime minister in waiting.

Meanwhile, Australia's trade figures began to decline as Gorton finally had to pay the price for more than twenty years of unremitting coalition hostility towards China. Canada extended diplomatic recognition to China and was immediately rewarded with a large wheat purchase. Because China took approximately one-third of Australia's annual wheat crop, the loss of such a market weighed heavily on rural producers. The fruit of decades of coalition vilification and abuse was a Chinese preference for wheat from countries that had, at least, extended diplomatic recognition. The existing Australia–China wheat agreement expired in October 1970, and the Chinese did not renew it.

Events moved to their climax for John Gorton in 1971. John McEwen, the Country Party leader retired, and his successor did not feel so strongly antagonistic to the idea of a McMahon-led coalition. Then, the minister for Defence, Malcolm Fraser, resigned from Cabinet and launched a stinging attack on the prime minister for his autocratic management of Cabinet and his imperious manner in demanding his own way. By these characteristics, Fraser claimed in the House of Representatives, Gorton had seriously damaged the Liberal Party and shown himself unfit for office: 'I do not believe he is fit to hold the great office of Prime Minister, and I cannot serve in his government'.[6]

The opposition announced its intention of moving a no-confidence motion on the next day, and Gorton called a meeting of the Liberal Party before the House of Representatives sat. At that meeting a vote of confidence in Gorton's leadership was proposed, and the meeting split 33 for and 33 against. Gorton, as chairman, then declared that the vote of confidence had failed to pass. He immediately resigned as leader and, in the ensuing ballot, William McMahon became the prime minister of Australia. Gorton was elected as his deputy. Malcolm Fraser, who had precipitated these dramatic events, went to lurk on the backbench. John Gorton became the only Australian prime minister to, in effect, vote himself out of office, but he was not to be the only leader or prime minister to suffer from one of Malcolm Fraser's ambushes.

William McMahon—failing fortunes

The new prime minister seemed to be destined for disaster. He had finally fulfilled his political ambitions at a time when the electoral cycle appeared to be moving inexorably against the coalition. Moreover, McMahon was a cartoonist's dream. Small, balding, with a high-pitched voice and a slight speech impediment, he made an unfortunate contrast to the tall and prepossessing Whitlam. He proved quite unable to reverse the drift in coalition fortunes, and the two years of his prime ministership were a litany of mistakes and small disasters. The media soon christened him with nicknames such as 'Silly Billy', 'Wingnut Bill', and 'Billy Big Ears', and respect for the office disappeared with respect for the man. He proved to be no match for Whitlam and probably had been handed a poisoned chalice when he won the leadership. Perhaps no leader could ever have reunited so divided a party.

His task was made all the harder by the fact that he had come to office as the first effects of the world recession of the 1970s began to affect the Australian economy. Unemployment and inflation were steadily rising throughout the world and, after thirty years of prosperity, Australian electors showed little patience with a government manifestly unable to deal with the problems. For the rest of McMahon's term in office, inflation and unemployment proved to be intractable—although, later in the decade, 2% unemployment and 6% inflation would have brought joy to the heart of any Australian government!

The McMahon government also demonstrated weakness on racial issues. In 1971 a rugby team from South Africa toured the country and provoked an outbreak of public demonstrations, pitched battles between demonstrators and the police, and invasions of the playing pitch when matches were in progress. McMahon made the Royal Australian Air Force available to carry the team and break a boycott organised by the transport unions, but the prime minister could do nothing to halt the scale of demonstrations. The government's attitude towards Aboriginal Australians also caused concern. Aboriginal leaders set up an 'Aboriginal Embassy' on the lawn in front of federal parliament to protest against the government's failure to grant land rights or protect them from eviction from their traditional lands by pastoralists. Police were sent in to remove the 'embassy', but the demonstrators were soon back and proved to be a great domestic and international embarrassment to the McMahon government. Urban Liberals in the capital cities seemed quite happy to make concessions to Northern Territory Blacks, but the Country Party and rural Australia was not, and rather than threaten the stability of the coalition, the government did nothing.

Labor ends the barren years

By the time of the next federal election in December 1972, McMahon had become a figure of ridicule, and the 'Silly Billy' nickname was widely used in the media. A faction-ridden and dispirited government faced a buoyant and supremely confident ALP which ran a very professional campaign on the theme that it was time for a change. Where the government vacillated, the ALP offered firm policies and a well-constructed program that had been carefully put together by Gough Whitlam. On 2 December 1972, the first ALP government since 1949 was voted into office. The ALP secured a majority of seven in the House of Representatives but, with ominous overtones from 1931, the opposition retained control of the Senate. McMahon did not stand for the leadership of the Liberal Party, which replaced him with Billy Mackie Snedden, the treasurer in the former government. McMahon retired to the backbench where he remained until he resigned his seat in 1982.

The first Labor government for twenty-three years raised expectations throughout the community. But, although the electorate had voted for change, a majority of seven seats did not constitute an overwhelming mandate. Whitlam's failure to recognise the limited nature of his mandate certainly contributed to the tumult of the next three years. As leader of the opposition, Whitlam had presided over the formulation of a program for change, and he was impatient to begin its implementation. Rather than wait for a meeting of the ALP caucus to select the ministry, Whitlam and his deputy, Lance Barnard, had themselves sworn in as a two-man ministry, holding all the portfolios between them. This was unusual, although constitutional, and thus it was that for the first fortnight in office, the new ALP government consisted of two individuals who speedily set about inaugurating momentous change. Events were set in train for the diplomatic recognition of communist China and for the speedy withdrawal of all Australian servicemen from Vietnam. Neither decision caused any surprise,

Edward Gough Whitlam in messianic mode at the launch of the 'It's Time' campaign in 1972. (Taken from Ross McMullin, *The Light on the Hill: The Australian Labor Party 1891–1991*, Melbourne, 1991)

as they had long been elements of ALP policy.

Crash through or crash

The pace of change did not slacken appreciably after the election of the full ministry on 19 December, although the new ministers found some respite over the Christmas break and the public service had a breathing space to adjust to a new and impatient style of government. Only three of the ministers had been members of parliament when the Curtin and Chifley governments had been in office, and they had not been ministers then. The prime minister himself was without experience in government and had already displayed a temperamental impatience which Whitlam himself later described as a 'crash through or crash' approach. His earlier tendency, as leader of the opposition, to announce new developments or policy changes publicly and then to defy caucus to overturn them, was translated into a tendency to ride roughshod over opposition in Cabinet and to throw tantrums when unable to have his own way. This characteristic antagonised some of the strong personalities in Cabinet, and the prime minister's lack of manipulative skills and Cabinet diplomacy have been described as attesting to his managerial naivety.[7]

The inexperience and ineptitude of the new administration

was demonstrated by the attorney-general, Lionel Murphy, when, on the morning of 16 March 1973, he actually mounted a police raid on the headquarters of the Australian Security Intelligence Organisation (ASIO) and seized documents and files. Because ASIO was under Murphy's own control, the resultant publicity brought no credit to the new government. The image of the attorney-general raiding his own department and failing to produce any supporting evidence of a plot to withhold information from him, proved to be very damaging. Whitlam himself later admitted that this fiasco was probably his government's greatest mistake.[8]

Murphy's raid does highlight a major difficulty encountered by the new government. The public service had become used to, and comfortable with, conservative administrations after twenty-three years of coalition government, and sometimes proved obstructive or slow to implement the changes desired by the ALP government. Moreover, there is some evidence that public servants in some departments actively sabotaged and subverted the new administration. Charles Perkins, by now a senior member of the Department of Aboriginal Affairs, commented: 'If only the Labor Party knew how much the public service personnel in many areas deliberately undermine their programs they would not sleep at night'.[9]

Wages policy

One of the early actions of the two-man interlude was a request to the Arbitration Commission to reopen the recently concluded National Wage Case, in order that the submission made by the previous Liberal–Country Party government could be withdrawn and a new submission entered by the ALP government. The Arbitration Commission agreed and later handed down an historic wage decision making it mandatory that females in the workforce receive equal pay for work of equal value. More than 50 000 female public servants were awarded wage increases under this ruling, and it flowed through the whole economy during the next few years. The Whitlam government was using the civil service as pacesetters for improved wages and conditions, which then could not be withheld from workers in other sectors of the economy. This reversed the traditional ethos which had maintained that the public service traded high wages and improved conditions against the certainty of employment, and had resulted in the service following the lead of the private sector rather than providing the lead.

The structural effects of this new policy approach can be gauged by the rise in average weekly earnings. In 1973, average weekly earnings rose by 13.6% and this was accompanied by an inflation rate of 13.2%. In the following year, average weekly earnings jumped by 30.8% and an inflationary wage–price spiral became inevitable. An across-the-board tariff cut of 25% on all imported goods was made in July 1973, and this had a deleterious effect on protected Australian industries which began to shed labour. The combination of rising unemployment, rising inflation, and rising wages created a recipe for severe economic dislocation, and placed great strain on the entire edifice of ALP economic policy. The entire structure collapsed into chaos in October 1973 when the OPEC countries of the Middle East suddenly quadrupled oil prices, causing economic collapse and recession in all industrialised capitalist countries. Again the ALP found itself in office, without a majority in the Senate, at a time of massive economic dislocation.

Given the general international economic malaise, an inexperienced government with a determination to produce change as quickly as possible might have attempted to achieve too much too rapidly. When the pursuit of change endangered the economic security of the electorate, a more experienced administration might well have become more cautious. But the ALP was led by a man who believed in, and practised, a 'crash through or crash' philosophy of government, and caution did not come naturally to him. Besides, the Scullin government had opted for a policy of caution during the depression of the 1930s and had still been dumped unceremoniously from office.

Women under Labor

Of all the areas of change embarked upon by the new government in 1973, probably the most symbolic was in women's affairs. Feminists had become increasingly important in the late 1960s and the early 1970s as shapers and movers of established Australian attitudes towards women and their role in society. Behind the froth and ridicule meted out by a hostile media to female activists who demanded that the ethic of the 'fair go' be extended to include women, and who campaigned for changes in abortion law, for equal pay, and for a radical reappraisal of relationships between males and females within Australian society; there lay a slow shift in attitudes. Societal attitudes were altering and, in recognition of this, Whitlam appointed a special adviser to the prime minister on women's affairs. The new appointee, Elizabeth Reid, operated in an advisory capacity and her brief was to examine all Cabinet submissions and advise on their impact on women. The prime minister publicly endorsed this approach, but real progress did not keep pace with the symbolic. Elizabeth Reid originally had no staff—although assistants were provided later on—and ministers were not obliged to consult her unit or involve her in their formulation of policy and decision-making. The prime minister was far ahead of his party on the question of women's issues, and it could be said that he was out of step with majority opinion in the ALP and the trade union movement. After 1974, when it came to the question of providing resources for childcare for working mothers, which Whitlam had pledged specifically during the election of 1974, the government refused to fulfil the promise. Aside from supportive rhetorical flourishes, the government made women's affairs one of the first areas to experience the chill winds of economic cutbacks when the recession really began to bite.

Political rough seas

By April 1974, Whitlam had accumulated four pieces of legislation that had qualified for securing a double dissolution of parliament by being twice refused passage in the Senate. When Billy Snedden forced an election by having the Senate fail to pass the government's Appropriation Bills, Whitlam triggered the double dissolution. The coalition fought the campaign on the issue of inflation and the government's incompetent handling of the economy, whereas Whitlam went to the people requesting that the ALP government be given a 'fair go'. Despite a volatile electorate, the ALP was returned to office with the loss of a single seat in the House of Representatives—but the party failed again to gain a majority in the Senate.

The aftermath of the election blended farce and high interest. Billy Snedden provided the Gilbertian element by refusing to admit that he had lost the election. He maintained that to agree that the coalition had indeed lost would be to admit to failure, whereas he claimed not to have failed. The result had been very close, and therefore the opposition had not lost, it just had not been successful. With this bizarre behaviour Snedden set the scene for his own political downfall at the hands of Malcolm Fraser, who had accounted already for one Liberal leader, the former prime minister, John Gorton. Fraser's supporters watched and waited throughout the remainder of 1974 as the hapless Snedden was systematically destroyed in parliament by Prime Minister Whitlam. In March 1975, Snedden's position had been sufficiently eroded for Fraser to stand against him for the leadership, and Snedden was ignominiously disposed of. The new leader of the opposition proceeded to distance himself from Snedden by proclaiming his belief that a government that had been elected twice in less than two years was entitled to govern for its full term. Fraser promised that he would never force an election (as Snedden had done) by denying the government supply in the Senate—unless extraordinary and reprehensible circumstances should occur. The hollowness of this undertaking was soon to be demonstrated.

Two other aspects of the political situation also changed dramatically as a result of the 1974 election. First, the DLP had lost all its seats in the Senate, and was destined never again to gain parliamentary positions. Second, as provided for in the constitution, the first ever joint sitting of both houses of the federal parliament took place in August 1974, and the ALP's legislation that had triggered the double dissolution was passed triumphantly into law. Because all the participants recognised the historic significance of the event, the joint sitting was filmed for the national archives, and excerpts were transmitted for broadcast over the nation's television stations.

Cultural affairs

Australian cultural life had benefited enormously from the large infusion of migrants from Europe after 1947 and, by the 1970s, the narrow Anglo-Celtic ethnocentrism of pre-war society had undergone a sea-change. Wine and coffee consumption had soared, and eating habits had broadened into an acceptance of basic European and Mediterranean cuisine, in addition to the ubiquitous Chinese restaurants. The world of high culture, especially painting and literature, also reflected a lessening of the national sense of isolation. Whitlam was tremendously supportive of the creative arts and, in return, enjoyed a tidal wave of goodwill from this influential sector of the community. As prime minister he supported and appreciated the work of local landscape artists such as Arthur Boyd and Fred Williams. He approved of the work of novelists such as Morris West and Patrick White who extended the coverage of literature by dealing with universal themes and a broader psychological canvas, even if they were sometimes in non-Australian settings. He also took advantage of being in office when cultural events occurred in which he had played no direct part.

For example, he presided over the opening of the Sydney Opera House by Queen Elizabeth II in 1973, amid a surge of national and international publicity. Similarly, when author Patrick White received the Nobel Prize for Literature in 1973. Some of the gloss rubbed off on the prime minister who was effusive in his congratulations. His support for modern art was demonstrated by his purchase of Jackson Pollock's *Blue Poles* for the collection of the Australian National Art Gallery in Canberra, and the catholicity of his tastes emerged when he made a cameo appearance as himself in a raucous comedy film *Barry Mackenzie Holds His Own*, written by the comedian Barry Humphries. Whitlam undoubtedly had become a major patron of the nation's cultural life, but his identification with the Arts was to carry a high price as the economy slid into crisis.

The loans affair

The second Whitlam government became the first elected Labor government ever to be re-elected in the federal parliament, but the joint sitting marked the high point of its existence. The world economic climate continued to deteriorate, with the OPEC countries steadily increasing the price of crude oil to keep place with inflation and thereby raising inflation levels rapidly in all industrialised countries. Domestically, unemployment and inflation continued to pose serious problems, and the government lurched from crisis to crisis, while Malcolm Fraser continued to circle like a vulture, in a desperate search for the necessary extraordinary and reprehensible circumstances that would allow him to deny supply in the Senate and force an election. Eventually, the government gave him the issue in the so-called 'loans affair'.

The loans affair stemmed from the anxiety of Rex Connor, the minister for Minerals and Energy, that Australia should regain control over the nation's oil and mineral deposits, the rights to which had been cheaply passed over to foreign companies in the years of coalition rule. To 'buy back the farm' would cost millions of dollars and, in the current economic climate, the only real source of such funds was the oil-rich countries of the Middle East. Labor's policies of re-establishing Australian ownership of resources provoked a response from foreign corporations that has been described as an 'investment strike'—although this probably owed just as much to the international emergence of recession and high inflation.[10] The withholding of investment gave an added fillip to the search for a Middle East loan, and the government intended to use the loan monies to finance new government-owned energy projects that would provide jobs for the rising numbers of unemployed and help to make Australia less dependent on unstable sources of supply in the Middle East.

There was nothing inherently wrong in this policy, but the non-traditional source of the sought-for loan caused concern. The traditional avenues through which international borrowing had normally been conducted were thought to be inadequate and, in December 1974, Connor secured Cabinet and Executive Council approval to attempt to raise a loan of US$4000 million. In fact, no loans were ever raised and no money ever expended in this search, but certain businessmen of dubious reputation, attracted by the possibility of large commissions, became involved as go-betweens, and therein lay the seeds of electoral disaster. The government policy of bypassing the formal apparatus for raising money overseas was leaked to the opposition and to an increasingly hostile media, and allegations of 'funny money' began to be made. Despite the best efforts of the opposition, however, no evidence of substantial wrongdoing or criminality was uncovered, and the affair looked likely to peter out when one of the dubious financiers, Tirath Khemlani, was found to be still attempting to raise money on behalf of the government. Because, by this time, both Prime Minister Whitlam and his minister Rex Connor had assured the House of Representatives that all authority to raise loans had been withdrawn, this amounted to a very serious charge of a deliberate deception of parliament. Connor was forced to resign in disgrace, and Fraser had at last obtained the required circumstances in which the opposition could deny supply in the Senate. An election had become inevitable.

Additional complications

That the Senate would obey the behest of the leader of the opposition had been placed beyond doubt by the extraordinary behaviour of the anti-Labor premiers of New South Wales and Queensland. ALP senator Lionel Murphy resigned from parliament to take up an appointment to the High Court, and Tom Lewis, the Liberal premier of New South Wales, refused to follow the established convention and replace Murphy with a nominee proposed by the ALP. Instead, he appointed a nominee of his own, thus shattering the convention that the democratically expressed wishes of the electorate should be respected by replacing a departing senator with a person from the same party. When the Queensland ALP senator Bert Millner died, that state's premier, Joh Bjelke-Petersen, the leader of the Country Party, emulated Lewis' breach of democratic convention by appointing a non-Labor replacement named Pat Field. The ALP was thus denied two Senate seats to which it was entitled and, although Bunton and Field (for different reasons) did not vote against the government's budget, the crucial distortion of votes in the Senate was to prove fatal to the government in the constitutional crisis that was soon to come. Strictly speaking, both premiers were within their constitutional rights to make such appointments, but the days when the Senate had truly been a states' house had long passed, and up to this time all political parties had observed the convention of allowing the party concerned to nominate a replacement when a casual vacancy occurred in the Senate. Clearly, the deck was being stacked against Labor.

The Whitlam government also suffered from a series of smaller disasters. Frank Crean, the first treasurer, was forced by Whitlam to resign because of his inability to manage the economy. Crean was replaced by Dr Jim Cairns, but his complicated personal relationship with his female private secretary, Junie Morosi, attracted much lubricious publicity, and Cairns also resigned after misleading parliament. The policy of using the public service as a pacemaker for improvements in the workplace—such as shorter hours, flexi-time, higher pay, maternity leave, and so on—became increasingly unpopular as the declining economy put people out of work. But the final nail in the coffin was provided by the resignation of the deputy leader, Lance Barnard, to take up the position of ambassador to Sweden. Barnard's safe Labor seat of Bass in Tasmania was lost by the ALP in a massive swing against the government which had lost its way and was drifting without purpose or direction from one disaster to another.

Nor was the Bass by-election the only electoral straw in the wind. In December 1974, Queensland had held a state election and the ALP received a heavy setback with a strong swing in favour of the Bjelke-Petersen government. In the following year, the popular ALP premier of South Australia, Don Dunstan, only just managed to hang onto office, and did so by pointedly disassociating himself and his government from the federal Labor government. The tide was running strongly against Labor and gathering momentum as 1975 progressed, and it was clear that the Whitlam government's days in office were numbered. It was no longer a matter of whether the opposition would win the next election, but only of when it would be held.

Crisis

In this climate of opinion, Malcolm Fraser decided to use the loans affair as the justification he needed to deny supply in the Senate and thereby force another election. The ALP was in desperate trouble and appeared to have isolated itself from the world of everyday Australians. Millions of dollars expended on subsidising the arts and so-called élite culture—epitomised by the opening of the Sydney Opera House in 1973 and the purchase of Jackson Pollock's 'Blue Poles' for the National Gallery in Canberra in 1975—did not sit well with people struggling to get by on the dole while inflation steadily eroded the value of their incomes. Any opposition worth its salt would have forced an election if it were able.

The Senate denied supply in October and precipitated a major constitutional crisis. Fraser and his followers possessed a majority in the Senate sufficient to refuse assent to the government's money Bills. The prime minister resolved to stand firm and not give in to the blackmail offered by Fraser—to pass supply in return for a general election. Fraser was asking the government to cut its own throat, and Whitlam declined. The prospect was that the government would run out of money late in November and would then be unable to pay its bills or public service salaries. Whitlam offered an election for half the Senate in the hope that the result would favour Labor and give him a majority in the Senate. Given the climate of the times, such hopes were pipedreams and Fraser demanded a full general election to resolve the issue. At this stage the governor-general, John Kerr, intervened.

The governor-general's role

Kerr had been appointed by Whitlam to replace Paul Hasluck in 1973, and was well regarded by most people on both sides of politics. He had risen to the post of chief justice of New South Wales and was considered to be a sound constitutional lawyer. That he had once, briefly, been a member of the Labor Party, and had more recently considered accepting preselection as a Liberal Party candidate for federal parliament, made him generally acceptable, although his support for the ALP industrial groups in the 1950s caused many left-wing Labor politicians to regard him with suspicion.[11]

These suspicions proved to be well founded, when Kerr secretly consulted the former Liberal Party minister, Garfield Barwick, by then chief justice of Australia, regarding Kerr's proposed course of action to resolve the deadlock. Another convention thus breached was the convention that the chief justice of the High Court should be above the political fray. It is at the heart of Australia's system of government that the judiciary and politics are separate from one another, but the former chief justice of New South Wales and the current chief justice of Australia ignored the doctrine of the separation of powers, and Barwick approved the plan. Kerr arranged for both Whitlam and Kerr to be present at the residence of the governor-general on the afternoon of 11 November 1975. Fraser arrived first. His car was hidden from view and he was taken to an ante-room where he waited while Kerr delivered the coup-de-   grâce to the prime minister. When Whitlam arrived he was shown into the governor-general's presence and was handed a letter removing him from office. Once the former prime minister had departed, Fraser was marched in and given a commission as caretaker prime minister—provisional upon his agreement to recommend a dissolution of both houses and a general election. The Senate immediately voted supply for the caretaker government and the country embarked upon one of the most divisive political campaigns of the twentieth century.

Labor supporters were furious that unilateral action by an unelected official such as the governor-general could ensure the demise of a properly elected government which had two years of its term still to run and a comfortable working majority in the House of Representatives. It made a mockery of the 1974 double dissolution election. Whitlam was further enraged by the alleged duplicity of the governor-general in dismissing him from office without giving any warning that such drastic action was contemplated. Kerr argued that he had to ambush the prime minister to avoid Whitlam's replacing him by a more pliant personality before the governor-general could carry out the threatened dismissal.

The governor-general's action was unprecedented and extreme, and it provoked extraordinary reactions. The former prime minister urged his supporters to maintain their rage and throw out the caretaker government, thereby repudiating Kerr's actions and Fraser's policy of forcing an election via a fabricated constitutional crisis.

On the other hand, Fraser and his supporters argued that the governor-general had acted with complete propriety and legality. All they were doing was forcing an election at which the Australian people could express their opinion on the Whitlam government's performance. How could this be undemocratic? Fraser's stony-faced strength, and his stubborn refusal to admit that he had been responsible for unleashing a highly damaging crisis by his refusal to observe accepted political conventions, contrasted with the frantic excitement of Labor supporters who made the slogan 'Shame Fraser Shame' their theme for the election campaign.

Fighting for government

Whitlam seemed transfixed by the events of 11 November and was unable or unwilling to move the election campaign onto other issues. Fraser, in contrast, refused to concentrate on the constitutional issue and stubbornly fought to switch the emphasis onto the Whitlam government's inept performance in office and its fiscal irresponsibility. The wages explosion and high inflation and interest rates were sheeted home to the Whitlam government, and the former prime minister's delight in overseas travel was pilloried by Malcolm Fraser's statements that Australians did not want a tourist as prime minister. The stress on economic performance and the opportunity to express a judgment on the Whitlam government's management of Australia proved to be extremely popular with the electorate. Public opinion polls showed that the considerable levels of sympathy for the dismissed prime minister had quickly dissipated, and the narrow focus of the ALP

J. Malcolm Fraser. (Australian History Museum, Macquarie University)

on the issue of the dismissal permitted Malcolm Fraser and his followers to set the real agenda for the election and to retain the initiative throughout. The result was a landslide win for Fraser of such proportions as to put the rejection of the ALP beyond doubt. The Liberal–Country party coalition won the biggest majority ever received since federation, picking up 91 seats in the House of Representatives to the ALP's 36, and gaining an absolute majority in the Senate. Malcolm Fraser became prime minister and Gough Whitlam was re-elected by the ALP as federal leader and leader of the opposition.

The bitter lees

The electoral arithmetic appeared to be overwhelmingly in Fraser's favour, but the result should not overshadow the exceptional bitterness injected into Australian political affairs by the events of 11 November 1975. When the new Fraser government voted Kerr a salary increase of 71% in its first budget of 1976, ALP suspicions regarding the governor-general seemed to be amply justified. Kerr's continuation in office constituted a persistent affront to the ALP and to many Australians who regarded his actions as quite improper. It also helped to stimulate the growth of republican sentiment which had received a major stimulus from the dismissal. Moreover, Kerr's public behaviour on occasions, when he seemed to be the worse for liquor, embarrassed the Fraser government, and his departure in 1977 was mourned by no one as he slipped out of the country and effectively into exile in Europe.

Malcolm Fraser, the new prime minister, must also accept a measure of responsibility for the acrimony he had helped to unleash. All the portents were for the Whitlam government to suffer a disastrous defeat when the next federal elections were held in 1976 or 1977. All Fraser had to do was to curb his ambition for the prime ministership and wait for the office to drop into his lap like a piece of ripe fruit. Accession to power would then have been legitimate and unarguable. As it was, Fraser tainted himself and his government in the minds of many Australians by the indecent haste and overwhelming ambition demonstrated by the events of October and November 1975. For the next decade, Australian politics revolved around the personalities of the protagonists in this great drama. Only after they had all departed the political scene did Australian federal politics shed some of the bitterness and personal animosity which characterised the Liberal government. But permanent damage undoubtedly had been done to any sense of trust between both sides of the political divide, and for the rest of the century mistrust and personal vilification became the norm—constituting Fraser's lasting legacy to Australian politics.

That the rejection of the Whitlam government amounted to an electoral judgment on the performance of Whitlam himself was demonstrated by Fraser in 1977 when he called an early election and focused the entire campaign on Whitlam's personal failings and performance as prime minister, and on the spendthrift policies of his government. Fraser won a second landslide victory. Whitlam accepted the inevitable and resigned from the leadership and the parliament. He was succeeded by his deputy, the former Queensland policeman, Bill Hayden.

The Fraser years

The focus of Malcolm Fraser's time as prime minister of Australia owed much to his distaste for anything that carried reminders of the previous government. A great deal of effort was put into dismantling the elaborate apparatus of commissions and 'quangos' through which Labor had sought to spread the message of centralism and increased Commonwealth involvement in many aspects of life. Severe cutbacks in expenditure in the fields of Aboriginal affairs, women's affairs, education, the arts, and social welfare were quickly put in place by a government intent on retrenchment in spending. This was accompanied by selective financial incentives to the government's rural supporters and to businesses to increase production and assist the country to trade its way out of the economic quagmire into which it had strayed.

The previous Labor administration had antagonised many state governments by its increasing use of tied grants to control developments in particular areas. The Fraser government relied much less on tied grants and, under the label of 'New Federalism', attempted to pass some income-taxing powers back to the states. The revenue-sharing system envisaged under the new federalism involved a two-tiered income tax regime that permitted states to add a surcharge on personal income tax rates for the residents of that particular state. The Commonwealth would assess and collect this additional revenue as part of the normal collection of income taxes, and return it to the state together with the annual grant made from federal funds. The system never actually came into operation because the state premiers followed the lead of the New South Wales Labor premier, Neville Wran, who adamantly refused to implement the scheme on the grounds that any state government which introduced an additional income tax would be swept out of office by infuriated voters at the next election.

Malcolm Fraser also reversed the practice of using the federal public service as pacemaker for wages and conditions throughout the workforce. The new government quickly imposed staff ceilings on all federal departments and effectively limited the growth in the numbers of civil servants. In December 1976, the government introduced legislation allowing it to force redundancy on public servants on the grounds of excess numbers, and to redeploy other staff to areas of greatest need. The following year further legislation permitted the government to stand down without pay public servants who were unable to work due to trade union activity taken by fellow workers, whether in government or in private employ.

Rising unemployment

The inevitable consequence of fighting inflation by rigorously pruning expenditure was an increasing unemployment rate. Government policy embraced the belief that a high level of unemployment was necessary in the short term to reduce inflationary wage expectations in the workforce and, ultimately, to curb inflation itself. The prime social effect was an increasingly demoralised and steadily growing pool of unemployed workers and, eventually, an assumption that the chronically unemployed really did not want to work. The term 'dole-bludger' entered the language at this time to describe someone who allegedly preferred to live in poverty rather than work for a living—an injustice given the state of the economy that the government nevertheless perpetuated with avidity. The establishment of such a mentality meant an acceptance of a higher level of unemployment than had ever been experienced, apart from the depressions of the 1890s and the 1930s. The Fraser government could effectively reduce living standards without incurring the obloquy that such a policy would hitherto have earned. In 1961 an unemployment rate approaching 2% had almost caused the defeat of the Menzies government. From the late 1970s onwards, Australian governments survived electorally with overall unemployment rates hovering around 10%, and with youth unemployment well above 20%. The measure of the Fraser government's negative achievement in this area is demonstrated by the increase in unemployment from 275 400 in December 1975, to 439 200 in January 1980, and to 674 000 by the end of 1982.

Multiculturalism

With unemployment running so high, immigration policies that added to the number of unemployed persons on social services came in for scrutiny, and care had to be taken to ensure that communal tensions were not aroused. It must be said, however, that Malcolm Fraser was an enthusiastic supporter of multiculturalism. Between 1950 and 1971, Australia's population had risen from 8 million to 12.7 million, and immigrants and their Australian-born children accounted for 53% of the increase. Migration patterns had also begun to produce ineradicable changes in the Australian way of life. European and Middle Eastern migrants brought with them their national customs and found that, for the most part, these transplanted readily to their new country. Many of these exotic influences percolated through to the mass of the Anglo-Australian population. Foods became increasingly varied and imaginative, wine consumption grew, and footpath cafés, coffee bars, and continental delicatessens added to the quality of Australian life, especially in the large urban centres.

In the capital cities themselves, entire suburbs slowly developed into ethnic neighbourhoods in which English was a second language, and migrant-language presses maintained a steady output of newspapers and magazines. Cultural and sporting clubs grew up which reflected the ethnic divisions within the different cities and locales, while suburban shopping centres demonstrated the changes in ethnicity by a plethora of multilanguage signs in shop windows. By the end of the 1970s government financed immigration was abolished, but a rising tide of refugee 'boat people' fleeing from communist-controlled Vietnam and Cambodia were welcomed in Australia and added a further cultural complexity to an already diverse Australian society.

Although some verbal opposition was expressed by small extremist groups to these changes, the anti-discrimination legislation put in place by the Whitlam government in 1975 ensured that a resigned and occasionally sullen acquiescence seemed to be the usual reaction of most Australians to the influx of non-European peoples. The country could no longer isolate itself from international events and the world community, but it took a lost war in Vietnam and a severe worldwide economic recession before this became apparent.

Fraser's political demise

In October 1980 the Fraser government again stood for election against the ALP now led by Bill Hayden. Again the coalition played the personal-attack card, and attempted to campaign on the premise that Hayden was merely Whitlam recycled. The electorate did not buy this argument and, although the government was returned, the ALP picked up thirteen seats from the coalition and was now within striking distance of victory. The government had also lost seats in the Senate to a new party, the Australian Democrats, led by a former Liberal Cabinet minister, Don Chipp, who had been driven from the party by Fraser's arrogance and conservatism. The Democrats now held the balance of power in the Senate, and Chipp and the new party had hit a nerve with the electorate when the party campaigned on a policy of 'keeping the bastards honest'. The decline in public respect for politicians of all parties can be seen in the extent to which the new party's policy resonated across the electorate. Nobody was in any doubt that the 'bastards' included the members of all three major political parties. From then on, the Australian Democrats received consistent support from a section of the voting public that voted for one of the major parties for the lower house, and then cast a vote for the Democrats in the Senate—a voting pattern which demonstrated that sophisticated disenchantment and cynicism was another permanent outcome of Malcolm Fraser's period in politics.

Meanwhile, all was not well in the ALP where the leader, Bill Hayden, had come under sustained pressure from the followers of an impatient rising star, the former president of the Australian Council of Trade Unions, Robert James Lee Hawke. Bob Hawke had only been in parliament since 1980, but his supporters felt that they had to force Hayden out before the next election because he might actually win it and be impossible to remove as prime minister. Hawke's people argued that, whereas Hayden *might* win, only Hawke could *guarantee* a win—because of his extraordinary public profile. Hawke was widely known throughout Australia for his abilities as a mediator between employers and employees during intractable industrial disputes. His conciliatory abilities stood in marked contrast to Malcolm Fraser's confrontational approach, and it was generally accepted—not least by Hawke himself—that he was Australia's most charismatic politician.

Malcolm Fraser sensed the danger posed by Hawke, and determined on a snap election before Hawke's supporters could marshal the numbers to overthrow Hayden as ALP leader. On 3 February 1983, Fraser stole a march on the ALP and secured a double dissolution of parliament on the grounds that the Senate had become so obstructive as to make government impossible. Fraser had anticipated pre-empting the move against Hayden and propping him up as leader of the ALP to ensure another three years in office. Hayden, however, seeing the writing on the wall, voluntarily withdrew as leader of the ALP in favour of Hawke, and where the government had hoped for savage internecine wrangling in the opposition, it found instead that it was confronted by a united party led by its nemesis Bob Hawke. Fraser had expected that he would catch Bill Hayden with his pants down (a jibe that

Fraser had previously used against Whitlam), only to find himself publicly exposed in the same predicament. The government never recovered from this and, on 5 March 1983, the ALP won a resounding victory with a majority of twenty-five seats in the House of Representatives. Labor had campaigned on a policy of reconciliation and reconstruction after eight years of what was described as the most divisive government Australia had ever experienced.

When the result was announced, television cameras focused on a modest and magnanimous victor, and then on a bitterly disappointed and weeping Malcolm Fraser. It was impossible not to feel some sympathy for the normally granite-faced Fraser, even though he had come to power via a Faustian route over the ruins of constitutional convention and remained one of the most disliked leaders the country had ever produced. Others looked at the new prime minister and detected in him the seeds of arrogance and an impatience to have his own way that would prove to be the equal of anything Australia had yet experienced. Would conciliation and consensus bring the country together and bind up the deep wounds after the communal strife of 1975 and its aftermath? Would the departure of Malcolm Fraser finally allow the wounds to heal and a new start to be made? Kerr, Whitlam, and Fraser had all left the stage; now there were new protagonists and different problems to be encountered. By rejecting Malcolm Fraser the electorate had also voted to put the events of 1975 behind it and to get on with the business of bringing Australia into the period of its bicentenary and, thereafter, into the twenty-first century.

Hawke had looked constructively to the future and had talked about his hopes of making Australia a better country to live in. He had come to personify the 'fair go' and the electorate perceived him that way and swept him into office on a wave of goodwill and national sentimentality. Whether any political leader could live up to those expectations, and to what extent the substitution of consensus for traditional ALP policies would be acceptable to party and people in the long run, provided the subtext for the next decade.

10

Economic Rationalism and Ideological Deconstruction

If ever a government in Australia came to power on a tide of optimism and goodwill, it was the first Hawke government. The parallels with the early Whitlam period are inescapable, but Hawke's arrival in the promised land had not been preceded by such a long time in the wilderness and he resisted the helter-skelter pace of reform that had been so exhilarating and so characteristic of the previous ALP administration. According to the Hawke agenda, consensus was to replace confrontation, and delay was inherent in the very nature of that process; consensus requires time to emerge. Any government that embraced consensus could not be other than a slow-paced and reformist administration, cautious in outlook and non-radical by temperament. The prime minister's background in the ACTU and his factional base within the right wing of the ALP was evidence of this innate conservatism. This was no wild-eyed bunch of revolutionaries intent on overturning Australian society and abolishing capitalism, but a sober and besuited group of politicians who prided themselves on their professionalism and managerial competence. There was no 'crash through or crash' philosophy espoused by this team. For his disinterested magnanimity, Bill Hayden received his reward in the Foreign Affairs portfolio—despite his comment at the beginning of the election campaign that even 'a drover's dog could lead the Labor Party to victory' against Malcolm Fraser.[1] And a brash Paul Keating went to the Treasury.

The Hawke ascendancy

From the earliest days of the Hawke period, unmistakable links between the state of the economy and the performance of the

Bob Hawke and his lieutenant Paul Keating made a dynamic duo for most of the 1980s. (Taken from Ross McMullin, *The Light on the Hill: The Australian Labor Party 1891–1991*, Melbourne, 1991)

government emerged. The new treasurer devalued the Australian dollar by 10%, deregulated the currency by floating the dollar, and announced with the prime minister their discovery that the country's finances were in a parlous state. As justification for failing to honour their election promises they used the allegation that the outgoing Fraser administration had deliberately hidden the precarious state of the economy and the level of Australia's international debt. This admission that the country could not afford the policies that the government had been elected to implement brought Hawke great kudos among the business sector and from Labor's traditional enemies. They saw it as evidence of firm and decisive leadership whereas, for many ALP supporters, it merely demonstrated the new government's appalling readiness to jettison inconvenient promises once it had attained office. It certainly did little to improve the credibility or reputation of politicians. Fortunately, economic indicators soon brightened when, within a few days of the election, a prolonged El Niño drought cycle ended, and the rains brought renewed optimism to Australia's primary producers whose exports during the oncoming wet cycle were expected to reduce the high level of the deficit quickly.

In search of consensus

The prime minister did move promptly to call together the economic summit meeting between employers and union organisations that had been a major component of his plan to heal the deep wounds caused by the years of confrontation under Malcolm Fraser. The former Liberal leader facilitated consensus by quietly resigning as leader and retiring from parliament to his farm 'Nareen'. From there he watched as Andrew Peacock, his successor as leader, and John Howard, the deputy leader, spent more time and energy fighting one another than in attacking the new ALP government.

The economic summit meeting between the representatives of capital and organised labour might have demonstrated the bona fides of the new prime minister's search for a lasting accommodation between capital and labour, but it also highlighted the entrenched prejudices and difficulties that such a process could encounter. The summit produced a plethora of patriotic and high-sounding generalisations about the partnership between capital and labour, and the necessity for cooperation and better communication between management and workforce. However, once the conference moved beyond such vague well-intentioned themes, old responses reappeared. The two major construction unions, the Building Workers Industrial Union (BWIU) and the Builders Labourers Federation (BLF), both announced that they had no intention of exercising wage restraint in the interests of the economy and the wider workforce. The leaders of both unions determined to pursue the best deal they could extract from employers for their members. This attitude was perfectly understandable; it was what trade unions were supposed to do, but it put the more militant unions out of step with the new industrial climate of consensus, and more especially with the Prices and Incomes Accord negotiated between the ALP and the ACTU before the 1983 federal election.

The Accords

The Prices and Incomes Accord, usually referred to simply as 'the Accord', dominated the whole period of the Hawke and Keating governments. In Hawke's time alone, it went through six versions that were ratified by either the Arbitration Commission or its successor the Industrial Relations Commission (IRC), and each of these agreements became the centrepiece of the government's wages and incomes policy of the time. The Accords were designed to bring a measure of control over the economy and to ensure that economic recovery was not jeopardised by wages breakouts, with militant unions driving up inflation by winning large salary increases that flow through to the rest of the workforce, irrespective of the economy's ability to absorb them. The Accords gave employers the advantage of being able to plan more efficiently, because they knew the policy framework and economic settings within which the government operated. They could not be taken by surprise by union ambit claims because such claims would be outside the Accord and therefore unacceptable to the government and unratified by the IRC. Wage restraint was accepted by the ACTU throughout these years as the price to be paid for rising levels of employment. Improvements in workers' standards of living were pursued through alternative means such as taxation reform, improved social welfare, and superannuation. The Accords not only secured a broad consensus over wages policy but also made the ACTU a virtual partner with the government in establishing the structure of general economic policy. The industrial labour movement enjoyed unparalleled access to government circles, and observers recognised the disciplined way in which organised labour cooperated in the process of economic management. This was one area in which consensus appeared to enjoy a signal success, yet the question of how the new system fitted into Australia's version of the Westminster system of government remained unclear. After all, parliamentarians could be called to account at elections, but what redress did those disadvantaged by the new system have against the ACTU?

Deconstructing party financial orthodoxy

The innate financial conservatism of the Hawke–Keating government (as it became known due to Keating's dominant role as treasurer and powerbroker within the government) manifested itself again in July 1984 at the ALP's national conference, where the treasurer sought and won approval to reverse years of ALP economic orthodoxy, thus allowing the government to deregulate the banking system and allow foreign banks to operate in Australia. Since the 1890s, Labor had been suspicious of the banks and had come to regard them as parasitical barnacles on the country's economy. The private banks had reciprocated with distrust of the ALP and financial support of the party's opponents. The Chifley government had fallen from office in 1949 partly as a result of the sustained campaign waged against it by the banks. The necessity for a measure of central control over the banking system had received bipartisan endorsement from all Australian governments since the 1940s. The deregulatory steps undertaken in 1984 were therefore apparently radical in contemporary terms, but they actually demonstrated how much the 'party of controls' had been taken captive by an even older ideology—that of free trade and economic deregulation. The reliance on market forces sat uneasily within the ALP, given the party's historic interests in regulation and industrial protection. However, despite misgivings from the left wing, the conference endorsed the proposal to renounce its traditional views and free up the Australian economy. This began a process that resulted, during the following decade, in the sale of all the government-run state banks, and the full privatisation of the Commonwealth Bank shortly thereafter. Government banks had given the authorities the competitive ability to control banking charges and fees, because the private banks could not afford to charge in excess of their government competitors. In relinquishing any role in banking, governments effectively made the community hostage to the greed of the private banking sector, and the decision taken by the ALP in 1984 thus marked a real watershed. The policy change also amounted to a demonstration of the extent to which the Hawke–Keating government had occupied the middle ground in Australian politics that had previously been the exclusive province of the Liberal Party. The transition of the ALP from a party of workers dominated by outmoded ideological constraints to a party formulating a conservative policy more acceptable to the upwardly mobile denizens of the business world was well under way.

The economy declines

In December 1984 Hawke seized the opportunity to go to an early election. As part of the election campaign, the prime minister promised to call another summit—this time a 'taxation summit'—to consider the modernisation and rationalisation of a cumbersome and old-fashioned system. By this time, economic indicators had begun to show that Australians were entering troubled times. Despite the Accords, a serious downturn in the level of real wages paid to Australian workers began in 1984, and this ran consistently through to 1989. There was a clear and sustained decline in domestic household savings during these years, as the falling real wage level forced Australian families to use up more of their disposable income for living expenses.[2] Yet the Hawke government managed to remain in office despite producing a state of affairs that, in normal circumstances, would have ensured defeat at the hands of an incensed and irritated electorate. In part, this was due to the disarray and internal divisions within the Liberal Party, as Peacock and Howard jostled for supremacy, but it was also due to the fact that the Accords trapped the ACTU into supporting a government that directly damaged the welfare and living standards of its members. It was no coincidence that this period of ALP government, from 1983 to 1996, witnessed a continuing decline in the membership of both the ALP and the trade union movement as disillusioned members withdrew from both organisations.

Taxation summit

The search for consensus via a taxation summit of 1985 proved to be a humiliation for the re-elected government. The treasurer, Paul Keating, planned to reduce income tax levels for individuals and for corporations. Revenue thus forgone would be made up by a new consumption tax to be levied on all goods and services. The prime minister committed himself to the new tax and, in partnership with the treasurer, attempted to sell the scheme to the representatives of workers and business assembled at the summit. The plan aroused a storm of opposition. It was regressive and would hurt those least able to protect themselves; it would make life bleak indeed for welfare recipients; and it would increase inflation as the new tax raised prices across the board. Keating and Hawke argued that it would be fairer because the new tax could not be avoided: the more a person consumed, the more tax would be paid, so the rich who consumed more would pay more whereas those who lived modestly would pay less. Besides, the scheme contained an inbuilt compensation mechanism in lower income tax levels. The summit resisted, and ultimately refused to be persuaded by these arguments. Hawke then struck his colours and informed his treasurer that he had withdrawn his support for a consumption tax. Paul Keating, bitter and betrayed, realised that because Hawke lacked the courage to take the hard decisions necessary to overhaul and modernise the Australian economy, he would have to take the leadership himself if his plans were ever to come to fruition. Consensus had been shown to produce compromise, and the treasurer believed that only root-and-branch restructuring would suffice. In the meantime, economic indicators showed a country slipping deeper and deeper into trouble.

Deregulation and overseas debt

The economic malaise eventually caused repercussions on overseas financial markets. Australia's increasing indebtedness indicated that the country was living beyond its means. The national government's failure to rein in this rising level of debt largely stemmed from its inability to control the activities of a few large corporate buccaneers who took advantage of deregulation to borrow billions of dollars. In most cases these borrowings were not used to increase productivity. Rather, they were used for unproductive corporate takeovers and mergers. Early in 1986 the value of the Australian dollar suddenly collapsed by about 20%, which effectively raised the level of foreign debt by a comparable amount. The extreme seriousness of the situation dawned on most Australians when the treasurer declared on radio that Australia was in danger of becoming a 'Banana Republic'.

'Deregulation' and 'economic rationalism' became the watchwords of an essentially bipartisan policy framework at the national level, and the consequences were a shared responsibility. The reduction of financial regulation and the reluctance of the Reserve Bank to oversee foreign borrowings (let alone adequately supervise the lending policies of the local banks and the new overseas entrants as they fought for market share) meant that extensive credit was readily available. The so-called corporate excesses of the 1980s were directly attributable to this easy access to credit in a deregulated financial market. The Reserve Bank restricted itself to the use of high interest rates as its only response, but high interest rates damaged productive enterprises which could not afford to expand in such an environment. Nonetheless, the corporate predators remained unperturbed and continued borrowing. Again, large quantities of overseas capital flowed into Australia attracted by the high interest rates, and the old familiar pattern of speculative boom followed by recession seemed all too likely to reappear. Clearly, the Reserve Bank could and should have done more than fiddle with interest rates. But, with the opposition parties supporting the basic thrust of government policy, it would have taken a brave governor of the Reserve Bank to fly in the face of such consensus. Both sides of federal politics therefore must share responsibility for the massive growth of Australian debt, both internally and internationally, and for abdicating responsibility for the national interest, even if this had have been at the cost of unpopularity with the banks and the financial freebooters. By abandoning the economy and the general population to the mercy of market forces, both the ALP and the opposition parties betrayed the country. As unemployment grew, and recession deepened, the prime minister and the treasurer kept reassuring Australians that they were really better off than they had been before deregulation, but ordinary Australians had their doubts. The 'Banana Republic' comment by Paul Keating tapped into, and articulated, an inchoate but deeply felt uneasiness concerning the direction in which the country was headed, but the bipartisan acceptance of the new direction meant that there was little political choice between the economic policies of either side. That the ACTU had become an accessory to government economic policy removed even that traditional avenue of bringing limited pressure to bear on a government causing pain to an increasing proportion of the Australian people.

In the federal elections of July 1987, the ALP sneaked back into office for an historic third term. No previous federal Labor administration had ever been returned for a third time, and one of the reasons for this success lay in the bipartisan approach to the economy. The ALP under Hawke had pirated the traditional Liberal ideology on free trade and economic deregulation and, with the electorate increasingly unwilling to swallow the old anti-communist fear campaigns, the opposition experienced considerable difficulty in establishing a distinct and separate identity for itself in a post-Cold War environment. The erosion of support for the opposition had become so alarming that, during early 1987, the Queensland branch of the National Party—the successor to the Country Party—had attempted to stake out its own subdivision of Australian conservatism by presenting the Queensland premier, Joh Bjelke-Petersen, as a 'serious' alternative candidate for the office of prime minister in place of the then Liberal leader, John Howard. Ironically, it was the resultant split between the Liberals and the Nationals, and the temporary fracturing of the coalition, that facilitated the return of the Hawke government for the third time in 1987.

The sharemarket crashes

Hawke's timing in calling the 1987 winter election proved to be fortuitous. Less than three months later the national economy reeled in disarray when, without warning, the international sharemarket collapsed. The value of Australian stocks and shares fell by nearly 40% in a couple of weeks, and the recipe chosen by financial interests to promote international recovery had a pernicious effect on an already unstable Australian economy. To avoid another worldwide depression like that of the 1930s, the central bankers of the world agreed to work together to maintain business confidence by ensuring a high level of credit availability. Although such a policy might well have been correct for the world at large, increasing credit for Australian entrepreneurs was the financial equivalent of pouring petrol on a fire. The collapse of the sharemarkets provided only a temporary interruption to the rising tide of borrowing. Soon, bigger and bigger corporate takeovers occurred, financed by huge borrowings both at home and abroad, as banks—with hysterical, manic prodigality—flung money at dubious businessmen. The ready availability of loan funds meant that Reserve Bank attempts to curb the cycle by continuing to raise interest rates proved ineffectual, as businesses took advantage of the flood of easy credit by borrowing even more. Bank lending to business grew by 24% during 1986–87, and by 29% during 1987–88. When high interest rates finally did begin to slow down the economy, they not only affected the corporate paper-shufflers but also destroyed many orthodox and productive enterprises. Good and bad companies collapsed and asset values plummeted.[3]

Venality and corruption

With its transition from a party of the lower orders to a party of the upwardly mobile bourgeoisie, the ALP at both state and federal levels had formed close links with some of the more disreputable denizens of the corporate sector and had indulged in unconscionable business practices designed to retain business support for ALP administrations. During the third Hawke government a number of scandals came to light that caused serious affront to the party's traditional constituency and cast grave doubts on ALP claims to superior managerial ability and competence. These were not short-lived political emergencies, but long-running cancers. By the end of the decade such practices were to bring down ALP state governments in Western Australia, Victoria, and South Australia. The prime minister's enthusiastic acknowledgment of his friendships with failed (and eventually jailed) entrepreneurs such as Alan Bond or Laurie Connell, and his continuing relationships with businessmen such as Sir Peter Abeles and Australia's richest man, the media magnate Kerry Packer, kindled a quickening uneasiness as public inquiries in several states brought to light associations between ALP functionaries and businessmen that were unwise, sometimes improper, and occasionally illegal. Moreover, the prime minister and the federal government became tainted through guilt by association when these financial irregularities were exposed.

In Western Australia, the ALP government was revealed in evidence taken by a royal commission to have engaged in criminal activities by demanding donations from business in return for government favours; and the premier, Brian Burke, later served time in prison for theft and misuse of party funds. Although Burke was replaced in time for a temporary political respite, the scandal inevitably led to the ultimate demise of the state Labor government at the hands of a revitalised coalition led by Richard Court. In Victoria, the Labor government led by John Cain caused financial mayhem through its incompetence, and presided over the destruction of the State Bank of Victoria which had overextended credit to entrepreneurs and found itself hopelessly overexposed when the sharemarket collapsed. The government had also managed to produce a debt of $4.2 billion attempting to run an accident insurance scheme known as Workcare. To top things off, a large financial trust organisation named Estate Mortgage, that had advertised widely and had attracted investments from people all around Australia, suddenly went bankrupt, thus ruining thousands of investors. Moreover, the Pyramid Building Society also collapsed, jeopardising the life savings of hundreds of thousands of ordinary Victorians. It was like the 1890s all over again, although this time the cause was basic incompetence and, in Victoria at least, there was not the criminality associated with affairs in Western Australia. At the next Victorian elections in 1992, the coalition, under Jeff Kennett, swept triumphantly into office over a demoralised ALP. The situation in South Australia also highlighted the financial incompetence of the ALP state administration. The state bank was shown to be in debt to the tune of more than $1 billion in non-performing loans, and investigations revealed a cocktail of inefficiency and incompetence similar to that of Victoria. The government led by John Bannon retained office in 1989 as a minority administration with the support of two independents, but the ALP lost office at the following election. In all three states, the financial collapses forced the sale of government-owned state banks as governments attempted to claw back some of the revenues lost as a result of mismanagement during the boom.

Just as financial policy was bipartisan during these decades, so too was the prevalence of corruption at the state level; and Queensland and Tasmania provided ample illustration that coalition politicians were as well practised in criminal activities as were their ALP counterparts in the other states. In Queensland, the National Party government led by Premier Bjelke-Petersen became notorious for the irregular activities of ministers (including the premier), and for the venality of the police. After much resistance, the Bjelke-Petersen administration was forced to establish a Special Committee of Inquiry into allegations of widespread corruption in the Queensland Police Force. The inquiry ran for several years and, by turns, kept the Australian public amused, saddened, astounded, and dumbfounded at the extent of institutionalised corruption unearthed. In 1991, the (by then) former premier, Bjelke-Petersen, faced criminal charges for perjury before the inquiry, and another high-profile minister, Russell Hinze, avoided criminal charges for accepting bribes only by dying. A prominent business tycoon, George Herscu, received a five-year jail sentence for bribing Russell Hinze, two former ministers ended up with short terms of imprisonment, and the commissioner of police also went to jail for perversion of justice. Joh Bjelke-Petersen's admission that businessmen seeking favourable treatment from his government would sometimes leave brown paper bags containing thousands of dollars on his desk, aroused disgust and repugnance. The conservative forces in Australia were irretrievably tainted by the seemingly endless revelations of malpractice that flowed from the inquiry, and this robbed complaints of ALP corruption and incompetence of much of their force. At the same time, bipartisan corruption increased the general contempt and hostility that many Australians felt for politicians of all persuasions.

In Tasmania, the Liberal premier Robin Gray lost office to a combined ALP–Green government in 1989, and responded to the defeat by seeking to bribe one of the ALP members to cross the floor. The amount offered was $100 000 and the speakership of the Tasmanian Legislative Assembly. The ALP member approached the police and reported the offer and, eventually, a prominent businessman, Edmund Rouse, received a sentence of ten years in jail for his involvement in the charade. A royal commission implicated Gray personally and accused him of improper conduct for his role in the affair, and also drew attention to Gray's careless habits in retaining for his personal use thousands of dollars of political donations to his party. Gray seemed unable to understand that he had behaved in an unacceptable fashion or to accept that the criticisms of his involvement in a bribery attempt and the mishandling of party funds amounted to anything other than a biased attack on him by the royal commission. His intemperate attacks on the commission and on the members of the composite ALP–Green government alienated public sympathy from the conservative side of politics and robbed it of the advantage of the high moral ground.

Deregulation and the rural sector

In March 1990, the Hawke government won an unprecedented fourth term of office by a margin of just eight seats, due mainly to a flow of preferences from various parties and independents with strong environmental policies. Hawke had shown firm leadership towards the end of the previous year when the domestic airline pilots went on strike for a 30% pay increase. Hawke had used the Royal Australian Air Force and foreign international airlines to defeat the strike, although such strike-breaking actions on the part of an ALP government were never satisfactorily explained. It certainly made life difficult for the opposition, which was left with little alternative but to call for Hawke to try consensus rather than to coerce the pilots back to work. The pilots' strike did serve to demonstrate how far Hawke had moved the ALP to the right of the political spectrum, all the while dragging the ACTU with him, and this might help to explain why the government received such tender treatment from the media. No coalition government could have acted in a more hostile fashion to a legitimate trade union campaign to raise the wages of its members, and the use of the armed services as strikebreakers left a bad taste in the mouths of many traditional ALP supporters. In an attempt to differentiate itself from the ALP, the Liberal–National Party coalition had embraced an even more extreme form of deregulation by opposing the whole concept of centralised wage-fixing as embodied in the Accords. Under the coalition policy, workers would be encouraged to negotiate individually with their employers to produce their own individual workplace agreements and contracts, and trade unions would have no place in such a system. It was freedom of contract '1890s style' that they offered.

Deregulation also flowed through to the primary industry sector, and produced a deleterious impact on the national economy as Australia's farmers succumbed to tumbling world prices which brought many to ruin. The price of wool collapsed to the point where foreign buyers made up only 10% of purchasers and the government-funded Wool Corporation actually purchased and stored the bulk of the annual wool clip. That Australia was selling wool to itself was a Gilbertian situation, and the National Party found itself on the horns of a dilemma because, in theory, it espoused opposition policy in favour of deregulation while, in practice, the party recognised that its implementation would bring havoc to wool producers. In the deregulatory climate of opinion of the 1990s, Australian primary producers were to be forced to compete on the open market or go under. The decline in the contribution of wool to the country's export earnings was dramatic. By October 1991, wool prices had fallen to their nadir, regressing to below the level of 1890, and more than $3.5 billion in overseas income had been lost.

Since the nineteenth century Australian wool had been competitive with the rest of the world, and there seemed little doubt that after reconstruction the wool industry could again resume its primacy in the rural exports of Australia. The same could not be said, however, for the wheat industry, and therein lay an anomaly. Australian wheat could compete successfully on an open international market if other countries played by the deregulation rules. In such circumstances the terms of trade favoured Australia's wheat growers. But, in 1991, Australian growers lost market share to subsidised wheat sold by the United States of America, Canada, and the European Community. Australian wheat farmers went to the wall as the Australian government refused assistance to them and their chief competitors refused to compete without subsidy. It made little difference that, in June 1991, Paul Keating resigned as treasurer after an unsuccessful attempt to dethrone Bob Hawke, and was replaced by the former minister for Primary Industry, John Kerin. By this time the ideology of free trade and economic rationalism had become an article of faith with all the mainstream political groups in Australia. The rider might change, but the horse continued to gallop in the same direction.

In the outback, as in the cities, the chief villain of the piece was identified as the banking sector. It was not only corporate Australia that had been corrupted by financial deregulation and the flood of speculative capital that flooded into Australia during the 1980s. When the corporate collapses began, the banks looked for ways to recoup their losses. High interest rates and ruthless foreclosures in rural Australia became policy as the financial institutions attempted to recover the losses they had incurred during the years in which they had funded the buccaneers. The managers of country bank branches pointed the finger of blame at top management and claimed that they had no authority any longer over bank lending and repossession policy at ground level.[4]

Estimates of farm debt varied between $300 000 and $500 000 per property and, as farm incomes declined precipitously the banks declined to extend more credit and the value of rural properties plummeted. The rising generation of young farmers began to sell up and leave the land, and the properties fell into the hands of large agribusinesses involved in corporate farming. The move was to huge properties owned by companies in pursuit of economies of scale. The historic desire of White Australians to own a piece of rural Australia and to wrest a living from it came openly into conflict with the new economic reality that innovative agricultural technology had become too expensive for most individual farmers. The statistics of the rural decline of the early 1990s indicate the stark reality:

Farm incomes were slashed by 67%, with 38% of farmers receiving no income at all, 75% of farmers owing $225 000 or more, financial returns per hectare down 92%, farm sector spending cut by $5 billion, total losses to the economy totalling $10 billion, and the margin for wheat growers between costs and prices down to 2%.[5]

The ALP government and the economic institutions that unleashed this financial reign of terror managed to escape the consequences because the opposition espoused the same policies and an identical ideology. As the former prime minister and farmer Malcolm Fraser pointed out, deregulatory bipartisanship meant that the Liberal Party stood by and applauded as the ALP initiated policies that were to cause so much damage.[6] In November 1991 the Hawke government altered the welfare regulations to permit primary producers to go on the dole without having to sell their farms.

Aboriginal policy

Such concerns were far from the minds of most Australians on 26 January 1988 when the nation celebrated the bicentenary of White settlement. It was a day of patriotic pride and goodwill for most Australians, although descendants of the Aborigines held a day of mourning and a large pro-Aboriginal demonstration—at the end of which they castigated both federal and state governments for 200 years of neglect and racial prejudice. Prime Minister Hawke had hoped to sign a 'treaty' or 'compact' with the Aborigines that would symbolise a new era of respect and tolerance; but such a process could not be rushed. The government, in pursuit of consensus even here, opted for the widest possible discussions with representatives of the whole spectrum of Aboriginal organisations, even though this could extend over several years. The opposition flatly refused to accommodate the government with a bipartisan stance over the proposed treaty. Indeed, the coalition with the National Party made such a position impossible for the Liberals, even had they wished to proceed down that path. The opposition felt that there were serious social and political dangers in creating a nation within a nation, and the potential divisiveness of a treaty with one group in Australian society outweighed any advantages that might be gained by securing Aboriginal goodwill and agreement to a process of healing and reconciliation.

On 12 June 1988, the prime minister and the minister for Aboriginal Affairs sat down with a group of Aboriginal lawmen at Barunga in South Australia to discuss Aboriginal issues. The result, known as the 'Barunga Statement', committed the government to a treaty-making process. The opposition and some media commentators took a position of unrelenting hostility from the very beginning, concerned not only about splitting the community into separate nations, but also about possible large land claims that could result from any legal recognition of Aboriginal ownership of Australia prior to White settlement.

The question also arose of just what groups of Aboriginal people should be included in the process. A very real fear existed among Aborigines who still lived a more or less traditional lifestyle concerning the activities of urban Aboriginal activists. It was also unclear just who had a right to be called an Aborigine. The generally accepted definition by both state and federal governments was that an Australian Aborigine was a person descended from the original inhabitants who chose to identify as an Aborigine and was accepted as such by his group. Anyone who could claim descent from an Aboriginal forebear—and given the misuse of Aboriginal women in the nineteenth century by station owners and their workers there were many such—could legally describe themselves as an Aborigine. This definition maintained that Aboriginality is a question of race. But traditional Aborigines do not accept this definition. For them, an Aborigine is one who knows his own Aboriginal traditions and laws and lives by them. In other words, the crucial determinant of Aboriginality is culture not race. Much of this culture is secret and is passed on as part of traditional initiation ceremonies. Such lore, especially as it refers to relationship with country, can be imparted only by one who knows, and has little or nothing to do with racial identity, save that it is usually withheld from Whites. The governmental definition, which is still widely accepted, gives priority and status to urban Aborigines who are articulate in English, with the consequence that urban Aborigines, usually of mixed descent and often uninitiated into traditional Aboriginal culture, have become the spokespersons on behalf of all Aboriginal Australians. It was precisely to meet this difficulty that Charles Perkins, the Aboriginal activist, announced in February 1992 his intention of undergoing the traditional initiation rituals of his people in order to come to a fuller comprehension of traditional Aboriginal lore and customary beliefs. Such divisions certainly complicated the treaty-making process and helped to explain the lack of progress.

Aborigines and mining

Aboriginal rights and ALP policy came into conflict over the question of mining in Northern Australia. When some Aboriginal groups wanted to open uranium mines on their land, they soon ran into the ALP's notorious 'three mines policy'. Drawn up as result of an unsatisfactory compromise among the various factions of the ALP, this policy did not permit an increase in the number of mines beyond the nominal three, When Aborigines in 1988 reached agreements with mining companies to undertake large-scale uranium mining projects in the Kakadu area at Jabiluka, and at Koongarra in the Northern Territory, the issue again came to life. The existing Ranger uranium mine and the smaller Nabarlek mine together earned more than $300 million a year in exports, in addition to providing Aboriginal land councils with more than $12 million a year in mining royalties. Aboriginal enthusiasm for uranium mining and for a change in the restrictive ALP policy was understandable. Nevertheless, all attempts to alter the policy at the 1988 federal conference failed. The irony of Aboriginal support for increased uranium mining grew even richer when the Hawke government moved to consider reopening the mine at Coronation Hill on the fringes of Kakadu National Park.

Coronation Hill had been a successful uranium mine during the 1950s and 1960s, and recent geological exploration had shown that it possessed deposits of platinum and gold that could easily be mined and would earn Australia hundreds of millions of dollars. Reopening mining there was opposed vociferously by a loose confederation of environmental pressure groups on the grounds of potential ecological damage to Kakadu, and by the local Jawoyn Aborigines who first agreed that mining could take place but later reversed their decision. Aborigines believed mining would disturb Bula, a local deity said to be asleep beneath the surface. Bula had the reputation of being capable of enormous mischief and destruction. The mining industry, for its part, demanded access to

Coronation Hill and pointed out that it had already been extensively mined without 'awakening' Bula. The deposits of platinum and gold carried high international earning potential, and Australia could ill-afford to turn its back on such a considerable sum of money.

With the 1990 election safely behind him, the prime minister moved to tackle the intractable Coronation Hill issue early in 1991. Despite rising unemployment and a deepening recession, the government ruled against renewed mining on the grounds that to proceed would result in a violation of Jawoyn spiritual sensibilities. The mining industry and the opposition reacted with great bitterness and complained that the decision to permit the religious rights of a very small number of people to override the welfare of the entire nation would drive potential investors to other countries which were more self-interested and less self-indulgent.

The environment lobby

The Coronation Hill decision also demonstrated the growing power of the environment movement. The ALP had come to depend on the flow of 'Green' preferences in elections, and, in Tasmania, had actually governed in coalition with elected Green representatives. But the refusal of the environment lobby to compromise, and the zealous conviction with which they embraced the cause of the environment, angered many traditional politicians from both sides of politics. It appeared to many observers that the environmentalists were opposed to any and all resource development projects, irrespective of their merits. At a time when unemployment had risen above 10%, it seemed beyond belief that any government would so consistently defer to a single sectional pressure group. The ALP under Hawke found itself trapped between the demand for jobs of its traditional blue-singlet constituency and its perceived need to retain 'Green' support electorally.

Multiculturalism

One of the great defining issues that separated the ALP government from the opposition during the Hawke years was the symbolic area of immigration policy. The Liberal leader John Howard, proved to be a backward-looking conservative who felt most uncomfortable about the changing identity of the Australian community. He attempted to stem the growth of a multicultural and cosmopolitan Australia by stressing that incoming migrants should assimilate into the mainstream community, and he made such a position part of the policy position of the coalition under the rubric 'One Australia'. Howard abandoned the bipartisan tradition on immigration that had marked the administrations of Gough Whitlam and Malcolm Fraser and the early Hawke years, and attempted to tap into a core of dissatisfaction and unhappiness revealed by an official report on Australian immigration policy that had been presented to parliament during 1988. The 'FitzGerald Report', named after the chairman of the committee, the former ambassador to China Dr Stephen FitzGerald, advocated increasing the number of skilled immigrants and emphasised the establishment of an Australian identity. But what was such an identity to be? The report had also revealed that genuine consensus did not exist over multiculturalism, and it was this underlying uneasiness that Howard attempted to capture for the Liberals.

A rising tide of concern about Asian immigration levels had emerged during the Fraser years, and the zealotry of the government-funded institutions and organisations that had been set up to ensure that migrants did not become victims of discrimination aroused considerable resentment. Fears were expressed that multiculturalism meant, in practice, the denigration of Australian culture and the ridicule of those who expressed pride in an Australian identity. It was even suggested that the underlying rationale of the multicultural lobby lay in a belief that all cultures were worthy of respect except Australia's; and that such an outlook amounted to a new version of the cultural cringe that had been characteristic of Australians when they encountered the social and cultural pretensions of the English in earlier years. FitzGerald recognised that multiculturalism caused uneasiness and some hostility as did the outrageous and slanderous attacks made on any Australians brave or foolhardy enough to question whether multiculturalism was the right direction for Australia to travel.

Howard plunged into this emotional vortex when he proclaimed 'One Australia'. The government brought on a debate on the subject of immigration policy in August 1988, and Howard was caught in an impossible position. His concern lay in those wider community tensions to which FitzGerald had alluded and he worried about the nation's ability to absorb large numbers of Asian migrants. In May 1989 Howard was replaced as Liberal leader by Andrew Peacock, the former leader whom Howard had previously overthrown. Peacock held more liberal views on immigration and multiculturalism and, at his first press conference after the coup, he announced the restoration of bipartisanship in this area. When Peacock lost the 1990 election, the Liberals, in an effort to avoid the endless recycling of Howard and Peacock, replaced him with a former professor of economics named John Hewson.

Two bulls in the same paddock: Hawke vs Keating

Reconciliation and healing were also sorely needed within the Labor government from 1988 onwards as the rivalry between the prime minister and the treasurer began to affect government performance. When Paul Keating introduced his sixth budget on 23 August 1988 he believed it would be his last; that Hawke would retire before the next election and leave him in the Lodge as prime minister. Keating had always understood that once Hawke had won his historic third term and his place in the history books, he would retire gracefully. When Hawke refused to stand down, the association soured rapidly. The relationship between the government's two main performers became so poisoned that it could not be allowed to continue and, in November 1988, the two men met at the prime minister's official residence in Sydney, Kirribilli House. At this meeting Hawke, before witnesses called by both men, promised to retire as prime minister and leader of the ALP in favour of Keating after the 1990 elections. The blatant impropriety of such a compact in a democratic country and in a democratically based party seemed not to concern either man. The promise, when it came to light in 1991, proved that Hawke had lied throughout the 1990 election when he promised specifically that he would stay on as prime minister. If he had meant to keep that undertaking, it could only have been done by violating the pledge he had made to Keating in 1988. One way or the other, the prime minister had been exposed as a liar, which did little to restore the credibility of politicians from the abyss into which it had continued to sink.

The whole unsavoury mess emerged in 1991 when Hawke reneged on his promise to Keating and the treasurer challenged him before the ALP federal caucus for the leadership. At first glance, it would seem nonsensical that any party member should challenge the most successful leader the ALP had ever produced, especially when that person was still the incumbent in the highest office in the land. But Paul Keating was a paradox in Australian politics. His economic policies of deregulation and economic rationalism had brought undoubted hardship to countless ordinary Australians and had impacted heavily on the traditional working-class constituency of the ALP. By mid 1991 he had caused the Hawke government to be 18 points behind the opposition in public opinion polls. Despite all this, he was also the dynamo of a tired Hawke administration, and was far and away its best parliamentary performer. Paul Keating as a teenager, had spent a great deal of time around the former depression premier of New

South Wales, Jack Lang, and Lang had influenced the young man's development. He had become, like his mentor Lang, a warrior whom the opposition rightly feared for the ferocity of his enmity and for his capacity in parliament to leave them speechless and demoralised. Menzies had dominated parliament with his wit and intellect, whereas Keating dominated it with his scalding invective and contempt for conservative social policies and politicians. The cynicism of his views on political leadership in Australia had been revealed in September 1990 when he had responded to a suggestion from critics that that he could never hope to turn around his huge personal unpopularity in the electorate:[7]

> If the day comes that I have to throw the switch to vaudeville, I'll do it, understand? I mean, if one has to be all-singing, all-dancing, that's what we'll be. But all in due time. There's a more substantial agenda.

So the challenge to Hawke in June 1991 was not one that the party took lightly. When that challenge failed and Keating retired from the ministry to the backbench, the government, lacking anybody on its frontbench of comparable ability, floundered badly in parliament.

From the backbench Paul Keating continued his campaign to destabilise the prime minister by publicly calling for a revision of policies he himself had formulated and for a return to a traditional ALP concentration on the provision of jobs for the unemployed. The prime minister's cigar smoking image and his obvious preference for the company of business tycoons such as Alan Bond, Kerry Packer, and Sir Peter Abeles provided the outer signs of an inner shift within the ALP to a new identity as a party for middle-class bourgeois Australia. The various inquiries and royal commissions into ALP state administrations illustrated the way in which special deals for 'mates' in the business world had become the prevailing ethic and had replaced the old dictum of ensuring that all Australians received a 'fair go'. The ALP under Hawke showed all the signs of a tired and out-of-touch administration, and the 'them-and-us' double standard of the government towards its supporters was reflected in an enormous decline in party membership. When Hawke had led the ALP back into office in 1983, ALP membership had risen to around 50 000. By 1991, this had dropped to below 40 000, and was continuing to fall steadily. In that year, the party's national secretary attributed the fall-off in morale and numbers to a growing perception among blue-collar members that they had become irrelevant to the new-look ALP and that they were increasingly alienated from the party and its policies.[8]

The figures starkly mirror this alteration in the structural basis of the ALP. In the 1940s, one in 40 manual workers had been a member of the party; by the 1980s this had become one in 275. By the middle of 1991, the ALP had been transformed into a party in which the dominant group consisted of professionals and tertiary students. These people had not joined the ALP to fight the evils of capitalist exploitation, but to pursue an interest in implementing the policy ideals of the new social movements of feminism, peace, and the environment.[9] It had been a very long time since a train driver or a coal miner had led the workers' party.

The opposition recognised that Hawke was vulnerable on this issue of grass-roots alienation, and their new leader John Hewson exploited his advantage in parliament with telling effect when he accused the Hawke administration of finally extinguishing the 'light on the hill'—that beacon of idealism that had activated Ben Chifley's Labor government. Hewson's charge was that Labor under Hawke had forfeited any legitimate claim to be the party of ordinary Australians. 'People don't want any more special deals to help Labor's rich mates', he told parliament. 'They want a realistic plan to make this country prosperous again.'[10]

Hawke gets the sword

In August 1990, Hawke decided—without even bothering to call a Cabinet meeting—to commit three warships of the Royal Australian Navy to support an American-led international blockade of Iraq. The blockade would interdict all shipping to Iraq as a punishment for that country's invasion and occupation of Kuwait. The ensuing war caused no Australian casualties and brought a short-lived boost to the prime minister's fading popularity, as had his decision in 1989 to permit Chinese students marooned in Australia after the Tiananmen Square massacre to stay on as residents, But it was short-lived popularity, and when John Hewson announced the details of the coalition's new taxation package, which included sweeping reductions in personal income tax, the abolition of all wholesale tax, and the imposition of a new goods and services tax (GST), the government found itself in real danger. Hawke and his frontbench proved quite incapable of responding to Hewson's challenge, and the ALP resorted to a scare campaign against a policy its leaders had supported and attempted to introduce at the ill-fated taxation summit of 1985. The government's chances of surviving the elections due in 1993 seemed next to impossible. In desperation, on 19 December 1991, the federal caucus of the ALP made the only decision available to it if the malaise was not to prove terminal. By a margin of five votes, 56 to 51, the caucus voted for Paul Keating to replace Bob Hawke as leader of the ALP and prime minister. The vote was yet another historic first for Hawke as it marked the first time the ALP had unseated a sitting prime minister. The newspapers of 21 December 1991 carried photographs of a serene governor-general, Bill Hayden, swearing in Australia's twenty-fourth prime minister, and the irony that Hawke's victim of 1983 should be the one to anoint Hawke's executioner of 1991 was not lost on the observers. Hayden refused to make any comment when reporters brought this to his attention, thereby increasing his reputation for mellow tact and integrity. Hawke departed most unwillingly to the backbench, publicly shedding tears as he officiated at his final function as prime minister.

Thrills and spills of the Keating ascendancy

With the ALP apparently dead in the water at both state and federal levels, Paul Keating's assumption of power in 1991 seemed to be a poisoned chalice. The Hawke government had given the impression that it expected to be defeated in 1993, and its ministers were said to be actively canvassing alternative career options for the post-election years. As the *Sydney Morning Herald* was to comment later:[11]

> It was not so much that they thought their re-election was unlikely, though that was true, as that they couldn't imagine why they should be re-elected or what they would do if they were. Hawke had run out of puff. He had reached the terminal stage of accommodation with his officials where their initiatives were his. The Canberra bureaucracy is a wonderful machine and one of Australia's most valuable assets, but it should not be relied upon to do the politicians' job of seizing the initiative and prevailing over political opponents.

At the state level, ALP governments fell like dominoes, beginning with Tasmania in February 1992, then Victoria in October 1992, then Western Australia early in 1993, followed by South Australia in December 1993. It seemed more than clear that at the state level the electorate, ravaged by recession, was intent on punishing ALP administrations for the corruption and incompetence they had demonstrated during the 1980s. It was in this unfavourable climate of opinion that Paul Keating cemented his place in ALP mythology by reversing the trend of events and reinvigorating and inspiring a government that had appeared to be in the terminal stages of decay.

The first major response to John Hewson's 'Fightback' taxation package came in February 1992 when Keating launched his 'One

John Hewson. (Macquarie University Photographic Unit)

Nation' alternative. Keating had noticed what Hawke had failed to observe, that the projected revenue from the proposed GST had been allocated to eliminating petrol taxes and payroll taxes. This meant that the promised reductions in income tax that had been used to sweeten 'Fightback' were coming out of the same government revenues, especially income tax revenues, as were available to the ALP administration. Therefore, it followed that the government could offer equivalent income tax cuts to those offered in 'Fightback', but without a GST.

By offering, in broad terms, the same income tax cuts as were being offered by the opposition, but without an unsettling adventure into the unknown, Keating's 'One Nation' package effectively robbed the coalition of its major attraction.

Keating also fused the twin themes of idealism and nationalism into a potent appeal to the younger members of the electorate. This was nowhere better demonstrated than in the furore over the visit of Queen Elizabeth II to Australia in February 1992. Not only did the prime minister infuriate conservative Australians by putting his hand gently on the queen's back while introducing her to dignitaries in Canberra, but also, in his speech of welcome, he contrasted the Australia of 1992 with the Australia of the sovereign's first visit in 1954. Keating clearly enunciated a vision of two countries that had once been very close but that were now drifting apart as each pursued a regional destiny—Great Britain's in Europe and Australia's in the Asia–Pacific region. The opposition overreacted to this reasonably accurate description of the reality, with Hewson and his frontbench attacking the prime minister for being undignified and disrespectful to Australia's head of state. Three days later they wished they had somewhere to hide when, in the House of Representatives, Keating addressed them directly and painted an unequivocal picture of the differences between Labor and the coalition on the issue of nationalism and the British:[12]

> I was told that I did not learn respect at school. I learned one thing: I learned about self-respect and self-regard for Australia—not about some cultural cringe to a country which decided not to defend the Malaysian peninsula, not to worry about Singapore and not to give us our troops back to keep ourselves free of Japanese domination. This was the country that you wedded yourselves to, and even as it walked out on you and joined the Common Market, you were still looking for your MBEs and your knighthoods, and all the rest of the regalia that comes with it. You would take Australia right back down the time tunnel to the cultural cringe where you have always come from . . . You can go back to the fifties to your nostalgia, your Menzies, the Caseys, and the whole lot. They were not aggressively Australian, they were not aggressively proud of our culture, and we will have no bar of you or your sterile ideology.

The speech galvanised the ALP and delighted the dispirited parliamentarians who had hoped for just such leadership when they had disposed of Bob Hawke. It had been a long time since ALP backbenchers had cheered their leader's sallies in debate, but they found plenty of occasion to cheer over the following weeks and months as Paul Keating established an undoubted ascendancy over the coalition frontbench. But it was done at a heavy cost in terms of the destruction of personal civility and respect in parliament and the complete eradication of the former club-like atmosphere that had been characteristic of federal parliament for most members since 1901.

Regional ties

Apart from redefining the past to the discomfort of the opposition, the Keating-led ALP also wrong-footed its opponents with an enunciation of a clear vision of an Australian future inevitably linked with Asia, especially South-East Asia. Keating saw the dynamism of Asian economic development as an exciting opportunity for Australia, and he visited Indonesia and Japan very early in his term of office, and well before he travelled to Europe or to Britain. In so openly embracing a regional involvement for Australia's future direction, the prime minister antagonised many Australians who had supported John Howard and his 'One Australia' policy, together with many older Australians who were nostalgic for the days of their youth and for an overwhelmingly White Australia that no longer existed outside their memories. Although the policy setting chosen by the prime minister apparently appealed to the idealistically inclined generation of younger Australians, it was risky in a time of massive unemployment. It was very easy for minority groups opposed to any Asian immigration to portray their opposition in terms of protecting the jobs of 'real' Australians. Paul Keating's new direction certainly inspired some Australians, but it was also deeply divisive.

The opposition countered that the prime minister's overt republicanism and enthusiasm for Asia amounted to a policy of buying new friends by disloyally disowning old ones. This charge seemed to be somewhat credible late in 1992 when the United States of America was fighting a trade war with Japan to gain access to closed Japanese markets. Keating visited Japan where he carefully articulated the government's position that Australia was wholly behind Japan. He reminded the Japanese that they were Australia's most important export market, taking almost one-third of all Australian exports. In any confrontation between America and Japan over trade, Keating made it clear that Japan could rely on Australia to continue to supply raw materials. This was more than mere rhetoric, because Keating knew from his time as treasurer that Australia enjoyed a $6 billion trade surplus with Japan and, with the Australian economy in the doldrums, no prime minister could afford to place that in jeopardy. However, such constraints did not affect the opposition, and Hewson and the leader of the National Party, Tim Fischer, attacked the prime minister for deferring to Japan and getting nothing tangible in return.

The first GST election

That Paul Keating had been successful in wresting back the initiative from the opposition became clear by the end of 1992

Paul Keating. (The office of the Hon. Paul Keating)

when John Hewson felt constrained to make changes to his 'Fightback' package by removing food from the proposed 15% GST impost. This amounted to a backdown of monumental proportions because, ever since 'Fightback' had first been unveiled, Hewson had gloried in the fact that he was different from all other politicians. He had been adamant that he would never change any part of it. He had stated that it was more important to be correct than to compromise merely to win power. 'Fightback', he had declared, would not be altered because it was right and because he was a new sort of politician who would fight for what he knew to be right, even if it meant political defeat. By December he had been forced to change tack by public anger at the prospect of increased food prices under a GST, and by a shrewd tactical decision from Keating that, if the ALP lost the next election, it would allow the GST passage through the Senate. Voters were to be faced with the starkest of choices—either vote for the coalition and get a GST, or vote for the ALP and avoid the GST. Keating announced the policy in November and, within a month, Hewson had lost his nerve and had recanted on the GST on food. As soon as news of the backflip emerged, Keating moved in mercilessly, describing Hewson as a 'flim-flam man' who obviously stood for nothing other than what might win him votes at the next election.[13]

The election itself was bitterly fought, with considerable personal animus on both sides. The new coalition state government in Victoria had embraced standard coalition industrial policies to abolish the system of industrial awards and the centralised system for setting wage levels and working conditions. It had also abolished annual leave loadings and holiday pay, together with penalty loadings in all state awards. The result had been demonstrations and street protests the like of which had not been seen since the days of the Vietnam War. Paul Keating was quick to point out that the policies being implemented in Victoria would apply nationally if the coalition won the election in March 1993. As if the prospect of a GST were not enough, a victory for the opposition would also involve the possibility of an out-and-out war between the incoming government and the ACTU.

The primary focus of the campaign, however, remained the GST, and the government took the position that the election amounted to a referendum on the new tax proposals. The coalition made much of the prime minister's personal culpability for the recession in which more than one million Australians were out of work. It became accepted conventional wisdom that no government could hope to survive in the face of such high unemployment and, although the polls showed that the opposition was being overtaken by the government as the election proceeded, John Hewson and his party believed that they would win a handsome victory—that, in essence, the election was 'unloseable'. Most professional tipsters agreed, and duly forecast a close election with a coalition victory. In the event, they were wrong. The Keating government not only won the election but actually increased its majority in the House of Representatives. On election night, Paul Keating described the win as 'the sweetest victory of all', while a disconsolate Bob Hawke unsuccessfully attempted to look pleased that his rival had snatched victory from the jaws of apparently inevitable defeat. The press, which had been extraordinarily hostile to the government and had touted for a coalition victory throughout the campaign, saddled Hewson with complete personal responsibility for the defeat. The *Sydney Morning Herald* described the result in these terms:[14]

> The election victory by Mr Keating and the Labor Party is one of the most remarkable in Australia's political history. It was achieved against the gravity of history and most of the conventional wisdom about elections . . . A million people unemployed had been supposed, in another mantra of conventional wisdom, as an impossible leg-iron on any government. But voters around Australia showed that they were prepared to accept the terrible troubles and problems of their current situation rather than undertake a leap in the dark over the massive restructuring of the tax regime.

11

Vaudeville and the Conservative Resurgence

In the aftermath of the 1993 election, Paul Keating set about repairing some of the damage the decade of ALP government had inflicted on the fabric of the party. Economic rationalism could not be jettisoned in an increasingly global economy, and there could be no returning to the comfortable pattern of inefficient industries sheltering behind a tariff wall and providing safe employment for the community. What could be done, however, was to put in place policies that would ensure that when economic recovery did take place, the unemployed would not be left behind. The prime minister was determined to avoid the creation of an underclass of impoverished workers and their families, and the new ALP administration set about establishing a framework whereby unemployed workers would be offered retraining and education to upgrade existing skills or to acquire new ones. The traditional ethic of the 'fair go' was disinterred, and the government promised that those currently unemployed would not be left to stagnate. A measure of the success of this policy could be seen as early as the end of 1994 when the number of unemployed had dropped under the million mark, the economy had a growth rate of 4–5%, and the economic upturn had already produced more than 320 000 additional jobs.

Native title

It was in the area of Aboriginal affairs, however, that Paul Keating applied the 'fair go' ethic in its most radical form. Hitherto, the ideal that every Australian was entitled to a 'fair go' had not usually applied to Aboriginal Australians. Until the so-called 'Mabo judgment' handed down by the High Court of Australia in June 1992, Aborigines had no legally enforceable title to the country in which they had lived for millennia. The Mabo decision recognised for the first time that a form of native title still did exist in certain parts of Australia, and that the indigenous inhabitants had been the legal owners of the soil when European settlement took place. How was the government, now led by a man who was on record as believing that there was no point in attaining power if nothing was done with it, to respond to this new situation?

The prime minister laid out his intentions in the month following the elections when he delivered the H.V. Evatt Lecture to members of the party. In Paul Keating's view, the Mabo judgment offered a priceless opportunity to break the mould and to rethink and rework the relationship between Aborigines and the rest of the community. The relationship was to be based, for the first time, on the principles of justice and fair dealing. Accordingly, in June 1993, the government released a set of principles that it hoped might produce an acceptable compromise between the rights of indigenous people to native title and the need to protect pastoral and mining operations on contested land. It was proposed that national legislation to secure mining and pastoral leases be introduced, and that compensation be paid to Aborigines who had lost title to land by the issue of such leases. In contested areas it was proposed that a non-adversarial system of tribunals be established to determine where legal title lay and, finally, that the government would establish a national land-acquisition fund that would provide money to assist Aborigines who had lost their traditional links with the land to obtain freehold land of their own.

The mining industry attacked the proposals as unwieldy and

unworkable, and the newly elected coalition governments in Western Australia and Victoria refused to cooperate in any national system. The Mabo judgment had made it clear that, wherever Aborigines could show that they had maintained their traditional links with the land—by residing on it and carrying out the ceremonial and religious rituals associated with the land—they still possessed native title to that territory unless it had been disposed of as freehold title or as mining or pastoral leasehold. In Western Australia, a large proportion of the state (variously estimated as being half to two-thirds of the state) theoretically became subject to native title claims, and the coalition government led by Richard Court refused to countenance such a prospect. He was supported by Jeff Kennett and John Fahey, the Liberal premiers of Victoria and New South Wales respectively.

This fundamental antagonism—between the states' rights to control their own land and the federal right to bring in enactments on behalf of indigenous people—boiled over at a special meeting between the Commonwealth and the states to consider matters arising from the Mabo decision. One matter of special concern to the premiers was the prime minister's contentious view that Aborigines should possess the power of veto over land use in areas determined to have native title. It was feared that such an outcome would dramatically reduce overseas investment which would then be redirected to countries whose governments provided more supportive and compliant environments.

At the federal level, the coalition fully supported the attacks on the Keating proposals and took a position that virtually amounted to a refusal to accept that the High Court had made a decision—one consequence of which was to signal the need to establish some mechanism to give effect to that judgment. The coalition found itself divided between, on the one hand, genuine liberals in the Liberal Party and, on the other hand, the mining companies and more extreme pastoralists who were the natural constituency of the conservative parties, and who demanded nothing less than complete and untrammelled opposition. The necessity of implementing the High Court judgment and giving Aboriginal Australians a belated recognition as the original possessors of the soil might conform to abstract notions of justice. However, when such desires came into conflict with the vested interests of the traditional supporters of the coalition, justice for Aborigines went out the window. The government's Native Title Bill contained provisions to validate existing land titles placed in doubt by the Mabo judgment, to set up the tribunals to adjudicate in contested claims for native title, and to set guidelines for compensation payments where these were appropriate. The key principle underlying the legislation was the unambiguous recognition that native title did exist and had to be protected in law. When the government first introduced the Native Title Bill to the House of Representatives, the coalition declared that it was a day of shame in Australia's history.

Aboriginal groups generally responded favourably, and the National Farmers Federation supported the legislation because of the protection it extended to pastoral leases. The mining industry and the Business Council of Australia maintained that it would render the country's land-tenure system unworkable and would inhibit investment. Tim Fischer, the federal leader of the National Party, called for a referendum to be held with the intention of overturning the High Court's decision, and his position was endorsed by a number of prominent members of the Liberal Party including one frontbench member of the shadow cabinet.

Paul Keating attacked John Hewson for his abject failure to show leadership on this issue and to offer bipartisan support. In Keating's view, this was a moral not a political issue. The prime minister declared that the legislation embodied:[1]

> . . . an unashamed appeal for justice—a fair go—for Aboriginal Australians . . . We owe it to Aboriginal Australians, to all Australians, we owe it to our fair and democratic traditions and to future generations of Australians, to recognise this native title.

The Bill passed through the House of Representatives without a problem, but stalled in the Senate where two Green senators from Western Australia held the balance of power. After a number of Green and Australian Democrat amendments had been accepted by the government the Bill finally passed the Senate on 21 December 1993, despite a failed attempt by the coalition to filibuster. The historic passage of the legislation was greeted with applause by Aboriginal leaders watching from the public gallery, and was hailed by a jubilant prime minister.

The Native Title Act illustrated one of the major characteristics of Paul Keating's time as prime minister. Keating held the view that there was no point in the ALP being in power if it did nothing with it, and his government had all the reforming zeal of a new administration. This was anything but a tired administration and, by 1993, Keating had sacked or disposed of nearly all Hawke's ministers. The fatalism of the final Hawke years had been left far behind as Keating led a proactive government that shrewdly blended idealism and nationalism into a formidable and heady brew. It did not merely respond to the drift of events, but provided firm and decisive leadership.

Most Australians accepted without demur that the Native Title Act was a significant move in the reconciliation between Black and White Australians, and the prime minister had successfully tapped the idealism of the rising generation who generally seemed happy to see an historic injustice addressed in this fashion. The government had manoeuvred the opposition into a position where it was seen to be implacably destructive, and its leader's stance as shameful. The tactics of the opposition in opposing the Native Title Bill outright, and failing to move or support amendments to strengthen the position of industry, demonstrated a bumbling ineptitude that was the hallmark of Hewson's leadership.

The republic

The republican issue provided a further example of the essentially reactive nature of the coalition in national politics. In April 1993 the prime minister, in keeping with an election pledge, announced the establishment of a broadly based committee of eminent Australians to consider the options for a change to a republican form of government before the bicentenary of federation in 2001. Although the former Liberal premier of New South Wales, Nick Greiner, agreed to serve on the committee, along with prominent media personalities, academics, and the chairperson of the Aboriginal and Torres Strait Islander Commission (ATSIC), the coalition refused to participate and to nominate a representative to the committee. From this point onwards, coalition policy towards the issue of a republic placed the opposition offside with the rising generation who largely supported the republic, and locked it into the age group of 55 and over who generally supported the monarchy. This remained the position of the leader of the coalition right through until the referendum on the republic in 1999, no matter who held the office.

The coalition staggers

John Hewson's leadership had remained a bone of contention with senior Liberals from the time of his loss of the 'unloseable' election. The former prime minister, Malcolm Fraser, had repeatedly called for Hewson to resign after the election, and members of the party complained of his stubborn refusal to take advice or listen to his colleagues. His problems were compounded by open jockeying within the Liberal Party to take over his job. The former leader, John Howard, had challenged for the leadership shortly after the defeat, but had lost by 17 votes. The ambitious but vacuous Senator Bronwyn Bishop refused a shadow portfolio unless it elevated her to the coalition frontbench, and when Hewson refused to cave in to such pressure and left her fuming on the backbench, she openly began to stalk him and to attempt to establish her own credentials for his job.

More importantly, senior sections of the extra-parliamentary wing of the Liberal Party began to demand a greater say in the policy-making process. Michael Kroger, the former president of the Victorian branch of the party, pointed out that had the party branches and the party's salaried officials possessed a greater degree of input into policy, the Liberal Party would never have gone into the 1993 elections with a GST as its main platform.[2] Similar suggestions emanated from the federal president of the party, Tony Staley, and were, of course, echoed by Bronwyn Bishop sniping at her leader from the sidelines.

By May 1994 Hewson's tenuous hold on the leadership had slipped. Business withheld donations as a way of pressuring the Liberal Party to dispose of so unsuccessful a leader, and there was a rapid decline in the party's financial position. Eventually, the federal president and the party's administrative officers orchestrated a move against Hewson by a combined leadership team of Alexander Downer from South Australia and Peter Costello from Victoria. This dynamic duo failed to bring about the destruction of the Keating Labor government and, after a series of extraordinary gaffes and errors of judgment from Alexander Downer over course of the following year, the Liberals turned in desperation to the only man with the staying power to match Keating in parliament. In 1995 the party elected John Howard as leader of the Liberal Party for the second time. An ebullient Howard described himself as being like 'Lazarus with a triple bypass', but he had demonstrated grit and determination to stage a comeback from political oblivion, and time would show that he had what it took to turn Labor out of office.

Fitting into the region

One of the hallmarks of the Keating government was its policy of integrating the Australian economy into Asia, where two-thirds of the country's exports already went. When Paul Keating became prime minister, there had been no meeting between the heads of government of Australia and Indonesia for almost a decade. He speedily set about changing that, and the depth and warmth of his personal contacts with President Soeharto of Indonesia over the next few years became legendary. He also established close bilateral relations with the governments of South Korea, Japan, China, Vietnam, and Australia's neighbours in the South Pacific.

In 1994 Keating convinced the president of the United States, Bill Clinton, that it was in that country's interest to support his move to establish a forum to be known as the Asia–Pacific Economic Cooperation (APEC). A number of very successful leaders' meetings was held at which major moves were made to abolish trade barriers between the countries of the region. As a foundation member of APEC, Australia began to exercise a powerful influence to move the region into a progressive embrace of free trade that was mooted to be completed by the decade 2010–20. The prime minister's dictum that Australia had to find its security *in* Asia rather than *from* Asia, was soundly based in economic realities, but it was deliberately misrepresented by the coalition in Australia as being a policy to make Australia a part of Asia, and to reconstitute Australians as Asians. In December 1993, the prime minister responded to this falsehood in a speech in which he made his position crystal clear:[3]

> Australia is not, and can never be, an 'Asian nation' any more than we can—or want to be—European or North American or African. We can only be Australian and we can only relate to our friends as Australian.

Only in the case of Malaysia did this move meet opposition. The rejection of Keating's policy by the Malaysian prime minister, Mahathir Mohamad, was largely caused by his contempt for Australia's claim to be considered a legitimate participant in the region's affairs. Mahathir considered that Australia's European culture and history disqualified the country from full participation. The Malaysian media echoed the Mahathir line that Keating's alleged bad manners were the result of his descent from convict stock, and the Malaysian government orchestrated a campaign against Australia's more prominent role in the region. Mahathir went on to argue that only Asian countries could rightfully participate in regional forums such as APEC, and his government did everything in its power to ensure that Australia was excluded. Paul Keating was incensed and responded in kind. If Australians were to be excluded on racial grounds from a full participation in the region's affairs, Australia would feel obliged to reconsider the defence relationship with Malaysia. After all, Australian servicemen and servicewomen had met their deaths in protecting Malaysia from Chinese communist insurgents during the 1950s and from Indonesian invasion during the 1960s, and if it was good enough for Australians to die for Malaysia then it should be good enough for them to be accepted as equal partners. Australia would also reimpose dormant exchange controls on Malaysia to stop capital flows from Australia being used to underwrite Malaysian development. Faced with such a damaging prospect, Mahathir backed off, but his resentment against Australia continued to smoulder. By his appeal to history and his economic pressure, Keating had amply demonstrated that Australia had a right to claim a role in the region, and the strength to back up the demand if necessary. Aside from Malaysia, all other countries in the region welcomed Australia's obvious desire to be included, and the integration of Australia's economy with Asia continued apace. Even the later slowdown of the Asian economic boom in the late 1990s did little to set back this process.

The Keating roller-coaster

In the meantime, the attacks on Keating became more hysterical and vituperative than ever. In the Senate, some of the coalition's chief muckrakers, Liberal senators Michael Baume and Richard Alston, decided to attack the prime minister's business practices, especially his investment in a commercial piggery that began in 1991 and ended in 1994. It was claimed that the transaction made several million dollars profit for Paul Keating, and it was implied that there was something improper in a Labor leader making money in a business venture, especially if the interests to which the business had been sold came from Indonesia. No evidence was ever brought forward to justify these claims and racist insinuations made under the cloak of parliamentary privilege, but some of the mud undoubtedly stuck.

The prime minister's personal attacks on the opposition in parliament for their old-fashioned and backward-looking attachment to England and the empire, resulted in a sustained reaction of character assassination that undermined his reputation for honesty and accused him of arrogance in his public and private conduct. The fact that he wore stylish Italian suits, collected antique French clocks, and preferred classical music to popular bands was said to demonstrate his alienation from the common people. The costs of upgrading the prime ministerial residence in Canberra, the Lodge, were alleged to indicate his profligate nature, as was the allegedly extravagant cost of a $23 000 teak dining table that the prime minister desired to purchase. Untruths were peddled that Paul Keating and his family wished to air-condition a kennel for their dog, and to waste copious amounts of money in renovating and improving the Sydney harbourside residence known as Kirribilli House. News reports concentrated on these claims, and on the prime minister's fighting performances during Question Time in the House of Representatives, to reinforce the view that he was both profligate and unduly combative, and that the alleged fall in the standards of parliamentary conduct, as discerned by commentators, were not the fault of irresponsible operators such as Michael Baume and Richard Alston, but were somehow the responsibility of the prime minister.

The refusal of the prime minister to apologise for the recession or the continuing high unemployment caused much gratification among

John Howard. (Auspic Photos)

the members of the coalition who had decided to focus their opposition almost entirely on the personality of Paul Keating. Their new leader, John Howard, gave a public assurance that he would improve the standard of parliamentary behaviour, would establish a code of ethics to ensure that all ministers behaved with propriety, and would lead an honest and transparent administration. John Howard, as treasurer in Malcolm Fraser's govern-ments, had permitted some very questionable transactions to proceed in the area of tax-avoidance schemes for the rich and influential. In recognition, he had been tagged with the ironic cognomen of 'Honest John' by the media, but public memory had faded of the ironic intent of the title, and people only remembered the nickname itself. Being 'Honest John' Howard became a real electoral advantage and a way of distinguishing himself from the tainted reputation of Paul Keating. As part of this understanding with the Australian people, John Howard gave an unequivocal undertaking that the lesson of 1993 had been learnt by the coalition, and that it would `never ever' contemplate trying to implement a GST again.

The election of 2 March 1996, proved to be a landslide victory for the opposition with a handsome majority of 29 seats. Paul Keating experienced a massive personal rejection by the electorate after a campaign in which John Howard had made the arrogance of the prime minister the key issue. The issues on which Keating stood—globalisation and the economic integration with Asia, the move towards a lasting peace with the Aborigines, the economic recovery that had taken place during the three years between 1993 and 1996—all of these counted for little in the end. Paul Keating became the victim of a revulsion by the community against the rapidity and extent of change. He had also become a paradox, in that he was simultaneously loathed by a majority of the electorate, yet loved and admired by a substantial minority. The comprehensive reaction against thirteen years of Labor government could no longer be held at bay, and there seems little doubt that it was only the campaign against the GST that had enabled the ALP to win against the odds in 1993. Howard had rejected a GST, and he had offered a better behaved parliament, a willingness to continue the reconciliation with the indigenous people, and an acceptance of a multicultural Australian community. He had even promised a constitutional convention on the question of the republic. In other words, Howard offered reassurance on all the issues that were acknowledged strengths in the Keating program and, by so doing, he allowed an angry community to scapegoat a prime minister whose notoriety for overbearing arrogance had become well established while his reputation in other areas had become ambiguous. Three weeks later, Paul Keating resigned from parliament, and the job of rebuilding the ALP fell to the former deputy leader from Western Australia, Kim Beazley.

The coalition in government

John Howard was a conservative, and the party he led looked back to the Menzies' era for its ideological underpinnings and its social policies. The new government established its lasting reputation for hypocrisy very early in its term, when Howard announced his discovery that there had been 'core' promises and 'non-core' promises made by him during the election campaign. The 'core' promises were those that he intended to keep, whereas the 'non-core' promises amounted to lies that had been necessary to win an election, but which he felt no necessity to implement. 'Honest John' certainly ensured that Australians were rapidly reminded of the ironic intent of his nickname.

Because the restoration of integrity to government had been one of the promises that had brought him to power, Howard moved quickly to introduce a new ministerial code of conduct, under which ministers were required to make a declaration of their ownership of shares and properties. In the next three years, a series of ministers and staffers failed to pass Howard's integrity test and were consigned to political oblivion, but Howard reacted very badly when his code of conduct threatened to end the careers of his old friend Warwick Parer, who was caught with a significant holding of coal shares that he had neglected to declare, and the Queensland Liberal Warren Entsch, who also transgressed the code of conduct. Howard then declared that the code was really only a collection of guidelines, and that proven criminal activities alone would result in ministers' being asked to resign their portfolios.

Enjoying the spoils

The 1996 election campaign had concentrated on the degree to which Paul Keating had become arrogant and out of touch with the lives and aspirations of ordinary Australians. Howard had identified the 'battlers' as a constituency to which he could successfully appeal. 'Battlers' were former ALP supporters who had been left behind by the pace of change and had become frightened and resentful of an ALP that had so clearly abandoned them to their fate. In casting their votes for the coalition, they had looked for an end to extravagances such as $23 000 diningroom tables for the prime ministerial residence when they were suffering economic hardship. But Howard's concern for the views of the battlers apparently disappeared soon after the election when he announced his intention to move his family into Kirribilli House in Sydney rather than live in Canberra on a full-time basis. The coalition advocated that the unemployed should move to areas where work was available or lose their dole, but this was a rule for the 'battlers', not for the prime minister who had no intention of moving to his place of employment in Canberra.

Kirribilli House had been designated over the years to house visiting heads of state and foreign dignitaries, as well as to act as a Sydney residence for the prime minister when federal parliament was not sitting, but Howard elected to maintain it entirely for his own use so as not to disrupt his family or the education of his children. The arrangement included an upgrade of the security arrangements at a cost of well over one million dollars. Nor did his occupation of the residence end once his children had completed their education. He clung on to Kirribilli House as his primary residence while also making use of the Lodge in Canberra when parliament was in session. The alleged extravagance of Paul Keating paled to relative insignificance alongside Howard's self-indulgence. New stairways were fitted to Kirribilli House, and bathrooms were renovated at a cost to the taxpayers of $155 000. New curtains for the loungeroom of the Lodge cost $30 000, new air-conditioning a hefty $162 000, and a gas fire fitted into the already centrally heated room cost $3320. At Kirribilli House, refurbishment of the kitchens and renovations of the staff quarters totalled $35 000, and approximately $40 000 was expended on doing up another bathroom, renovating wardrobes in three bedrooms, and purchasing artworks and expensive pieces of decorative Australiana. By the end of 2002, one of John Howard's major legacies seemed likely to be his incorrigible use of public monies for the support of the Howard family's personal comfort.[4]

Pauline Hanson's One Nation

During the 1996 election campaign, a little-known female candidate for the Liberal Party named Pauline Hanson stood for the Queensland seat of Oxley, centred on the town of Ipswich. A former proprietor of the local fish-and-chip shop, Pauline Hanson represented the small business wing of the Liberal Party. She made some prejudiced and racist remarks during the campaign about Aborigines and Asians, and the Liberals reacted quickly. In damage-control mode, they expelled her from the party. This engendered enormous public sympathy for her, and she won the seat as an independent. Her maiden speech in the House of Representatives touched on the problems of a multicultural Australia with particular reference to alleged special treatment for racial minorities at the expense of mainstream Australia. An enormous furore erupted, with most of the press and Labor politicians taking a hard line of opposition to what they regarded as a worrying revival of Australian racism. In contrast, the coalition government gave tacit support to Pauline Hanson's views and the prime minister revisited his earlier statements of concern about the pace of multicultural change, suggesting that people who opposed Pauline Hanson were seeking to impose their own brand of 'political correctness' on her and were endangering free speech in Australia. Howard's tendency to follow a populist course rather than show leadership on the racial issue reflected the opinion polls which showed that there was considerable sympathy for Pauline Hanson in the wider community. Howard refused to condemn her views, and the result was an explosion of bigotry as Aborigines, Asians, and other migrant minorities came under open attack. The residue of Australia's historic racism was stirred into life by the prime minister's inactivity which provided covert support for Hanson and her followers.

Later in 1996, Pauline Hanson formed a new political party known as One Nation, later Pauline Hanson's One Nation, which launched a populist campaign based upon Australians' increasing distrust of professional politicians. The new party was a paradox, in that it garnered support from an electorate on the basis that it was an anti-political political party and could therefore be trusted whereas the other parties, comprised of professional politicians, could not. One Nation won considerable support throughout rural and urban Australia by attacking welfare payments to Aborigines, the 'Asianisation' of Australia, gun-law reforms that outlawed automatic and semi-automatic firearms, and economic rationalism. Party branches opened in all states, and Pauline Hanson developed into an effective (although sometimes incoherent) media performer. Still John Howard and the coalition in Canberra did nothing, although Liberal state leaders such as Jeff Kennett, the premier of Victoria, recognised the danger posed by Hanson and actively campaigned against her. The ALP, in contrast, had opposed Hanson and One Nation from the outset, and announced that whenever state or federal elections might be held, One Nation candidates would automatically be placed last on all ALP how-to-vote leaflets whatever the political cost. Beazley and the ALP won great kudos from this decision, but Howard and the coalition remained obdurate in their refusal to condemn the One Nation party or its policies.

Early in 1998, a state election in Queensland shocked the coalition, when eleven One Nation candidates won seats in the Legislative Assembly, largely at the expense of Liberal Party and National Party members. The depth of electoral disillusionment with conventional politics was demonstrated by the success of the new party, and the National Party in particular began to fear the loss of many of its federal seats. To win back its waning support, the Howard government began to espouse policy positions that had more in common with One Nation policies than the normal bill of fare of Liberal-led coalitions since the time of Menzies. Aboriginal affairs was one area in which Howard made an unashamed appeal to recapture conservative rural votes from One Nation.

Reconciliation and the Wik judgment

Following the 1992 Mabo decision of the High Court, and the Native Title Act of 1994 (in which the Keating government acknowledged that native title had existed on all Australian land in 1788, and continued to exist on unalienated land), the Aboriginal people had continued to explore the new law, especially the limited criteria under which a successful native title claim could be made. It had been generally understood that the Native Title Act ruled out overlapping titles, and that wherever leases or freehold had been given to settlers, native title had been effectively extinguished. Nevertheless, when the High Court handed down its judgment in the *Wik Peoples v Queensland* case in 1996, the whole area was thrown open to question, for the judges ruled that native title and pastoral leases could coexist, and that a pastoral lease did not necessarily extinguish native title. The National Party was the major partner in the coalition in Queensland, and the northern pastoral interests had become a vital ingredient of the coalition support base. The so-called 'Wik judgment' became a cause of great concern to northern pastoralists, who argued that if native title had not been extinguished by the issuing of a pastoral lease, it might not have been extinguished by other forms of alienation either. Perhaps native title might be found to coexist with mining leases, or freehold title, or other forms of leasehold? The scaremongers even suggested that suburban backyards were now in danger of native title claims. The mining industry feared that the earlier difficulty over Coronation Hill could provide a template for a future that involved endless confrontation between mining companies and Aboriginal people; and the Howard government took the extremist position that the economic consequences of the Wik judgment could prove ruinous to all involved in pastoral and mining enterprises.

The One Nation party's well-known anti-Aboriginal prejudice meant that popular support for the National Party had begun to haemorrhage in rural districts, and the coalition had to act promptly if it was not to lose out to the new extremist party. The government spent the next two years in dealing with the Wik decision, and brought in legislation to provide certainty to the holders of pastoral and mining leases by legislating native title out of existence on all land that had ever been the subject of any form of leasehold tenure. John Howard commented that 'the pendulum had swung too far towards Aborigines and had to be reset'.[5] Aboriginal people and the ALP opposed this eradication of native title, but National Party leader Tim Fischer had promised his rural supporters that the government's Bill would provide 'buckets of extinguishment', and the Wik debate in the Senate generated enormous controversy throughout Australia. Fischer demonstrated the level to which the coalition would sink when he denigrated Aboriginal culture as so backward that it had not even developed a wheeled cart.[6] The final compromise between the government and the independent Brian Harradine from Tasmania in the Senate in July 1998 was in favour of the coalition and provided the certainty that pastoralists had demanded at the expense of the indigenous people. The enactment also stretched beyond the Wik decision and limited native title legislatively to land that had never been alienated. Furthermore, the government's attacks on native title and its determination to wind back the rights granted to Aborigines by the High Court weakened the growing appeal of One Nation by winning the coalition important support in the country areas and urban districts where people were feeling the pinch of privation.

Relations with Aboriginal people continued to decline throughout the Howard government's time in office, and the coalition's intransigence over the Wik issue was echoed during the government's second term by Howard's unwillingness to issue an apology to the nation's indigenous people for the injustices and policies of forced assimilation that had been inflicted upon them since 1788. The kidnapping of Aboriginal children had been government policy in most states of Australia until the second half of the twentieth century, and Aboriginal people mourned the loss of what they termed the 'stolen generations'. The trauma of forcible removal took an enormous toll both mentally and physically on the kidnapped children and their families, and was held to explain, in part, the high rate of suicide brought to light by the Royal Commission into Aboriginal Deaths in Custody which delivered its report in 1995. Very few Aboriginal families were unaffected by the abduction of children, and most Aborigines in modern Australia could point to at least one missing family member. The sense of outrage, therefore, was almost palpable when Howard's minister for Aboriginal Affairs, Senator John Herron, affirmed in parliament in May 2000 the government's view that there was no such thing as 'a stolen generation', because no more than 10% of any generation of Aboriginal children had ever been kidnapped. Howard and Herron stuck to this position, despite a chorus of complaint from Aborigines and academic professionals who argued that the real figure was much higher than this, and that even a 10% abduction rate was unacceptable in any free country. Australian Democrat senator Aden Ridgeway, himself of Aboriginal descent, accused John Howard of deliberate provocation of Aboriginal people for his own political gain.[7] When it later turned out that Herron's submission had actually been written in Howard's office, and that its intention had been to minimise any potential liability for compensation claims from the victims of the kidnappings or their families, Howard's credibility on the race issue was in tatters. On 28 May 2000, more than 200 000 people marched across Sydney Harbour Bridge, led by community leaders, politicians, and clergy, and including former prime ministers from both sides of politics, to show support for reconciliation between Aboriginal people and the rest of the community. John Howard refused to walk himself or to permit any of his ministers to participate, and he continued to withhold the apology that most Aboriginal people maintained was an essential prerequisite to any process of reconciliation. His position on an apology had been described by the conservative *Sydney Morning Herald* twelve months earlier as 'so obtuse as to defy reason'.[8] When the Aboriginal athlete Cathy Freeman, to enormous public acclaim, won the gold medal in the 400-metres sprint at the Olympic Games held in Sydney during September 2000, Howard was confronted by a popular icon who had herself lost relatives as part of the stolen generation. But even this proved incapable of shifting his intransigence.

The goods and services tax revisited

John Howard's statement that he would 'never ever' revive the question of a GST lasted about half-way into his first term as prime minister. Clearly, his undertaking had not been a 'core' promise, and the cynicism regarding politicians and their promises received a further stimulus when he revived the issue and made it the centrepiece of the next election campaign. His majority of twenty-nine seats gave Howard a comfortable cushion of risk, and he revisited the Hewson model for a GST with some confidence. Even if it did frighten the electorate, no government had ever lost an election with such a huge majority under its belt. Moreover, the level of the new tax was set at only 10%—significantly lower than Hewson's attempt to set it at 15%—and the abolition of wholesale taxes accompanied by large reductions in the rates of income tax would sweeten the package. The difference between introducing the new tax with the advantages of incumbency, rather than from opposition, was made plain in the election campaign when Howard's government looted a $70 million scheme that had been originally devised as a fund for worthy community cultural and heritage projects to celebrate the bicentenary of federation in 2001. To ensure transparency, an independent assessment process had been put in place to decide which of the hundreds of applications should receive funding. When 60 proposals had been selected, two ministers, senators Robert Hill and Richard Alston, then intervened to include 16 projects that had not been selected in the list of winners. At least 114 other applications had been ranked ahead of these 16. The intervention occurred three days before Howard called the election, and its overall effect was that three-quarters of the funding for projects in marginal seats went to seats held by coalition members. During the election campaign, 39 winners were announced, 33 of them in coalition seats. In contrast, most of the successful applications from ALP seats were not announced, and the losers were not informed until after the election. In view of the fact that the government's majority was reduced from 29 to 6 in an election that was won with a minority of the total votes cast, this doubtful use of patronage by 'Honest John' Howard might well have enabled the government to sneak back into office.

The electoral arithmetic shows that Howard came perilously close to losing to Kim Beazley's ALP. The coalition came within 1500 votes of losing office in the marginal seats, and could well have done so had it not been for the money doled out via the federation fund. In national terms, after the distribution of preferences, Howard lost the popular vote by more than 200 000 votes. The promise of large tax cuts for the middle and upper classes probably got Howard over the line, but the parties opposed to a GST actually won a majority of the votes cast. The Australian Democrats, however, opted to negotiate with Howard for improvements in the GST and, after the coalition agreed to exempt fresh food from the tax—another thing that Howard had pledged that he would never ever contemplate—the Australian Democrats supported the government's legislation in the Senate and voted the GST into law. The new tax system came into operation on 1 July 2000 and, in the run-up to its imposition, Howard and his treasurer, Peter Costello, spent well over $400 million of public money to fund a propaganda campaign that presented the dubious innovation as a positive achievement for the government. Ironically, it was the possibility of war with Indonesia, rather than the introduction of a new tax, that attracted most attention in the six months before the GST's scheduled starting date.

Relationships in the Asia–Pacific region

Australia's good relations with Indonesia date back to World War II when Indonesian nationalists worked in Australia to help the Allied war effort throw the occupying Japanese out of their country. Once the war was over, Australia supported the establishment of an independent Indonesian state, and resisted the reimposition of colonial rule by the Netherlands. Indeed, Australia was seen by Indonesia as its strongest supporter in its four-year struggle to achieve independence from the Dutch, and Indonesian appreciation of Australian support during their nationalist liberation period provided the basis for Paul Keating's policy of constructive engagement with Australia's largest northern neighbour. When the coalition came to power in 1996, Australia had a security pact with Indonesia, and the two countries undertook joint military exercises together. Indonesian soldiers were trained in Australia, and the close personal relationship between Indonesian President Soeharto and Prime Minister Keating was reflected by similarly close professional and personal relationships between the senior military personnel in both countries.

This was the situation when the Howard government came to office after the election in 1996, and the incoming coalition administration wasted no time in assuring Indonesia that it wished for a similarly close rapport between the two nations. Deputy Prime Minister Tim Fischer travelled to Indonesia soon after the election, and crowned his first official visit to that country by acclaiming President Soeharto at an official reception as 'perhaps the world's greatest figure in the second half of the century'.[9] Unfortunately, the cosy relationship was destined to founder on the rocks of Indonesia's annexation of East Timor, which the Whitlam government had supported in 1975.

The East Timorese had suffered terribly under the Japanese occupation during the war, but this had not stopped the Timorese from offering substantial aid and assistance to Australian commandos operating behind the Japanese lines. For their support of Australian forces, an estimated 60 000 East Timorese had met their deaths at the hands of the Japanese, and most Australians felt that they owed East Timor a debt of gratitude. When Indonesia invaded East Timor in 1975, and when the East Timorese resistance movement continued to resist incorporation into the Republic of Indonesia through a campaign of guerilla warfare, an irritant had been injected into the relationship between Australia and Indonesia. Moreover, official documents released in September 2000 made it abundantly clear that Australian governments of both political complexions had been complicit (although secretive) in accepting Indonesia's aggression during 1975, a matter about which the Australian public had been deliberately misinformed for the following 25 years.[10] As long as President Soeharto and the Indonesian armed forces remained firmly in control, East Timor remained a minor irritant. But, in 1998, Soeharto's grip on power began to slip and, eventually, he was replaced by an interim civilian president, B.J. Habibie. It was the decline of Soeharto and the influence of Indonesia's military that encouraged the East Timorese to agitate with renewed intensity for independence and, after considerable stalling from Indonesia and a great deal of thuggery and murder from Indonesian-funded militias in East Timor, the people voted overwhelmingly for an existence outside Indonesia.

Descriptions from Australian commentators and observers of Indonesia's violent attempts to retain East Timor as a province had raised considerable sympathy for the plight of the East Timorese, and the fall of Soeharto made a change in Australian policy towards Indonesia imperative. The existing accommodation with Indonesia had delivered considerable benefits to Australia in the form of increased trade, expanding educational and business links, and political stability between Australia and a nation of more than 210 million people. The rising tide of public support for East Timor, and the hostility directed towards Indonesian military violations of human rights in East Timor, required careful management at the Australian end if these gains were not to be placed in jeopardy. Unfortunately, East Timor collapsed into anarchy, and the Australian government found itself forced by public opinion into the leadership of an international peacekeeping force known as 'Interfet' (International Force for East Timor) comprised mostly of Australian soldiers that landed in East Timor to protect the people from the violence of the Indonesian-backed militias. The Interfet force deployed rapidly and, for the next three months, in a magnificent display of discipline and proactive soldiering, it held the militias at bay until a United Nations' peacekeeping force could be assembled and transported to East Timor to relieve the Australians.

The effect of Interfet on relations between Australia and Indonesia was disastrous, and Howard's use of the crisis to improve his political position in Australia became the immediate cause of a diplomatic crisis. Howard announced that Interfet was in East Timor to defend what Australia thought was right. The Australian public demanded a military involvement for reasons of morality, and Howard provided it. But the solution finally had to be found in a political outcome. Australia, with a population of 19 million people, could not afford a military conflict with Indonesia's 210 million people. Australia's best interests were served by peace and stability in the region, but Howard's enunciation of the conflict in cultural and moral terms of right and wrong was designed for a domestic Australian audience. Howard also described Australia as a 'deputy sheriff' for the United States, and Indonesia resented this description of the situation as a form of cultural arrogance involving a veiled threat. When Howard went further and pointed out that, in his opinion, previous Australian governments (presumably including the Fraser government in which he had served as treasurer) had been too interested in promoting a special relationship between Australia and Indonesia at the expense of what Australia knew to be right, the response was swift. Indonesia abrogated the security treaty, and a relationship based on years of careful diplomacy was lost. Mobs in Jakarta stoned the Australian embassy, and the Australian flag was ceremonially burnt and trampled upon in the streets of Indonesia's capital. One effect of the special relationship had been that Australia's expenditure on defence had fallen to the lowest proportion of gross domestic product for 60 years, so an immediate outcome from the fallout with Indonesia was a dramatic increase in military expenditure in the budget for 2000, with a similar increase projected for at least the next four to five years.

Relationships with Indonesia declined dramatically. The newly elected Indonesian president, Wahid, refused to visit Australia and, in May 2000, the Indonesian airforce scrambled warplanes to intercept and confront four unarmed Australian jet fighters and a refuelling tanker in mid air over the ocean off East Timor. What Indonesians saw as Australia's humiliation of the Indonesian military had produced a combustible situation. Despite the Australian fighters having the necessary clearances from Jakarta, the two countries were within a hair's breadth of a disaster. Howard's depiction of the disagreement as a cultural one in which only he of all Australia's leaders, both Labor and Liberal, was prepared to do what was right, played into the hands of Australia's most inveterate enemy in the region, the prime minister of Malaysia, Mahathir Mohamad, who described Australia's attitude to non-European societies as belligerent. In June 2000, President Wahid gave tacit endorsement to Mahathir's accusation when he pointedly informed Howard that it was Indonesia's belief that Asian countries needed to develop a common cultural identity and to act collectively. From 1996 to mid 2000, Australia's hitherto successful engagement with its East Asian neighbours faltered and collapsed in the hands of a prime minister whose focus on short-term domestic political advantage precluded any sense of vision concerning the country's long-term needs for stability and peace in a potentially dangerous part of the world. In June 2000, Howard and President Wahid met on neutral ground in Japan as they each attended the funeral of the Japanese prime minister, and the Indonesian president expressed a cautious desire for the relationship to be improved, although he refused to set any date for a visit to Australia, and Howard continued to refuse to visit Indonesia. The fragility of the former friendship between the two countries, and Indonesian suspicions concerning the Australian government's attitude to the Indonesian province of Irian Jaya—formerly Netherlands New Guinea—was demonstrated at this meeting by Howard having to reassure President Wahid that the Australian government did not desire to destabilise Indonesia and did not support the local independence movement in that troubled province.[11] This obvious mistrust contrasted markedly with the warmth of the welcome extended by President Wahid to the ALP leader Kim Beazley when he had visited Jakarta in the preceding month.

Extinguishing the republic

In 1995, when John Howard was resurrected as leader of the Liberal Party, he found himself facing a prime minister who was an avowed republican, and who had promised, if re-elected in 1996, to go to an indicative plebiscite on whether Australians wanted an Australian national as head of state or wanted to retain the British monarch in that role. Howard accepted the idea of a people's convention to discuss the republican issue which his predecessor, the hapless Alexander Downer, had made Liberal policy. Howard therefore promised that, if the coalition won office, he would call such a convention, and if it came up with a majority in favour of a republic he would place the issue before the public in a referendum. In February 1998, a half-elected, half-nominated constitutional convention met in Canberra, and eventually resolved in favour of a republic with a president who was to be elected by a joint sitting of the members of the federal parliament. Because it was an essentially undemocratic body, the convention's recommendation was flawed from the start, but it gave the monarchist Howard just the outcome for which he had hoped.

The ALP had promised to give the people a chance to make an in-principle decision on whether they desired to replace the British monarch with an Australian head of state. Such a question could easily have been put and, in the event of an affirmative response, a series of republican alternatives could then have been voted upon and the constitution altered accordingly at future referenda. But Howard determined to bypass the simple plebiscite on whether a change to an Australian head of state was desired, and insisted that voters had to say either 'Yes' or 'No' to a head of state appointed by politicians only. In other words, the referendum was rigged from the start to produce a negative result. Howard also knew that in the political history of Australia no referendum had ever succeeded if had been formally opposed by any serious political leader, and certainly no referendum had ever been passed that had been opposed by the prime minister of the day. He deemed such political chicanery to be necessary, however, because public opinion polls showed that there was overwhelming support for an Australian head of state, and any simple plebiscite along those lines would have produced a very large majority. By manipulating and undermining the entire process—from insisting that half the members of the convention be nominated, to making the voting for the convention purely voluntary, to forcing a referendum on a form of words that gave more power to politicians—Howard demeaned the process and his office.

In the event, the prime minister's spoiling tactics worked well, and the referendum failed in all states, attaining about 45% support nationally. The Australian people despise politicians, and any referendum that could be presented by interested parties as increasing the power of politicians was bound to fail. Howard gave aid and comfort to some of his right-wing ministers and to the conservative monarchists to mount a campaign of opposition that focused on the untrustworthiness of politicians, and electors were confronted by the outlandish spectacle of government ministers making public speeches to the effect that they could not be trusted, and even that Howard himself might connive in a deal with the leader of the opposition to make some crony president. The 'No' case, which Howard supported, could only increase the mistrust and discredit of politicians in Australia. Public opinion makes it clear that a republic will come inevitably at the hands of Howard's successors as coalition leader—the frontrunning Liberal heir, Peter Costello, is a republican—or from the next ALP government. Again, a trickster's short-term political advantage had triumphed over any sense of vision or feeling for the aspirations of the rising generations.

A 'Pacific solution' to a refugee problem

These themes were revisited and reinforced in the run-up to the federal election in November 2001. In March of that year, the coalition had lagged behind the ALP by twenty points in the public opinion polls, and seemed headed for a heavy defeat. However, things began to change rapidly in August when a Norwegian container ship, MV *Tampa*, rescued 234 Afghan and Middle-Eastern boat people from their sinking vessel in Indonesia's territorial waters. They had been part of a growing flood of illegal immigrants smuggled into Australia by people smuggling criminals based in Indonesia and throughout South-East Asia.

The Norwegian captain elected to sail into Australian waters and to attempt to land his unlooked-for cargo on Christmas Island off the northern coast of Western Australia. A major political and diplomatic emergency ensued which permitted the coalition to reverse completely the political momentum, and the prime minister to live up to his earlier self-description of being 'Lazarus with a triple bypass' by snatching victory from a seemingly impossible position.

The context for this miraculous recovery was an increasing tide of hostility over the previous decade in Australia's largest cities directed against immigrants of Islamic background. Much of this had been caused by popular reaction against gangs of young Muslim men who stood accused of a long list of antisocial behaviours, including a heavy involvement in the distribution of illegal substances, aggressive confrontations with police who attempted to enforce the law, deliberately targeting non-Islamic girls for pack rape attacks during which the victims were taunted with being 'Aussies', and subjecting police, schoolteachers, people of Asian appearance, and ordinary Australians to physical violence and attack. Members of such gangs amounted to a tiny minority of the total Muslim community in Australia, but the publicity accorded to their activities provoked a more general distrust of all people from an Islamic culture.

The arrival of the *Tampa* in Australian waters crystallised and focused this rising concern because the rescued people were all Muslims, and the government linked a harsh policy against 'boatpeople' to the revulsion in the wider community against what was perceived as Muslim lawlessness. The so-called 'Pacific solution' was the outcome of this process of political opportunism, and so strong had public perceptions become, that the ALP meekly offered full bipartisan support. The 'Pacific solution' prohibited the *Tampa* boatpeople and all boatloads of refugees thereafter, from landing (even temporarily) in any Australian territory. Instead, Australia searched for small Pacific nations that would, in return for a handsome fee, agree to offer temporary sanctuary to the boatpeople in internment camps while their claims for refugee status were investigated. Only after that process had been exhausted would those who passed the checks be permitted to request entrance into Australia.

To enforce the new policy, the Royal Australian Navy received orders to patrol the oceans to Australia's north to intercept illegal migrant vessels and persuade them to turn back to the Indonesian ports from which they had sailed. The *Tampa* was boarded by Australian Special Air Services commandos who then sailed the ship to the island of Nauru which, in return for a payment amounting to many millions of dollars, had agreed to become the first Pacific holding camp. Meanwhile, the government began to sound out other Pacific states such as Papua New Guinea, Fiji, Solomon Islands, and Kiribati, to ascertain whether they would be interested in following Nauru's lead. Beazley, the ALP leader, followed every twist and turn of Howard's government in this episode, and fully supported the policy of excluding all Islamic boatpeople who arrived illegally through the operations of the people smugglers.

When Muslim terrorists attacked the United States on 11 September 2001, the very real threats posed by Osama bin Ladin's international terrorist organisation reinforced the already combustible mix of anti-Islamic sentiment in Australia. Islamic terrorism abroad, Islamic crime within Australia, and illegal Islamic boatpeople came together in timely fashion on the eve of an election that John Howard hitherto appeared to have had no chance of winning. In response to the attack by terrorists on the World Trade Center in New York and on the Pentagon in Washington, Howard immediately offered America the unequivocal support of Australia and promised full military assistance to the extent of its capabilities. Beazley supported the policy on behalf of the opposition.

The election campaign began in October, and Beazley found it virtually impossible to gain traction when campaigning on domestic issues (such as education, public health, and aged care) while a war was going on in Afghanistan to which Howard had already committed Australian combat forces. The media concentrated their attentions on reporting the progress of the 'War against Terrorism', and Howard made frequent reference during the course of the campaign to the distinct possibility that there would be Australian casualties once the troops arrived in the war zone and engaged the forces of Osama bin Ladin's Al Qaeda terrorist network and the Taliban troops of the Afghan government. Incumbency proved to be a great advantage to the prime minister, as did the refusal of the ALP to do anything more than echo the policies of the coalition in the major areas of military support for

America and the exclusion of Islamic boatpeople.

During the campaign, illegal immigrant vessels continued to turn up in the waters off northern Australia. When one boat arrived off Christmas Island and the navy ordered it to return to Indonesia, the people on board allegedly threatened to throw their children overboard into the sea. They then sabotaged their vessel, causing it to sink. Photographs soon appeared, depicting naval personnel rescuing children in the water, and the government deliberately allowed the inaccurate impression to emerge that some of the boatpeople had actually carried out their threat to throw their children overboard. The 'children overboard affair', as it became known, contributed to the Australian public's growing sense of outrage at, and alienation from, an Islamic culture that would seek so cold-bloodedly to gain an advantage by putting its own children's lives at risk. The full extent of the subterfuge was not revealed until September 2002 when a Senate committee of inquiry reported that government officials had been informed, on more than ten occasions at the time, that the reports of children having been thrown overboard were inaccurate. In this case, truth certainly had become the first casualty of war.[12]

On 10 November 2001, Howard and the coalition secured a third term in office. It amounted to a personal triumph for the prime minister and afforded a wonderful endorsement of his gritty determination and refusal ever to admit defeat. The coalition not only retained government, but also secured a nationwide upswing in its support of around 2%, while the Beazley-led opposition lost a similar percentage. Labor's primary vote actually collapsed to the lowest level since the defeat of the Scullin government in the Great Depression of the 1930s, as many former supporters, reacting to Beazley's policy of full support for the government on boatpeople and the war, delivered their first preferences to minor parties and independents who opposed the current trends, and cast only their second or third preferences in favour of the ALP.

Howard had proved to be a formidable and ruthless campaigner who deliberately used the issues of race and war to his electoral advantage. The coalition's final week of advertising had saturated the media with images of the prime minister with a clenched and raised fist proclaiming that: 'We will decide who comes to this country and the circumstances in which they come!'. The policy approach was deplored by two former prime ministers—the Liberal Malcolm Fraser who commented that Howard's use of the race issue had put Australian politics back a century, and the ALP's Keating who claimed that Howard had stained the soul of the nation.[13]

The election result and the bipartisan policy of the 'Pacific solution' were greeted with considerable reserve in some parts of the world. The London newspaper the *Financial Times* editorialised that Howard's victory was 'squalid', and a top adviser to the Indonesian government commented that, for the nations of South-East Asia, the Howard win bore witness to the fact that Australia had revealed itself to be a deeply racist country that risked becoming a pariah throughout the region.

After the election dust had settled, the ALP quickly replaced Beazley with his deputy Simon Crean, the son of the former Whitlam treasurer Frank Crean, and elected Jenny Macklin to the deputy's position—the first woman to hold a leadership position in the federal ALP. Crean and Macklin inherited the difficult task of reforming the party

An ALP dynasty, Simon Crean, federal ALP leader, with his brother (now deceased), and his father, former Whitlam treasurer Frank Crean.

structures and revisiting the policy platform in an attempt to understand why the ALP had been abandoned by so many of its traditional supporters who had hitherto been regarded as 'rusted on'.

Entering the third millennium

As the third millennium of the Christian era begins, there seems to be very little common wealth left to be shared by the members of the Commonwealth of Australia. All the signs are of division and decline. In 1901, liberals, countryfolk, and members of the labour movement shared a common belief in the future of the new nation—a common belief that made them essentially optimists. The 'fair go' ethic had become embedded in the national culture and seemed to presage the realisation of the great Australian dream of the establishment of a democratic and egalitarian society. A century or more later, the optimism has gone, and the 'golden soil and wealth for toil' that are celebrated in the national anthem seem a cruel dream to many in the community. Australia's nineteen million people are more divided than they have been since the convict days, and the easy egalitarianism that rode on the back of national abundance has been replaced by a fearfulness about a future in which the class divisions of the old world—which many had hoped had been left behind in 1901—have been replicated and even strengthened in the deepening economic, racial, and social fragmentation of modern Australian society. In June 2000, the national newspaper, the *Australian*, led with a banner headline that announced 'The Death of the Fair Go', and highlighted the despair and alienation of those sectors of the community—such as the rural population and the urban working poor—who had become casualties of change and fallen behind the mainstream in the new privatised and economically rationalised economy. The divisions were highlighted during September 2000 by violent rioting on the streets of Melbourne by large crowds of people demonstrating against economic globalisation—as a result of which both police and demonstrators needed hospitalisation.[14]

Similar civil disobedience and confrontation with riot police occurred again in Sydney in November 2002 as unruly mobs took to the streets in protest against the World Trade Organization whose leaders were meeting to advance the cause of economic globalisation.[15]

Rural Australia is in a parlous state, and in the grip of the worst El Niño drought since records were recorded. In New South Wales, only 1% of the state is drought-free.[16] In October 2002, Queensland experienced the largest duststorm ever witnessed, in which millions of tonnes of priceless topsoil disappeared out over the Tasman Sea. Two out of every five remaining farmers are reduced to reliance on social welfare payments to survive, and a huge divide is opening between urban and rural Australia. Many regional and outer suburban areas are in danger of collapse if predicted interest rate rises cut into incomes and assets that have declined rapidly in real value. In one region that covers a third of New South Wales, the average value of the family farm had slumped from $500 000 in 1990 to less than $200 000 at the end of the twentieth century.[17] A decline in wool and commodity prices, the ravages inflicted by the cycles of El Niño, and large-scale land degradation and salination caused by inappropriate farming methods and tree clearances have devastated rural communities in all states. Many farmers have been forced into negative incomes by the decline, and rising indebtedness will force many of those who are still hanging on to walk off their properties. Nationally, over the past thirty years, the number of families able to wrest a living from a farm has dropped by 10 000, and a further 20% are expected to give up the struggle in the next decade.

The devastation of the farm sector has been reflected in the destruction of the social and economic infrastructure that is essential to maintain viable communities in the bush. In New South Wales alone, in the past decade of economic rationalisation, more than a hundred towns and communities outside Sydney have lost their last bank branches in a process that has resulted in the disappearance of almost a quarter of the state's rural bank branches.

The twelve postcode areas with the lowest average personal income in New South Wales are all in rural areas, whereas the five top areas are all in Sydney. From 1988 to 1995 rural New South Wales lost more than 5000 hospital beds, and thirty hospitals were closed, downgraded, or privatised. Schools, public transport, and other businesses were all affected by the decline, and they too have wound back or discontinued services. Internal migration bleeds the younger and more mobile population off to the larger towns and cities, and the average age of Australian farmers is now 56 and still rising. The stress of living in rural Australia is reflected in the increasing criminal assault rates, which are now outstripping those of the capital cities. For example, in Sydney in 1998, there were about 40 sexual assaults per 100 000 people; in the far west of New South Wales there are now 160 sexual assaults per 100 000 people.

Even within the capital cities, the economic chasm between the haves and the have-nots is closer to nineteenth-century figures rather than to those that applied for most of the twentieth century. In the well-to-do areas and those affected by high-tech investment and industries, average household incomes have continued to rise. But in those parts of the cities that have relied on small-scale manufacturing, textiles, and metal products—the so-called 'rust-bucket' industries—household incomes have barely moved in the past ten years. In 1999, the Australian Local Government Association issued a comprehensive report covering all 628 local government areas of Australia, and the story was the same throughout the nation. The loss of services and facilities affected cities as well as rural areas, and the falling morale and demoralisation was spread from one side of the country to the other. In all, since 1993, about 1800 bank branches have closed across Australia, with the concomitant loss of about 40 000 jobs. Most of these branches and jobs came from the cities. The situation is similar with the Telstra corporation. In March 2000 the chief executive of the partially privatised corporation announced that a further 10 000 jobs would be shed by the telecommunications giant, in addition to the 20 000–30 000 jobs that had already gone. Hatred for politicians of all parties is one of the by-products of a situation like this, as is the rising support in urban as well as rural Australia for parties such as Pauline Hanson's One Nation with its scapegoating of easy targets such as Aborigines, Muslims, and Asians as bearing responsibility for people's suffering. John Howard's flirtation with the populist bigotries of One Nation might have brought him some electoral advantage, but at incalculable cost to the fabric of the community.

Australia's division into two nations of haves and have-nots has resulted in a decline in the legitimacy of governments. Economic rationalisation has been practised by both sides of the political divide, and this has entrenched cynicism and disengagement from the political system. Add to that the shallow and unworthy behaviour of John Howard as prime minister and the combative arrogance of his ALP predecessor Paul Keating, and the disenchantment with electoral politics becomes understandable. The dislike of the community for the established political parties can be seen in their continuing decline in membership and the rising support for fringe groups such as One Nation and independents. The two largest parties are literally dying on their feet. Howard's Liberals are beset with a rapid decline in members, and the situation in New South Wales mirrors developments in the other states. In May 2000, more than 80% of Liberal Party members in New South Wales were aged over 55, and almost two-thirds of the membership was 65 or older. In 1975, the state branch had a membership of about 50 000 which, by the turn of the century, had fallen to a rump of only 6000 active members. When the Liberal Party held its national convention in Melbourne early in 2000, it was so short of money that it permitted the tobacco company Philip Morris to sponsor its convention dinner. Nor was the ALP in much better shape. The grassroots of the party lie in the trade union movement, but that now represents merely 25% of the workforce and is declining rapidly. The branch structure has been corrupted by wholesale branch stacking to produce private factional fiefdoms and safe preselections for favoured candidates. The rampant use of ethnic groups to stack a branch has angered and alienated traditional members who actually did the hard routine work of manning polling booths on election days and doorknocking and letterboxing on behalf of Labor candidates. They have withdrawn their labour and the party has increasing difficulty in manning its polling booths. Moreover, the ALP has long ceased to be a political party in which a coal miner or a train driver might one day become prime minister. At the beginning of the twenty-first century there were only three Labor members of the House of Representatives who had not previously worked as union officials, political staffers, or public servants, and two of these had been lawyers with well-established trade union practices.

Of the smaller parties, the National Party has been losing members to the One Nation movement as the party's representatives in Canberra embrace the economic rationalist dogma despite its enormous human cost in rural areas. The Australian Democrats still retain a comparatively large number of members who engage in democratic consultations before policy changes can be undertaken. It is also true, however, that the Australian Democrats' cooperation with the coalition to bring in the GST cost the party dearly in terms of membership numbers and support. The untidy disposal of a popular leader Senator Natasha Stott Despoja by a disaffected group of four Democrat senators in August 2002 robbed the party of credibility,. The Greens continue to gather strength. The party won an additional Senate seat at the expense of the Australian Democrats in New South Wales at the 2001 election and, on 26 October 2002, the party secured its first seat in the House of Representatives when it won the previously safe seat of Cunningham from the ALP. It continues to garner support because it is a party of strong convictions, the members and leadership of which are prepared to support policies they believe to be right rather than popular. So the Greens oppose the use of Australian troops in the Middle East, and have denounced the proposed American invasion of Iraq as being a ploy by the United States to gain control over some of the world's most significant oil reserves.

When the war on terrorism reached Australia's own back door with a terrorist bomb explosion in Bali, Indonesia, on 12 October 2002, a sense of deep shock and profound sadness marked the passage of Australia from being a spectator of events into a prime participant. The initial sympathy accorded to the more than one hundred dead Australian victims by our neighbours in the region soon mutated into a barely disguised conviction that Australia's Howard-led posture of disengagement from, and cultural hostility towards, Islamic countries in the region and in the wider world had brought its own reward in the form of Australian civilian casualties of Islamic terrorism. Howard's uncritical support of the United States attempts to disarm the Iraqi dictator Saddam Hussein and to restart the Gulf War with or without the sanction of the United Nations, his dispatch of troops to join the United States forces in Afghanistan, and his involvement in humiliating Indonesia and causing that proud people to lose the province of East Timor, all combined to make Australia and Australians a target for terrorist attack. His policies to exclude Islamic boatpeople only exacerbated the hostility. Howard always refused to acknowledge the connections between these various areas of international policy and his domestic migration policies, and insisted that each was a discrete entity to be handled separately from the others. The reality was brought home to Australia by Osama bin Ladin himself, in a special taped message that he prepared for broadcast over the airwaves of the Middle East:[18]

> What do your governments want by allying themselves with the criminal gang in the White House against Muslims? Do your governments not know that the White House gangsters are the biggest butchers of this age? . . . What do your governments want from their alliance with America in attacking us in Afghanistan? I mention in particular Britain, France, Italy, Canada, Germany and Australia . . . We warned Australia before not to join in the war in Afghanistan, and against its despicable effort to separate East Timor. It ignored the warning until it woke up to the sounds of explosions in Bali.

When Australian police and intelligence operatives raided the Sydney, Perth, and Melbourne homes of Islamic migrants suspected of having links with the terrorist networks, and when the government issued travel warnings advising Australians not to visit Indonesia and other parts of the region, the response was swift and unforgiving. President Megawati of Indonesia suggested that Australia had overreacted to the Bali bombings and ought be more sensitive to Indonesian feelings, while Australia's most inveterate critic, Mahathir Mohamad of Malaysia, proposed to issue a travel warning to all Muslims to avoid a country such as Australia where they would be in danger of attack and of having their front doors battered down by the Australian authorities.[19]

As the nation celebrated the centenary of federation and began the first decade of the new millennium, a sense of impatience with the status quo and a feeling that the country had become torpid became discernible. John Howard had been a stop-gap leader called upon by a desperate Liberal Party in a time of great failure and tribulation. His dour stubbornness, his cunning, and his shrewdness proved appropriate for that time, but he has clearly passed his use-by date, and the time has surely come for him to resign and make way for a younger and more dynamic generation of leadership. In July 2000, Howard led a large delegation of Labor and conservative politicians to London to celebrate the centenary of the passage of the Australian constitution through the British parliament. One hundred years earlier, an excited and exhilarated Alfred Deakin had watched over the passage of the Bill and celebrated the realisation of his vision for an Australian nation. A century later, yet another Liberal leader dined with the royal family and tugged the forelock in the approved fashion, while Labor premiers did the rounds of the London financial world touting for investment and demonstrating to their fellow Australians in the starkest possible manner how far out of step with their hopes and aspirations all political leaders had become. People understood that, at the national level, there could be no moving forward on domestic issues such as reconciliation with the Aborigines or the republic while John Howard remained prime minister. Nor could the vital rebuilding process be undertaken to repair the damage to our reputation as a tolerant non-racist country throughout South-East Asia. The prime minister's limitations make him a good wartime leader, but render him apparently incapable of vision or inspiration in normal times, and the community is already looking past him at his likely successors, both Liberal and Labor, to see who could most likely fill the leadership void in a way that will allow them to shed their cynicism and disenchantment and who might get the nation moving again in the direction of goals that encourage hope in place of despair, engagement instead of withdrawal, and true and effective conciliation of the interests of all members of the Australian Commonwealth. In the meantime, the country drifts, stagnates, and waits.

The picture is not entirely without hope, however, and the basic strengths of Australian society and the inherent decency of its people cannot be overestimated. It remains a strongly democratic country with a population that still responds to appeals to its idealism and generosity of spirit. The rising generation is well educated, sophisticated, and well aware of what needs to be done to actualise the potential of a land that the national anthem celebrates as abounding 'with nature's gifts, of beauty rich and rare'. Renewal, when generational change finally occurs, might well unleash an explosion of energy that will burst the logjam and permit the nation to resume its interrupted progress towards the vision of a tolerant, fair-minded, and decent society for all its citizens—a vision that so energised and activated the men and women of the six colonies who campaigned to bring the country together in the aptly named 'Commonwealth of Australia' in 1901. Australia needs to throw off the corrosive self-doubt and arthritic conservatism of current times and the recent past, and to recapture the free-flowing, radical, and inclusive self-confidence of 1901.

Notes

Chapter 1 Aboriginal Australia

1. Dampier, William, *A New Voyage Round the World*, vol. I, 1698. cited by Clark, M. (ed) 1971, *Sources of Australian History*, Oxford University Press, London, p. 26.

Chapter 2 In Search of the Great South Land

1. See McIntyre, K.G. 1977, *The Secret Discovery of Australia*, Souvenir Press, London. See also Fitzgerald, Lawrence 1984, *Java La Grande: The Portuguese Discovery of Australia*, The Publishers Pty Ltd, Hobart.

2. Harlow, Vincent T. 1952, *The Founding of the Second British Empire 1763–1793*, Longmans, London, vol. 1, p. 15.

3. Dampier, William, cited by Clark, M. 1971, *Sources of Australian History*, Oxford University Press, London, pp 24–7.

4. Purry, Jean Pierre, cited by Mackaness, George (ed.) 1943, *Some Proposals for Establishing Colonies in the South Seas*, Australian Historical Monographs, vol. XI, Review Publications Pty Ltd, Sydney, pp 15–20.

5. de Brosses, Charles, cited in Mackaness 1943, op. cit. (note 4 above), pp. 21–34.

6. Marchant, Leslie 1982, *France Australe*, Artlook Books, Perth, p. 64.

7. On the question of secret oral instructions to Anson and Britain's grab for new territory, see Steven, Margaret 1983, *Trade, Tactics and Territory*, Melbourne University Press, Melbourne, chs 1–2.

8. Steven 1983, op. cit. (note 7 above), pp 19–20. Spanish commentators were in no doubt that British colonisation of New South Wales constituted a military threat of major significance to Spanish America. See King, Robert J. 1990, *The Secret History of the Convict Colony: Alexandro Malaspina's Report on the British Settlement of New South Wales*, George Allen & Unwin, Sydney.

9. Viceroy to James Cook, 27 November 1768, *Historical Records of New Zealand*, vol. 2, pp 20 and 72.

10. Frost, Alan 1980, *Convicts and Empire: A Naval Question*, Oxford University Press, Melbourne, p. XIII.

11. Ibid., pp 1367.

12. Lord Sydney to the Lords Commissioners of the Treasury, 18 August 1786, *HRNSW*, vol. 1, pt. 2, pp 14–19.

13. Lord Sydney to the Lords Commissioners of the Treasury, 9 February 1785, cited by Frost 1980, op. cit. (note 10 above), p. 31.

14. Clarke, Frank G. 1998, *The Big History Question: Snapshots of Australian History*, Simon & Schuster, Sydney, pp 82–8.

15. Report of Select Committee of the House of Commons, cited by Frost 1980, op. cit. (note 10 above), p. 43.

16. Ibid., p. 132.

17. *Times*, 10 September 1786.

18. Phillip to Sydney, 15 May 1788, *Historical Records of Australia*, series 1, vol. 1, p.18.

19. *HRNSW*, vol. 1, pt. 2, p. 24.

20. McIntyre 1977, op. cit. (note 1 above), pp 196–7.

21. Tench, Watkin, cited by Clark, M. 1971, *Sources of Australian History*, p. 86.

22. Ibid., p. 86.

23. Collins, David 1798, *An Account of the English Colony in New South Wales*, A.H. & A.W. Reed, London, vol. 1, p. 8.

24. Tench, op. cit. (note 22 above), p. 85.

25. Ibid., p. 69; and Collins 1798, op. cit. (note 24 above), pp 53 and 496.

26. Butlin, Noel 1983, *Our Original Aggression*, George Allen & Unwin, Sydney, p. 20.

27. See Clarke, Frank G. 2000, *The Big History Question: Snapshots of Australian History*, Simon & Schuster, Sydney, vol. 2, pp 10–14. See also debate between Noel Butlin and Charles Wilson in *Quadrant*, March 1985, June 1985 and July 1985.

28. The economic structure of early New South Wales has been exhaustively outlined in Hainsworth, D.R. 1972, *The Sydney Traders*, Cassell, Sydney.

29. Governor King to CO, 8 November 1801, *HRA*, series 1, vol. 3, p. 322.

30. The work on alcohol consumption is by Butlin, Noel, 'Yo, Ho, Ho and How Many Bottles of Rum?', *Working Papers in Economic History*, ANU, 1982, Working Paper No. 3. For the work on women, see Robinson, Portia 1985, *The Hatch and Brood of Time: A Study of the First Generation of Native-Born White Australians 1788–1828*, Oxford University Press, vol. 1, ch. 3. See also Robinson, Portia 1987, *The Women of Botany Bay*, Penguin, Ringwood, passim.

31. Perrot, Monica 1983, *A Tolerable Good Success:Economic Opportunities for Women in New South Wales 1788–1830*, Hale & Iremonger, Sydney.

32. Phillip to Grenville, 17 July 1790, *HRA*, series 1, vol. 1, pp 195–7.

33. Tench, op. cit. (note 22 above), p. 100,

34. King to Hobart, 9 November and 23 November 1802, *HRA*, series 1, vol. 3, pp 698–9 and 737.

35. Memorandum of a proposed settlement in Bass's Straits, nd, *HRA*, series 3, vol. 1, pp 1–3.

Chapter 3   Australia All Over: Completing the Conquest

1. Ellis, M.H. 1973, *John Macarthur*, Angus & Robertson, Sydney, p. 260.

2. Bligh to Sir Joseph Banks, 7 February 1807, cited by Evatt, H.V. 1965, *Rum Rebellion,* Angus & Robertson, Sydney, p. 71.

3. Macquarie to Bathurst, 27 July 1822, *HRA*, series 1, vol. 10.

4. Robson, Lloyd 1976, *The Convict Settlers of Australia*, Melbourne University Press, Melbourne, ch. 5.

5. Hirst, J.B. 1983, *Convict Society and its Enemies*, George Allen & Unwin, Sydney, pp 57–69.

6. Clark, M. 1980, 'The origins of the convicts transported to Eastern Australia 1787–1852', *Occasional Writings and Speeches*, Fontana/Collins, Melbourne, pp 94–143. See also Chesney, Kellow 1970, *The Victorian Underworld*, Penguin, Harmondsworth, passim.

7. *Australian*, 19 January 1826.

8. *Australian*, 12 January 1826.

9. *Monitor*, 14 July 1826.

10. *Sydney Gazette*, 18 July 1826.

11. *Times*, 17 January 1829.

12. Stannage, C.T. 1979, *The People of Perth*, Perth City Council, Perth, pp 19–23.

Chapter 4 Agrarian Ideology vs Pastoral Reality

1. Clarke, F.G. 1977, *The Land of Contrarieties:British Attitudes to the Australian Colonies 1828–1855*, Melbourne University Press, Melbourne, pp 120–44.

2. Ibid., p. 124.

3. *Sydney Gazette*, 28 April 1835.

4. Stanley, A.P. 1846, *The Life and Correspondence of Thomas Arnold*, B.T. Fellowes, London, p. 386.

5. Glenelg to Bourke, 30 November 1835, *HRA*, series 1, vol. 18, p. 202.

6. Gawler to Glenelg, 22 January 1839, *Despatches of the Governor of South Australia to the Secretary of State for Colonies.*

7. Glenelg to Bourke, 13 April 1836, *HRA*, series 1, vol. 18, p. 379.

8. Figures from Burroughs, Peter 1967, *Britain and Australia 1831–1855: A Study in Imperial Relations and Crown lands Administration*, Oxford University Press, Oxford, Appendix 2.

9. Stanley to Gipps, 5 September 1842, CO 202/45.

10. Clarke 1997, op. cit. (note 1 above), p. 94.

11. Serle, Geoffrey 1963, *The Golden Age*, Melbourne University Press, Melbourne, p. 168.

Chapter 5 The Long Boom

1. *Empire*, 21 October 1861.

2. *Sydney Morning Herald*, 16 September 1861.

3. Rutherford, J. 1961, *Sir George Grey KCB, 1812–1898: A Study in Colonial Government*, Heinemann, London, p. 493.

4. Clark, C.M.H. 1979, *A History of Australia*, vol. 4, Melbourne University Press, Melbourne, ch. 9.

5. Clarke, Frank G. 1998, *The Big History Question: Snapshots of Australian History*, Simon & Schuster, Sydney, pp. 43–6.

6. Rutherford 1961, op. cit. (note 3 above), pp 562–4.

7. Cusack, F. 1973, *Bendigo:A History*, Heinemann, Melbourne, pp 101–2.

8. This episode is described at length in Inglis, Ken 1985, *The Rehearsal:Australians at War in the Sudan 1885*, Rigby, Adelaide.

9. Clarke 1998, op. cit. (note 5 above), pp 72–6.

10. Butlin, N.G. 1964, *Investment in Australian Economic Development 1861–1900*, Cambridge University Press, Cambridge, p. 6.

11. Cannon, Michael 1966, *The Land Boomers*, Nelson, Melbourne, p. 34.

Chapter 6 Civilising Capitalism

1. Cited by La Nauze, J.A. 1965, *Alfred Deakin: A Biography*, vol. 1, Melbourne University Press, Melbourne, p. 131.

2. Hereafter the spelling 'Labor' will be used to designate labour in politics, whereas 'Labour' will be used to describe industrial labour. The spelling 'Labor' was adopted early in the twentieth century to distinguish the political Labor parties from the trade unions and the industrial labour movement, and it is a convenient distinction to carry back into the past.

3. Henry Parkes' Tenterfield address 1889, cited in Clark, C.M.H. (ed.) 1971, *Select Documents in Australian History,* Vol. 2, 1851–1900, Angus & Robertson, Sydney, p. 468.

4. Coleman, Peter and Tanner, Les (eds) 1967, *Cartoons of Australian History*, Nelson, Melbourne, p. 120.

5. Clarke, Frank G. 2000, *The Big History Question: Snapshots of Australian History*, vol. 2, Simon & Schuster, Sydney, ch. 2, pp 5–9.

6. Hughes, W.M. 1950, *Policies and Potentates*, Angus & Robertson, Sydney, pp 242–3.

7. Hughes, W.M. 1929, *The Splendid Adventure*, E. Benn, London, p. 236.

Chapter 7 A Land Fit for Heroes

1. Mr Justice Pike's Report on Soldier Settlement 1929, cited by Crowley, F.K. (ed.) 1973, *Modern Australia in Documents 1901–1939*, vol. 1, Wren, Melbourne, p. 449.

2. Robertson, John 1974, *J.H. Scullin: A Political Biography*, University of Western Australia Press, Nedlands, pp 103##5.

3. Edwards, Cecil 1965, *Bruce of Melbourne: Man of Two Worlds*, Heinemann, London, p. 195.

4. *Labor Daily*, 27 August 1930, cited by Crowley 1973, op. cit. (note 1 above), p. 475.

5. *Labor Call*, 11 December 1930.

6. *Australian Worker,* 27 August 1930, cited by Crowley 1973, op. cit. (note 1 above), p. 477.

7. Edwards 1965, op. cit. (note 3 above), p. 208.

8. *Australian Worker*, 23 October 1935.

9. Clarke, Frank G. 1998, *The Big History Question: Snapshots of Australian History*, Simon & Schuster, Sydney, pp 131–5.

10. *Age,* 27 April 1939.

11. *Sydney Morning Herald*, 4 September 1939.

Chapter 8 World War and Cold War

1. *Yorkshire Post*, 8 August 1939, cited by Hazlehurst, Cameron 1979, *Menzies Observed*, George Allen & Unwin, Sydney, p. 138.

2. Ibid., p. 140.

3. *Australian Worker*, 25 October 1939.

4. *Sydney Morning Herald*, 27 December 1941.

5. *Courier-Mail*, 3 April 1943, cited by Crowley, F.K.(ed) 1973, *Modern Australia in Documents 1939–1970*, vol. 2, Wren, Melbourne, p. 81.

6. Ibid., pp. 284–8.

7. Santamaria, B.A. 1964, *The Price of Freedom*, Campion, Melbourne, ch. 2.

8. Clarke, F.G. 1971, 'Loaves and Fishes: The financial Difficulties of the Democratic Labor Party in WA', *Politics*, May, 1971.

9. Crisp, L.F. 1961, *Ben Chifley: A Biography*, Angus & Robertson, Sydney, p. 394.

10. *Sydney Morning Herald*, 3 March 1951.

11. For a detailed account of the Roman Catholic Church's involvement in the 1955 split in the ALP, see Clarke, F.G. 1971, 'Labour and the Catholic Social Studies Movement', *Labour History*, no. 20, May 1971.

12. *Herald* (Melbourne), 30 April 1965.

Chapter 9 The Turbulent Years

1. *Age*, 21 January 1966.

2. *Commonwealth Parliamentary Debates*, House of Representatives, 8 March 1966, p. 26.

3. Ibid., p. 240.

4. Griffiths, Tony 1977, *Contemporary Australia*, Groom Helm, London, p. 100.

5. Hughes, Colin A. 1976, *Mr. Prime Minister: Australian Prime Ministers 1901–1972*, Oxford University Press, Melbourne, p. 175.

6. *Commonwealth Parliamentary Debates*, House of Representatives, 9 March 1971, pp 679–84.

7. Walter, James 1980, *The Leader: A Political Biography of Gough Whitlam*, University of Queensland Press, St Lucia, p. 154.

8. Daly, Fred 1977, *From Curtin to Kerr*, Sun Books, Melbourne, p. 198.

9. Cited by Lorna Lippman 1979, 'The Aborigines', in Patience, A. & Head, B. (eds) 1979, *From Whitlam to Fraser: Reform and Reaction in Australian Politics*, Oxford University Press, Melbourne, p. 177.

10. Smith, Gary 1979, 'Minerals and Energy', in Patience & Head (eds) 1979, op. cit. (note 9 above), p. 239.

11. Hall, Richard 1979, *The Real John Kerr: His Brilliant Career*, Angus & Robertson, Sydney, passim.

Chapter 10 Economic Rationalism and Ideological Deconstruction

1. Cited in Stubbs, J. 1989, *Hayden*, Heinemann, Melbourne, p. 253.

2. McGrath, Michael 1989, 'Economic Review', *Australian Quarterly*, Autumn 1989, p. 123.

3. For a full description and analysis, see Max Suich, 'Bank Ruptured', *The Independent*, May 1991.

4. *Sydney Morning Herald*, 30 March 1991.

5. *Weekend Australian*, 29–30 June 1991.

6. *Sun-Herald*, 15 September 1991.

7. *Sydney Morning Herald*, 1 June 1991.

8. *Weekend Australian*, 23–4 March 1991.

9. Scott, Andrew 1991, *Fading Loyalties*, cited by Richard Farmer, 'Labor's Lost Legions of the Working Class', *Australian*, 22 May 1991.

10. *Weekend Australian*, 11–12 May 1991.

11. *Sydney Morning Herald*, 20 August 1994.

12. *Commonwealth Parliamentary Debates*, House of Representatives, Question Time, 27 February 1992.

13. *Sydney Morning Herald*, 10 December 1992.

14. *Sydney Morning Herald*, 15 march 1993.

Chapter 11 Vaudeville and the Conservative Resurgence

1. *Age*, 16 November 1993.

2. *Weekend Australian*, 5–6 June 1993.

3. Keating, Paul 2000, *Engagement: Australia Faces the Asia##Pacific*, Macmillan, Sydney, pp 20–1.

4. *Sydney Morning Herald*, 12 February 2000.

5. *Age*, 9 June 1997.

6. *Sydney Morning Herald*, 10 July 1999.

7. *Sydney Morning Herald*, 4 April 2000.

8. *Sydney Morning Herald*, 7 June 1999.

9. *Sydney Morning Herald,* 10 July 1999.

10. *Sydney Morning Herald*, 13 and 14 September 2000; *Australian*, 13 and 14 September 2000.

11. *Sydney Morning Herald*, 9 June 2000.

12. *Sydney Morning Herald*, 28–29 September 2002.

13. *Sydney Morning Herald*, 16 November 2001.

14. *Weekend Australian*, 17–18 June 2000; *Australian*, 13 September 2000.

15. *Sydney Morning Herald*, 14 and 15 November 2002.

16. *Sydney Morning Herald*, 14 November 2002.

17. *Sydney Morning Herald*, 1 October 2000.

18. *Sydney Morning Herald*, 14 November 2002.

19. *Sydney Morning Herald*, 9–10 November 2002.

Index